120934
Leach Library
Londonderry, NH 03053

The Volleyball Handbook

Bob Miller

HUMAN KINETICS

796.325
MIL

05 Nov 18
B+T
1995 (1397)

Library of Congress Cataloging-in-Publication Data

Miller, Bob, 1945 Apr. 17-
 The volleyball handbook / Bob Miller.
     p. cm.
 Includes index.
 ISBN 0-7360-5610-6 (soft cover)
 1. Volleyball. 2. Volleyball--Coaching. I. Title.
 GV1015.3.M55 2005
 796.325--dc22

                                        2005014524

ISBN: 0-7360-5610-6

Copyright © 2005 by Bob Miller

All rights reserved. Except for use in a review, the reproduction or utilization of this work in any form or by any electronic, mechanical, or other means, now known or hereafter invented, including xerography, photocopying, and recording, and in any information storage and retrieval system, is forbidden without the written permission of the publisher.

Notice: Permission to reproduce the following material is granted to instructors and agencies who have purchased *The Volleyball Handbook:* pp. 208 and 217. The reproduction of other parts of this book is expressly forbidden by the above copyright notice. Persons or agencies who have not purchased *The Volleyball Handbook* may not reproduce any material.

Acquisitions Editor: Jana Hunter; **Developmental Editor:** Julie Rhoda; **Assistant Editor:** Carla Zych; **Copyeditor:** Andrew Smith; **Proofreader:** Darlene Rake; **Indexer:** Nan N. Badgett; **Graphic Designer:** Nancy Rasmus; **Graphic Artist:** Francine Hamerski; **Photo Manager:** Dan Wendt; **Cover Designer:** Keith Blomberg; **Photographer (cover):** © Getty Images; **Photographer (interior):** Mark Anderman, The Wild Studio unless otherwise noted; **Art Manager and Illustrator:** Kareema McLendon-Foster; **Printer:** United Graphics.

Human Kinetics books are available at special discounts for bulk purchase. Special editions or book excerpts can also be created to specification. For details, contact the Special Sales Manager at Human Kinetics.

Printed in the United States of America   10 9 8 7 6 5 4 3 2 1

Human Kinetics
Web site: www.HumanKinetics.com

United States: Human Kinetics
P.O. Box 5076
Champaign, IL 61825-5076
800-747-4457
e-mail: humank@hkusa.com

Canada: Human Kinetics
475 Devonshire Road Unit 100
Windsor, ON N8Y 2L5
800-465-7301 (in Canada only)
e-mail: orders@hkcanada.com

Europe: Human Kinetics
107 Bradford Road
Stanningley
Leeds LS28 6AT, United Kingdom
+44 (0) 113 255 5665
e-mail: hk@hkeurope.com

Australia: Human Kinetics
57A Price Avenue
Lower Mitcham, South Australia 5062
08 8277 1555
e-mail: liaw@hkaustralia.com

New Zealand: Human Kinetics
Division of Sports Distributors NZ Ltd.
P.O. Box 300 226 Albany
North Shore City
Auckland
0064 9 448 1207
e-mail: info@humankinetics.co.nz

This book is dedicated to my family—Margie, Julie, Brian, Heidi, and Brent—for the sacrifices, support, and encouragement over the years that allowed me to continue working with athletes in the sport of volleyball, and for the feedback they provided during the writing of this book.

CONTENTS

FOREWORD

Having been involved in the sport of volleyball for over 30 years, a few things have become clear to me. It is a fairly complex sport from a skills standpoint, and the perfection of the requisite skills can be difficult and time-consuming. Moreover, learning all of the rules, systems, and sequences that go along with the game can be overwhelming at times.

Bob Miller, the consummate educator and coach, has worked hard to develop a very comprehensive and easily understandable instructional model of the game. This is what you would expect from a coach considered by many to be a pioneer of the sport in Pennsylvania, who has established winning programs with both male and female volleyball players. Within the handbook, he has broken down this sport to a level that allows him to share his passion with new players and coaches alike. While instructing and coaching his athletes from the classroom and the sidelines for 35 years, he has continued to be a student of the game. He is constantly searching for new information to add to his comprehensive knowledge of the sport, and he shares all of this with you.

This book should find itself on every volleyball enthusiast's desk as it encompasses all of the concerns that a coach or player could encounter, from conducting tryouts and developing a coaching philosophy to game tactics, contest management, and goal setting.

Well known for his competitive nature, high expectations, and ability to draw the most from his athletes, Coach Miller provides instruction for mastering the physical skills and the mental and emotional aspects of the game. He conveys his belief in serving and receiving as the core skills of the game, from the middle school level to the Olympics, and in individual and team defense.

One of the key features of the book is Coach Miller's use of his "P Principles of Success." Applying these principles, he approaches all facets of running a program, incorporating players' viewpoints and especially coaches' viewpoints to address each area. He discusses Preparing, Polishing your Philosophy, Planning, Participating with Passion, Practicing, Performing under Pressure, accurately Processing observations, and the ability to Promote the game. I sincerely believe it was his attention to all of these items throughout his career that allowed him to achieve such tremendous levels of success, and I feel confident that you will benefit from his experience if you incorporate his approach to volleyball into your own game or program. Combining these P principles with skills, drills, game strategies and tactics, and advice on handling other day-to-day concerns, this book will help players and coaches put together a high-quality program.

Probably the greatest endorsement I can give Coach Miller is to say that I would have been proud to have had him work with my children. He not only talks the talk but also lives his philosophy on a daily basis, and the players who have played for him and the coaches who have worked with him have all been the winners!

Russ Rose
Head Women's Volleyball Coach,
Pennsylvania State University

PREFACE

Volleyball for male athletes has a short history in the United States when compared to team sports such as football, basketball, and baseball. Pennsylvania, which has sponsored a state championship since 1936, has been one of the leaders in boys' volleyball across the nation. And although the history of volleyball for boys and men dates back to 1936 in our country, it was played by only a small percentage of schools until the past few decades.

Title IX, the federal educational amendment approved in 1972, provided the impetus to develop female athletics in the United States. This gave volleyball a huge boost; it is now played by legions of girls and young women nationwide, in scholastic and in collegiate venues and in the Junior Olympics.

Volleyball for the male athlete also experienced a surge in the number of participants with the increase in scholastic programs, starting in the 1980s and continuing today. My playing experience in high school was limited to the instruction and games played in physical education class. My college experience was expanded to include competition in a fraternity league as well as participation in a co-ed league made up of students in teacher training for an education degree that featured physical education as a component. Student-athletes today have considerably more options.

From an early age I aspired to be a teacher, motivated by the guidance, support, encouragement, and positive role modeling provided by my high school teachers. During my 35 years as an educator, I was fortunate to have two modes of instructing young people—as a teacher in the classroom and as a coach on the volleyball court. I always considered coaching a team to be an opportunity to teach "an advanced placement" type of curriculum for the highly skilled, motivated, and self-disciplined athlete.

The game of volleyball in the 1960s was dominated by the basic skills that defined the sport in that era and could be considered developmentally primitive when compared to the fast moving, explosive rally score game of today. In fact, our early promotion of the sport emphasized the term "power volleyball" to distinguish it from picnic or gym class play. The word "power" was meant to indicate that each play was based on three contacts, with the final contact being a spike. Little did we anticipate at that time the evolution the sport would undergo to become today's game of quickness, finesse, dynamic defense, and explosive attacks.

Then as now, older, more experienced coaches took on leadership roles to promote the sport and help young coaches develop, providing demonstration clinics and individual instruction for both players and coaches. Each year, even today as I volunteer coach, my continued development stems from watching other coaches and teams, attending clinics and camps, asking questions, and monitoring the strategies and techniques taught by others to see what might be applied to raise the level of play.

The skill and movement of the game have increased dramatically since the 1972 Olympics. The defensive techniques and offensive attack speed were upgraded by the play of the Japanese Olympic teams. Rule changes that permitted penetration of the net while blocking, as well as the block not counting as a touch, had a huge impact on net and transition play. Subsequent Olympic Games saw the United States lead the way with the inclusion of primary passers, swing hitting, and the back-row attack. The proliferation of the jump serve, the play of the libero, and rally scoring have brought the game to its current form.

Life skills can be part and parcel of the training of individuals to function together as a solid unit. This book is a compilation of what I've learned over the past 38 years. My hope is that it will provide food for thought and cause you—whether you play or coach the game—to reflect on what you are currently doing and consider some of the options I've presented. I hope you enjoy reading the book as much as I have enjoyed putting it together.

ACKNOWLEDGMENTS

The accomplishments that have come my way are the results of the input, mentoring, and teaching of others. Just as it takes a village to raise a child, it took the contributions of many people to make my career in volleyball a successful one.

Thanks to all those who answered questions, put on clinics, involved me in camps, wrote books, made videos, ran tournaments, and gave back to the sport of volleyball. Some of the folks who were especially helpful include Don Geyer, Jack Quinn, Joe Silipo, Denny Patton, and Bruno Krsul in the 1960s; Tom Tait, Russ Rose, Rich Schall, Dan Brown, Mike Larko, and Doug Beal in the 1970s; Larry Bock, John Kessel, Al Scates, and Jeff Stork in the 1980s; and Mike Schall, Tom Peterson, Dennis Hohenshelt, Mark Pavlik, Laurie Lokash, and Tom Justice in the 1990s.

I also want to acknowledge those who assisted me at North Allegheny High School—Dick Krotzer, Bill Gallagher, Brian and Julie Miller, Lisa Failla, Dan Schall, and Heidi Miller. I cannot thank these individuals enough for dedicating themselves to the betterment of youth through the sport of volleyball.

Last but not least, to the North Allegheny athletes who listened so well, were so receptive to demanding training, competed so intensely, and who have given so much back to the game—thank you.

KEY TO DIAGRAMS

LB	Left-back player
DS	Defensive specialist
LFB	Left-front blocker
MB	Middle-back player
MF	Middle-front player
MFB	Middle-front blocker
MH	Middle hitter
OH	Outside hitter
P	Passer
RB	Right-back player
RF	Right-front player
RFB	Right-front blocker
RS	Right-side player
S	Setter
T	Tosser
(P)⟶	Player who is moving
⌒⟶	Two-step player movement

CHAPTER 1

P Principles of Success

There is no magic formula that separates one volleyball program from another when success is involved, but what many successful programs have in common is an established learning climate. In the right learning environment, there is a challenging, high-achieving atmosphere that pushes individuals to levels that they may not have previously believed they could attain.

In such an environment, coaches try to raise their players' expectations of themselves and help them formulate positive attitudes toward learning, responding, and competing. Coaches help players analyze their strengths and recognize and acknowledge their weaknesses so that they are better able to work to improve these weak areas. Players can also contribute to the learning environment by taking the initiative to work on their own weaknesses, bringing positive energy to the drills, and supporting the efforts of their teammates.

Achieving success at the individual, team, and program level is a worthy goal that can best be described in terms of a marathon race rather than a sprint. It takes time to accumulate and build on individual and team achievements, all of which come about through the structured and steady pace of practice. In this chapter, I identify some keys that I think are necessary for success in volleyball; I call these keys the P principles of success. When implemented, these principles result in a plan that can be flexible when appropriate and is as free as possible from a coach's assumptions about what a player already knows and can already do.

The eight P principles of success in volleyball include the following:

- Preparing by focusing on what you need to do to improve your game
- Polishing your philosophy
- Planning your season and practices
- Participating with passion
- Practicing
- Performing under pressure
- Processing observations about the game accurately
- Promoting the game in your district or community

Positive prior preparation, planning, and practice prevent poor performance.

Prepare for Success

The keystone of the P principles is preparation. Preparing for success means that everyone—coaches and players alike—contributes by focusing on what he or she considers success and determining how to get there. Coaches must mentally prepare for the challenges to come, and players must be physically conditioned and mentally ready to meet the daily trials they will face.

According to Robert Gilbert's paper titled "Daily Thoughts for Excellence in Leadership and Management," there are four surefire rules for success. These rules can be embraced as a part of each player's and each coach's daily participation in volleyball.

1. **Show up ready to learn.** Laying a foundation and building on it are fundamental to the learning and retention process. To develop and maintain a base and enhance their knowledge and ability, players must show up every day ready to perform the skill repetitions and face the intellectual challenges that will enable them to improve. At every practice, coaches must ask players to transfer their skills and knowledge into competitive situations at game speed. Missed practices in the formative years may well negatively affect learning. Therefore, it is imperative that even young players (and all coaches, for that matter) show up ready to learn.

2. **Pay attention.** Players going through the motions or coaches permitting players to use rote memory to get through practices can lead to a stagnation of individual skills and uninspiring team play. It is vital that players pay attention to the teaching points presented to them and that they attempt to duplicate training techniques. This kind of attention to detail, undertaken with an eye on improving individual skills, ultimately will raise players' skill level and the level of team play. As Mike Kzryzewski, coach of the Duke University men's basketball team, has so eloquently put it, "Every game is important for me and, quite frankly, every play is important to me. If you lose that, you don't have a chance to be as good as you can be."

3. **Ask questions.** Developing an atmosphere of respect, trust, and honesty is vital for creating the most comfortable, yet challenging, learning environment possible. When players don't feel that they can ask questions or raise concerns, both they and their coaches tend to make faulty assumptions. Asking questions and discussing issues allows both coaches and players to more fully understand the principles, strategies, and logic behind a particular drill or session. Players and coaches need to have an understanding of where they are going and how they are going to get there.

4. **Don't quit.** Rather than avoiding a problem or acting as if it doesn't exist, both players and coaches must muster the inner strength to work their way through tough situations and respond by moving forward. As Confucius wisely said, "A man who has committed a mistake and doesn't correct it is committing another mistake." Henry Ford pushed this point further: "Failure is the opportunity to begin again more intelligently."

Decide How You Measure Success

An important part of preparing for success, whether as a player or a coach, is deciding how to measure its achievement. Whether it is measured in terms of athletic wins, professional advancement, intellectual development, or personal growth, society is consumed with quantifying accomplishment. This phenomenon in and of itself isn't necessarily problematic, especially in the realm of sports. When a player leaves the gym after a practice or a game knowing that he or she has improved, that is success. When a coach's growth as a person and as a teacher enables him or her to better lead the team, that is success. When a team faces an obstacle that challenges its chemistry and values and subsequently handles that adversity with poise and dignity, that too is success.

More important than following a textbook definition of success is that coaches and players have a clear idea of what success means to them. Thoughtfully preparing and writing down goals before the start of the season are important parts of the process. One player may think that making the team is more important than being a major contributor or a starter, while another may consider himself or herself successful only as a starter. A few players may think their season is a success only if they make an all-star team or receive a college scholarship. Others may view the opportunity to compete in college, whether as a scholarship recipient or a walk-on athlete, to be the icing on the cake. Some players measure their success and that of their team in terms of wins and losses or the ability of the team to qualify for the playoffs.

What many players fail to realize (and therefore fail to appreciate) is that daily individual or team improvement, no matter to what degree, is just as important a measure of success as wins, awards, or scholarships. In fact, daily improvement may be of greater value than what most people regard as success. The discipline and sacrifice and the confidence that results from meeting the challenges in order to improve are vital components of success. Team members must discuss the importance of having dreams and put their individual and team goals into writing. They can refer to them periodically throughout the season and use them for motivation.

Winning games, awards, or scholarships cannot be achieved without consistent improvement. In fact, whether you receive such accolades is often out of your control. What you can control is your own performance. Thus, consistent improvement really must be the ultimate goal for each player and the team. Dean Smith, former basketball coach at the University of North Carolina, puts the idea of achievement into proper perspective when he says, "It is amazing what can be accomplished when no one cares who gets the credit."

A coach may determine that success means the ability to accurately assess talent and skill and to nurture his or her athletes in order to form them into a cohesive team. These achievements, rather than a record of wins and losses, awards, or the pursuit of a more prestigious coaching position, can be more valid measures of that coach's success. One can easily see a coach's influence on a team when he or she conducts practice sessions and directs matches that permit each player and the team as a whole to improve. Producing players

© Human Kinetics

A high-reaching attack with hitter coverage.

who go on to the next level and witnessing graduates who return and give back to the sport by coaching, officiating, or starting club programs are indications of the impact that a coach and the sport have had on those players. Providing opportunities for his or her players to grow as people and seeing the beneficial results of modeling positive leadership are also good examples of how a coach can measure his or her success.

It is also possible to evaluate team success by noticing the manner in which the team competes against other volleyball programs of similar strength and even teams of greater ability. Is the team able to score points against the other team? Is it able to dictate the speed and intensity of the game? A team's success can also be measured by whether the caliber of play meets expectations. The coach can observe in practice, for example, how well the team executes a special adjustment designed specifically for use against an upcoming opponent. Perhaps the team has been practicing a special blocking and coverage scheme designed to force the opponent's middle hitter to use shots he or she generally does not perform well or is not used to making. Is the team able to implement the practiced schemes? Do the players see the value of the intended adjustments? Whether the match ends in a win or a loss, the individual players and the team have established the framework for continued success.

Another component of success is measured by noting the way coaches are able to identify each staff member's or player's primary strengths and how he or she is best able to contribute to the team. Encouraging each person to use his or her unique abilities will generate an enthusiastic atmosphere and ensure that the staff and players contribute to the development of a climate conducive to success.

You can measure a program's success by the way it is perceived by potential student-athletes, the administration (or club governing board), its opponents, and the community. The ability of a club or team to "reload" itself each year by blending eager newcomers with more experienced returning athletes also reflects the success of a program—as does the ability to attract players; draw the interest of other clubs, teams, or coaching colleagues who want to watch practice; schedule exhibition matches; and be invited to invitational tournaments. Further evidence that a program is successful is provided, moreover, when opposing coaches approach the coach or members of the team to ask questions that will help their own program to improve, as well as when they compliment the coach on the determination and sporting behavior displayed by the team.

To be successful in these ways, one must have a plan and some good ideas regarding how to implement it. Having a vision and a motto that gets everyone involved with the program to expect great achievement is key. (My program's creed was "More is expected from you than you think you have to give and more often than you think you can give it.") Do not sacrifice the time you need to build a strong foundation for long-term success by instead focusing on winning immediately. Be patient and get involved at the developmental level of your program. Find ways to introduce as early as possible the skills and drills designed to produce efficient movement and ball control. Have a vision for how young players can develop, how their skills can best contribute to the team, and how they can be more effectively assimilated into the team as they move through the program.

Set Goals

Set smart goals—goals that are realistic, attainable, and measurable. Ideally, coaches and players set personal goals and then verbalize them in a way that allows them to measure their own success. For players, the ability to set smart goals involves understanding the philosophy behind the structure of training sessions and how the priorities behind the practice design develop individual players into a competitive group. (I discuss philosophy in the next section.) The program needs to develop a climate that permits hard-working players to thrive and thereby set a good example for their teammates. The players should train with the idea that the choice of who starts and at what position is based on the ability to play the game at the required level consistently and with poise. Solid team chemistry and unselfish support by each player for every other player can produce amazing results. Players who are truly committed to the team have the ability and confidence to police their peers. They don't hesitate to keep their teammates on task.

For some coaches, a long-term goal may be to maintain and enhance a previously established tradition, while for others it may involve establishing a program that can grow steadily over time and be attractive to potential athletes and the community. Goal setting by coaches should also carry over into the short-term goals of the team, even, for instance, influencing how particular drills are conducted. For example, my staff instructs players to strive for 10 "perfect" passes to a target, a predefined area where the setter runs the offense. Players, of course, need to be clear on what constitutes perfect.

A player's goal might be to improve his or her ability to control the ball when moving and playing balls hit to his or her left. In this respect, touching a ball that is three or more steps from the starting point may be an achievement. The next achievement may be to turn the ball back to the right so that it is directed toward the target. Finally, the player may strive to turn the ball and make a percentage of perfect passes to the target.

It is important to realize that there are multiple steps involved in attaining any goal and that accomplishing each step indicates success. Additionally, there are many drills in which the goal is to achieve ball control for a greater and greater number of positive individual touches each time. Players often can get to three or four consecutive touches but make a mistake before reaching the fifth touch. My staff and I found that having athletes shoot for higher expectations leads them to achieve goals that they thought were not attainable.

As my staff and I set coaching goals to produce consistently competitive teams, we incorporated a rolling five-year plan for training athletes. This allowed us to look ahead to where we wanted the current eighth graders to be by their senior (and final) year in the program. With this long-range view, we would view a sophomore who still had three more years of development differently than we might if we had assessed our team simply from year to year. We found ways for the players to develop over the long haul, thereby avoiding a quick-fix mentality. Over the years, we had many examples of late bloomers in our program. These players could have easily been cut as they progressed through their high school years. Instead, they were allowed to have an effect on the team and program in their own way.

Polish Your Philosophy

Once you have decided how you wish to measure success, it's time to determine how this measure melds with your overall volleyball philosophy. There are a number of sources that you can use to develop this philosophy. Perhaps the primary source is those people that have provided wisdom, knowledge, and guidance in your development in the sport of volleyball or in other sports or activities. Which of their characteristics should you embrace? What ideals or strengths can they contribute to your philosophy? What in your personal history can be brought to the table? Draw on your past participation in and observation of the sport and extrapolate from this to illustrate a style of play that will help players compete at a high level. Plant the seeds of this philosophy and permit them to germinate as players' performance and the program as a whole are observed by administrators, club management, spectators, and opposing teams.

Once you've taken these steps to shape a philosophy, step away from it to view it as an outsider would and see if it is really what you envision. At this point, you can refine it as needed while still (of course) adhering to your overall goals and manner of measuring success. Always remember that your own personality, and not someone you are trying to emulate, must come through.

Should ball control and defense be the cornerstones of your philosophy? If so, then you would want those traits to be observable by others watching your team play, not only in their physical style of play but also in their mental prowess during the match. Coaches, parents, administrators, and spectators would see that the team is well prepared, disciplined, and unselfish on the court, as well as enthusiastic, smart, aggressive, and fair.

A respected and trusted coach is a role model and a youth leader. Coaches can attempt to model their program after those that they admire, but their own knowledge, leadership skills, and personality will be major factors in the way they are viewed by participants. Moreover, players tend to adopt the demeanor and personality of their coach. If the coach remains poised in the eye of the storm, players are more likely to be poised. If the coach is a stickler for perfect technique, players will often also discipline themselves to do the same.

Another aspect of philosophy that coaches need to consider is whether to discourage athletes from participating in any sport other than volleyball or whether competing in multiple sports is suppported. They also must decide how to coach single- versus multiple-sport athletes. Today, it is much more common for coaches to strive to have their athletes focus on a single sport to the exclusion of other sports. What does a coach do when his or her philosophy of encouraging athletes to compete in multiple sports or activities is at odds with colleagues' philosophies? When all is said and done, who really determines what is best for a student-athlete? Input can come from parents, the player, coaches, teachers, and guidance counselors. Seek compromise, but even if a decision is made that ultimately does not favor the athlete's participation on the team, continue to provide support to the athlete in all his or her endeavors.

With regard to team size, a philosophy should take into account the number of players a coach can realistically instruct in an effective manner. Club programs often keep smaller squads that permit more individual playing time and exposure for each athlete to recruiters. The size of club teams is generally governed by the demand to provide maximum playing time for up to 10 players. Members of club programs must be able to pay dues in order to participate. Some players interested in a club program may not be able to be involved because of financial constraints, although many club programs have established scholarships or adjusted costs to include more players. Other factors governing club program infrastructure are the number of players available for each age group and the number of coaches available to coach multiple teams, if necessary, in a specific age group.

Some school districts mandate squad size or have a "no-cut" policy. Others require equal playing time for all players. Unless dictated by the school district or club program, a coach's philosophy concerning the number of players contributing to the style of the team's play will determine squad size and team composition. A coach may believe that size and strength at the net correlate more closely with success. Using these guidelines, taller players who jump well would receive priority over smaller backcourt specialists who might play better defense. Another coach might think that ball control and defense are what win matches. He or she might focus on having several backcourt specialists contribute by entering to serve and play defense. Yet another coach might like using the libero—a relatively new position that permits unlimited entry into the backcourt for one or two players. In today's rally-score games, the libero can save team entries and still permit the use of specialists. Finally, a coach needs to decide if his or her philosophy is more focused on giving a large number of players the opportunity to compete in a team sport or on enhancing the play of a few selected players—or on trying to accomplish both.

A coach's philosophy will be evident through the priorities emphasized in practices. Practices that promote athletes' abilities to process information and transfer their skills and knowledge to playing at game speed will help a team achieve its long-term goals. Based on the three-entry rules that guided my coaching style and the number of seasons that I had to perfect the system, I became very comfortable with a varsity squad of up to 20 players. When in my last year of coaching the rules changed to mandate 18 total team entries but unlimited player entries, I adjusted the squad down to 16 players and also changed the management of the team. My coaching staff and I adjusted our game tactics by alternating player entries by game rather than during a single game as before. I adopted the "team-first" philosophy in which my players were asked to buy into contributing to a team effort rather than a "me-first," starting-only role. Whether a player starts, subs into a game, or contributes more in practice is not the issue. Rather, how he or she makes a contribution to the team and program is of primary importance. In most cases, athletes were comfortable with their roles, but occasionally challenges did come from parents.

Players should be aware of their personal philosophy of competitive sports and how it fits into their lives. Players have had their competitive spirit nurtured by parents, friends, teammates, and coaches during their time participating on various volleyball teams and in other competitive endeavors. Players need to constantly evaluate how and why they are doing things the way they are doing them. Are they attempting to satisfy others, or are they taking part in volleyball for the pure enjoyment of participating and competing? As players grow in ability, they must also be ready to increase the intensity of their play and the time they are willing to commit as well as hone their work ethic. The pursuit of excellence in volleyball requires constantly seeking to improve one's speed, power, agility, and proficiency with "rebound" ball control (that is, the player cannot hold or catch the ball, but must use a hand or arm surface to direct it).

Some players relish the competition side of volleyball to such a great extent that they only pursue this one sport. Other players desire to continue their skill development by participating in several sports. Being able to mesh the demands of high-level competition with academics and other interests can make for some stressful times. After all is said and done, a player's actions and the way he or she competes will reflect his or her developing philosophy. An athlete's philosophy should be evident to those who have the opportunity to observe the player's actions.

You may be entering a program that has either a positive or a negative history. You can help to eliminate controversy by emphasizing moving on. As Chuck Noll, former head coach of the Pittsburgh Steelers, famously declared, "It is not where we have been, but where we are going together as a team that is critical." Identify the standards and expectations of the entire program and do your part to model them.

Plan for Progress

Once you have established goals and a philosophy, it's time to plan how to implement them. The keys to doing so lie in creating a workable timeline and assessing what realistic level of support you can expect to have in your long-term and short-term pursuit of them. Planning for progress covers a much more specific scope than just preparing generally to meet your goals. It involves laying out a conditioning plan and sequential practices while also establishing how those practices fit into the season as a whole.

Once long-term goals are established (see "Prepare for Success" on pages 2 to 7) coaches need to develop plans for off-season, preseason, and in-season training. This means taking a progressive approach to conditioning as well as movement and skill acquisition for the entire season. From here coaches can determine weekly goals for each phase of the season. For example, a team's long-term goal might be to develop its setters and middle hitter to be able to run a quick-attack offense. A fitting progressive weekly plan that would help to achieve this goal is to implement the 1-ball set attack in training (see pages 64 to 65 for more on this). In the beginning, the 1-ball set might only be hit in front of the setter at a slow pace. Once this tempo and the setter–hitter relationship are developed, the following week's goal might be to increase the distance between the setter and hitter. Next, the play-set could be made behind the setter. Finally, players could run combination plays, using the established rhythm with the middle hitter as well as additional players. Coaches can then develop flexible daily plans that allow them to review previous game play and enhance specific skills, tactics, and mental training as needed. Honest feedback that is consistent among all players and a solid strategy for improvement should be included in all sessions. Coaches need to put themselves in the players' shoes as they plan practices and develop a climate conducive to success.

I have coaching colleagues who have consistently produced high-achieving athletes and teams without ever realizing the dream of a championship. Other colleagues I know have gone 10 to 30 years before winning a championship. A coach's timeline for achieving excellence and qualifying for a championship may have to be extended. Be realistic when developing strategies for fielding a competitive team, and be willing to learn and grow daily with those who surround you. Together you can improve and meet individual and team goals. Break the program plan into manageable pieces with an estimated timeline for building on the established foundation. Put the players into practice and competitive situations where they can succeed. Coaches and players need to be ready every day to implement the plan through effective practice design (see chapter 10 for more on practice design). Players will face frustrations and self-doubt, but when they persevere, they will raise their abilities to a higher level and develop a positive attitude. This leads us to our next P principle.

Participate With a Purpose and Passion

A player's approach to being the best volleyball player he or she can be starts with passion and commitment to the sport. The player's coach and teammates can also influence his or her practice habits. Be aware, however, that passion can be a double-edged sword. With control, passion can stimulate awareness of the personal traits that can elevate an athlete's play. Training with a purpose increases a player's focus, self-discipline, and self-motivation. A player's resolve can increase his or her personal growth. But uncontrolled passion for the sport can cause a player to overemphasize one area of his or her development at the expense of his or her education, family, or personal health.

Players need to learn to keep volleyball in its place, alongside the other significant aspects of their lives. The way they balance volleyball with other important endeavors may be emulated by their teammates or younger players. Being a role model can be part of the experience, whether it is sought or unknowingly assumed. Keeping this in mind, a player can demonstrate mature behavior by adhering to academic and attendance guidelines at school and other established tenets that govern their lives.

College recruiters often ask whether a particular player is "coachable." This question refers not to the athletic ability of the player but to such intangible aspects as what sort of person he or she is and how he or she can fit with and contribute to a new team. Some of these intangibles, which are so important to being a successful player, include the following:

- **Passion for the game.** The work ethic, energy, and enthusiasm that both coaches and players display enhance the learning atmosphere for all members of the team. Displaying passion for the game means responding to peers and events around you with genuine emotion. Passionate players keep working hard to get to the next level, and their energy helps to bring teammates along with them.

- **Focus.** A player's ability to pay attention, concentrate during practice, ask questions when appropriate, and transfer instructions or modeled skills into calm and controlled play are all qualities of a coachable player. In a more tangible sense, focus also refers to a player's ability to understand where to visually center his or her attention during the sequence of ball contacts.

- **Self-motivation.** A player finds the game more rewarding if he or she takes the initiative to do the little things necessary to improve rather than relying on teammates or coaches to push him or her to reach his or her potential. Some little things that provide evidence of a player's self-motivation include scheduling time after practice to receive more ball contacts, being willing to work with teammates to enhance their development, and requesting time to watch themselves or opponents on video. A player needs to determine whether he or she is getting better when no one is watching. The ability of a player to accept constructive feedback and work through the frustrations of changing a motor skill provides a coach with a snapshot of that player's personality as well as his or her competitive nature and passion for the game.

- **Self-discipline.** The ability of a player to take responsibility for his or her actions on and off the court is another important intangible that makes a great player. A player who understands his or her role as part of the team and functions in that role even though it may be a secondary one shows self-discipline. A disciplined player can be trusted by coaches and teammates to expect the ball to come his or her way and to move into the correct court position while maintaining balance.

- **Encouraging others.** A player can help make those around him or her better by giving both physical and verbal cues that either provide the encouragement that teammates need in order to work their way through adversity or by playing balls that put their teammates into situations where it is easier to succeed. A team is only as good as its weakest link. Acknowledging others with accurate and well-timed feedback is not just the role of the coach but a tactic that each player can embrace to help strengthen the play and confidence of his or her teammates.

Perfect Your Practice

We've all heard that practice makes perfect. But according to Tom Tait, former Penn State men's volleyball coach, it's *perfect* practice that makes perfect—because practice makes the form you're practicing permanent. Practice can provide training repetitions for footwork and ball control, but if it is done without corrective feedback it can produce bad habits and mistakes. Therefore, coaches must establish measurable standards for a technique or a drill. Players need to be accountable for using the techniques that improve their ability to master the game. An example of a measured drill that helps perfect practice is the performance of 10 perfect consecutive passes to a target area. The target area must be defined before the start of the drill and the players must do the counting. By holding the players accountable for counting, they are forced to focus on each pass and respond by giving the pass an evaluation. What gets measured gets accomplished!

Another part of practice success is good practice design. I discuss this in detail in chapter 10 and provide some examples. Coaches need to implement the best practices for learning—practices here meaning identifiable, organized sequences with built-in checks to measure improvement. Coaches need to take into consideration the individual learning styles of team members in structuring practices and emphasize focus, self-discipline, and listening skills. They must pay attention to whether they have helped all players to improve their skills.

It's also important for coaches to make notes on the effectiveness of individual practice sessions and decide what drills or sequences work best. They should also adjust or eliminate any drill that is not accomplishing the desired goal. Several times during the season players should have the responsibility to design, explain, and implement a drill. This provides them with a greater sense of ownership of the team's improvement. Coaches can also remind players to communicate a technical or tactical need to them so that concerns or problems can be addressed.

Perform Under Pressure

The competitive intensity and attitudes of players are the most difficult character-istics for coaches to accurately evaluate because tryouts or practices really don't duplicate the pressure of a game or match point. Therefore, coaches need to work diligently to provide situations that challenge players' abilities to remain calm, controlled, and confident, yet still spirited during the intense and pressure-filled situations in matches.

Part of helping athletes perform under pressure involves addressing individual player behavior that is selfish or unsporting in nature. Should the team or an individual player develop negative patterns in response to errors or losing—such as holding back or giving up—a coach must re-create the proper level of intensity in practice and show the player or players how to respond with the poise neces-sary to break the faulty pattern. Successful teams are made up not necessarily of the most talented players but of those who can model a positive response to pressure and make good things happen in the heat of the match.

One way coaches can do this is by providing "pressure plays" throughout practice sessions so that players can experience stress while attempting to play with poise. Coaches can observe the players' reactions to mistakes to see how those who make an error respond as well as how their teammates react to it. My staff and I worked hard to raise our players' level of concern by using verbal challenges and demands for perfection during individual, small-group, or team drills. The player or group would have to continue doing the drill until the last play resulted in a positive touch.

A favorite pressure-play drill that teams can try is called Money Ball. To begin the drill, the coach puts a ball into play such that several volleys can occur after the ball's introduction. As the ball is being played during any one of the volleys, the coach calls out, "Money Ball!" Players on both teams try to end the rally with a positive play. The team that loses the rally receives a consequence. A consequence may be a set of skill drills at full speed, or it may constitute replacing the player that caused the error before the next rally begins. The replaced player would then spend two minutes working on the technical aspect that caused the error while reflecting on whether he or she will be given the opportunity to reenter the drill. I like to run this drill when players are fatigued to duplicate the game action after a long and critical rally. The only pressure that defies duplication is the pressure that results from a mistake that costs the team a game or a match. This is what playing Money Ball is intended to prevent.

Finally, it is important that players feel the coach's full support as they go through intense practice sessions that simulate the pressure of competition. Play-ers must be aware of the situations that frustrate them or make them doubt their abilities. They must honestly assess their effort and their use of learned skills. If players have done everything as well and intelligently as possible, then they can be confident that they will move forward. If players hold back or try to perform a skill that is currently beyond their skill level, they need to regroup and be smarter on their next opportunity. They must remain fully focused and ready to handle the next competitive test that comes their way. They must *want* the next ball and have the desire to personally take control of the situation and succeed as well as the discipline to maintain correct technique.

Coaches also have to perform under pressure as they are faced with putting a quality team on the court—a team that reflects their instructional abilities and how they have worked to form individual players into a cohesive unit. The team may be tested in as many as two matches per week plus a weekend tournament. Sometimes the pressure coaches feel is self-induced. They try to do too much or are unrealistic in evaluating where their team is at present and where it can be by the season's end. At other times, they receive pressure from administrators with respect to the number of players who get playing time or their record of wins and losses. On yet other occasions, they feel pressure from other coaches who are vying for a player's time to train for another sport or from disgruntled but well-meaning parents. Players and parents alike need to understand the dynamics of the team structure, the role that each player is to assume, and how players are to conduct themselves on and off the court. Since team participation is a privilege, player expectations on the court and in school are justifiably higher and normally more stringent than those placed on regular school students.

Coaches can improve their performance under pressure; they can assess player potential, determine which players to cut and which to keep, and make management decisions during a match in a professional manner. Communicating diplomatically with players and parents before and throughout the season can help make the player selection process and any playing-time issues less controversial. Being fair, firm, honest, and consistent enables a coach to prepare his or her athletes to perform at a high level and helps to eliminate any misinterpretation regarding how team issues are handled. Moreover, no coach can take lightly such concerns as school, district, state, or national guidelines with which he or she must comply to ensure player eligibility for matches and team eligibility for postseason competition.

Process Your Observation

As I look back on my own coaching career, I believe the aspect that was most valuable to our program's success was my ability to observe and listen. Coaches must constantly monitor and adjust drills, team play, and the composition of the team on the court based on what they see and hear. This applies not only to the technical and tactical aspects of a game or practice session but also to the more intangible parts of the game, such as mental toughness, player leadership roles, intensity, poise, and the ability of players to make those around them better. All of these elements are critical to the pursuit of excellence. A seasoned coach can develop the ability to make good instantaneous decisions about time-out strategies, player substitutions, and player responsibilities during the two- or three-hour daily training sessions; these sessions offer the chance to gain experience in dealing with these sorts of intangibles.

While I was working on my masters' degree at Slippery Rock State College (now University), I took a class taught by John Bunn, a visiting professor, on the efficiency of human movement. In the class, we learned how to isolate and analyze human movement while an athlete was performing a skill. We reviewed several still photographs that showed only one portion of an entire athletic movement. We looked for correct body position, including arm and leg angles and body balance during the movement, and then wrote our perception of the action. We noted why the movement was efficient or gave reasons why it was not correct. Using these photographs, we eventually developed the ability to create a snapshot in our own minds as we viewed actions. With videotaping and stop-action remote control, coaches today can perform this same exercise and teach themselves to be better processors of their observations. They can learn to break down their players' skills in order to help them improve.

Players and coaches can further increase their odds of success in volleyball if they develop the ability to watch the action of all team members on the court simultaneously. This takes time and practice, but it is similar to taking a visual snapshot of the action and knowing when one or more players need to be corrected. Coaches should learn to take visual snapshots of a player's technique during his or her performance of a skill or of a player's court position within the context of the entire team coverage out on the court, while also paying attention to the nonverbal behavioral actions projected by players. With these skills, a coach can immediately give feedback to players about court positioning, body position, or technique by using specific cues when a rally is terminated on a particular play. During our matches, my assistant coaches and I watched our team almost exclusively and made specific notes beside players' names so that we could relay information or teach again a particular play. We also acknowledged positive performances.

Coaches should try to relay information as soon as possible after a play—when play has stopped, during a time-out, or between games—in such a way that players can refocus quickly. Players must also observe, listen, and be able to effectively process the information or directions they are given. Should players have difficulty picturing their errors, they can be provided with a few minutes of video to study during practice. This will help them to identify or visualize what they were doing incorrectly. If a skill needs to be taught again, this should be done in the next available practice session. Providing immediate feedback and instruction gives players the opportunity to make skill adjustments more comfortably and gives them a greater chance to retain what they have learned.

Coaches must watch their players to detect facial expressions and other types of body language that can indicate a loss of the confidence and composure necessary to move forward successfully. During practices and timeouts during matches, coaches should place themselves in a position where the athletes are forced to focus on them and from which they can see their players' eyes. Body posture can provide clues as to a player's emotional state, but the eyes can reveal doubt, concern, confusion, or, better yet, focus, determination, and confidence. As a coach, I looked for players with intensely burning eyes that made it clear that they could handle whatever came their way and could carry others if necessary. As coaches read their players, it is essential that they make every effort to know each player's "buttons," or emotional triggers, and be able to review with them how to work through frustrating events. Comments such as, "Your movement and balance were excellent, but you must prepare your platform earlier," can provide support while at the same time telling the player how to correct a technical aspect of his or her game. Or a coach may say, "Your body language indicates that you know the cause of your error, so correct it yourself." Since volleyball is a game in which mistakes are regularly made, players must develop a positive attitude and mental toughness. By acknowledging and taking ownership of their errors, players can respond by refocusing on the next play and thereby moving forward. Players also need to be cognizant of the body language of their teammates and, if necessary, take leadership roles in working with particular players to help them deal with difficult situations.

Promote the Game

The sport of volleyball has to attract young female and male athletes from the same pool of students that baseball, soccer, track and field, basketball, softball, and lacrosse do. Introducing and exposing players under the age of 14 to volleyball is all the more difficult because it is very much a rebound sport. That is, to keep the game flowing, the ball must be kept moving with control, using techniques that are uncommon and more difficult to master than those required for other sports, especially for younger players. Play in volleyball can be terminated, positively or negatively, with the first touch of the ball by one of the six players on each side of the court. Thus, the game can very quickly become frustrating or boring for players. By the same token, players in other team sports are running the field or court while using a great deal of energy without the need for controlling or even playing the ball. Volleyball, at the early stages of players' development or in physical education classes, has too many kids standing around or one or two players knocking others down to play a ball out of their area of responsibility. The overaggressive play of a player without discipline is a detriment to that particular game, and it leaves a lasting impression on the young athletes who are trying to determine if volleyball is a sport that they want to continue playing.

What can attract young athletes to our sport? A tradition of success can make the sport more attractive to those who want to be involved in a winning program. At the same time, some young athletes will leave to play other sports if a program is not a winning one. Our program relied on several factors, including recruiting siblings of former players and developing over several years a tradition of successful team experiences. Coaches and players who help to promote the sport are perhaps the most critical cog in the wheel.

• **Be visible.** Coaches should attend athletic contests in the district in which younger athletes compete and that take place during the school year and the summer. They should go to soccer, basketball, softball, baseball, and field hockey games as well as track meets. They should seek to identify competitive athletes and determine what they do in their off-seasons without directly approaching them. Off-seasons are becoming rare, however. Many players are becoming one-sport athletes who play year-round or play two sports, each of which occurs during the off-season of the other. But coaches and even players on the junior varsity and varsity teams can become involved and make themselves visible by helping during community-sponsored programs or by teaching younger players when clinics are provided before tryouts.

• **Be a recruiter.** Coaches should talk up the sport with the physical education teaching staff and work with coaches of other sports in the district to communicate the benefits to athletes of playing mutually compatible sports. Playing several sports that have similar physical demands will benefit players and ultimately improve their individual play in each sport. If you are a teacher in the district where you coach, strike up a conversation with potential players in class as well as students in the hall and ask them to try the sport. Coaches can also ask current players if they know any athletes who aren't involved in school sports and seek them out personally or send them a letter asking them to give volleyball a try.

• **Be a promoter.** Here are some examples of activities or events that my staff and I did for our volleyball program that worked for us:

  • Put on assemblies with older players during activity periods or after school at the elementary and middle (or junior high) schools in your district.

  • Run a peer-tutoring program for the physical education teachers and their classes in the district as they begin to implement their volleyball unit. Having experienced players teaching younger or newer players benefits the squad members because they have to analyze the movements and techniques of newer players and provide appropriate feedback. My staff and I got the peer-tutoring program cleared with our administration, and our players were required to be released by their teachers either by turning in work (or taking a test) early or making arrangements to do so. We even had players return to the high school to take one or two classes before going back to the middle school to finish the day.

  • Host open gyms, clinics, or a day of tournament-style "pool play," in which four or five teams are assigned to a court on which they will play each other in a round-robin tournament.

- Provide volleyball instruction through a community-sponsored summer program. In our area, a program made up of two weeks or 10 straight weekdays of instruction, each lasting 90 minutes, was the best way to implement sequential learning and ensure retention of fifth- through seventh-grade students.
- Invite students playing intramural volleyball in grades five through eight to see your team's matches. Provide them with some sort of recognition before each match or between games.
- Have a volleyball kids club that invites younger students to clinics and also provides them with special seating area at high school matches.
- Host a match featuring local college teams using your facility.
- Take players to local colleges to watch matches. Players may even want to offer to retrieve balls during collegiate matches.
- Arrange for your team to go to a team summer camp.
- Encourage players to attend individual summer camps.
- Get involved with the state association.
- Attend Junior Olympic Club tryouts and offer to evaluate athletes or to help in other ways, such as offering the use of your gymnasium for practices.
- Get involved with coaching clinics by joining the state volleyball association. Join the American Volleyball Coaches Association (AVCA).

CHAPTER 2

Player Development

A player's perception of volleyball can take many forms, depending on his or her exposure to the game. Playing the game in physical education class or at a picnic is quite different from playing in a controlled, competitive atmosphere in which three contacts per side are preferred. Early recreational exposure to volleyball isn't always conducive to good competitive play. Such a setting lacks continuous action due to ball handling errors or bullying by one or more players. This results in players not learning the progressive skills like passing, setting, and attacking that competitive play requires. Developing a sense of what competitive play entails is a key component to bringing young athletes into the sport.

In this chapter I discuss the following four components of player development:

1. **Learning to play the game**. As in all sports, some young people have been exposed to volleyball by parents or siblings and show an earlier interest and aptitude for the game. But most young people aren't physically ready to hone their skills for the game until they are at least 12. This is a good age at which to teach them the basics.

2. **Learning positions and movements**. To be successful, players must understand their role in the framework of court coverage and team flow. The game requires court coverage on and off the net; for this to be done successfully players must understand how to develop court awareness. They must learn how to position themselves on the court and move to the ball during play.

3. **Learning to react.** It takes time, focus, and discipline for players to be ready to handle an opponent's sequence of ball contacts and the speed of the game as well as the individual and team strengths of their opponents. Since players can view the ball movement on both the opponent's side of the net and their own side, they must receive numerous balls to understand when, where, and how the ball will cross the net. The best reactions result from players being focused and disciplined enough to be where they can see the ball.

4. **Learning to compete.** The ability to compete begins with thorough preparation that addresses the strengths of each player and the team as a whole, as well as a review of the strengths, weaknesses, and tendencies exhibited by the next opponent. Anticipating how each player will react and respond to what occurs on the court is critical.

Developing players into a cohesive unit requires understanding the way each player learns the game and his or her role on the team. How can the coach best introduce skills, movements, and teamwork to players while at the same time providing the necessary repetitions for them to blend into one unit? Players must be given the opportunity to learn body positions for volleyball. They also must learn corresponding footwork movements that permit them to be in position to have the most success in playing the game in the air and on the ground. Players must develop an awareness of and the ability to react to what is happening on both sides of the court, which comes about through sequential preparation. How players react and respond during competition will depend on how they react to their own mistakes and to those of their teammates.

Learning to Play the Game

When working with younger players, coaches must take into account how much information they can process and whether a particular player approaches learning in a holistic manner, learns better by breaking down the various aspects of the game, or is most comfortable with a combination of the two methodologies. Many of the drills coaches use in practice sessions with younger players are initiated and controlled by the coaches themselves. This approach can necessitate limiting the number of repetitions that each player receives or cause coaches to reduce squad size to accommodate more reps for fewer players.

As the skills of the players improve both in technique and consistency, player-initiated drills can be incorporated. This can permit several drills to be run simultaneously, allowing the coach to observe and provide feedback. The players must now control the tempo and accuracy of the drill, which gives them a role in their own improvement. As players increase their prowess, coaches can challenge them to maintain higher standards—by achieving more consecutive positive touches or a better percentage of touches to a specified target area.

Determining a Player's Readiness for the Game

The issue of player development, how early it should begin and how often players should practice, is of prime interest to those charged with the physical, mental, and social growth of student-athletes. The idea of introducing a young athlete to a sport is to whet his or her appetite and to keep the fires burning. According to Dr. Colleen Hacker, a sport psychologist at Pacific Lutheran University in Tacoma, Washington, the top reasons for children to participate in a sport include the following:

To learn and improve skills	To experience competition
To have fun	To enhance physical fitness
To be with friends	To demonstrate their competence

Notice that the list focuses on why children choose to participate and not necessarily why *adults* want them to be part of a team or program. By the same token, children withdraw from an activity when the sporting experience fails to meet their primary motivation for participation.

It is certainly a challenge to determine the age at which it is best to introduce volleyball to aspiring male and female athletes. Because of the way volleyball is played and its small court area, introducing the game too early may push kids away rather than spark their interest. Ball tracking, player movement, and first-ball contact are vital to a team's getting three touches on their side and involving up to half of the team players in each volley sequence. Poor control of the ball results in short, one- or two-contact volleys. And even if *your* team is successful, there is no guarantee that the opposing team will return the ball or keep it in play.

Also, unlike such team sports as basketball, soccer, field hockey or lacrosse in which athletes can be continually moving and getting an aerobic workout regardless of whether they touch the ball or personally score, volleyball can quickly become boring for those who aren't in on the action.

Volleyball is also unlike most other sports in that mastering a set of skills is mandatory for beginning and continuing play; you must do A before you can do B or C, and then you may begin the same sequence again, all within the same rally. The progressive nature of the skills required in this rally sport first demands that a player be able to serve to initiate play. Without a good serve, there can be no forearm pass. Without a successful forearm pass, the setter cannot set. Without an accurate set, the hitter is at a loss. In basketball, on the other hand, many players—even young ones—need only be able to catch and throw to keep a ball in play, although at some point a team will need someone to shoot. But in volleyball, players must train each individual skill to the point that they can perform it legally to keep the action going.

Except for players who have grown up with volleyball by watching siblings play, I have found the junior high or middle school years to be the most appropriate time to begin a volleyball program. Depending on their mastery of the technical aspect of ball control, some girls with early exposure in the sport may choose to participate in Junior Olympic Club programs for 10- or 12-and-under age groups. Boys in states that offer boys' volleyball can join a team through Junior Olympic Club programs beginning with the 12-and-under age group, or in seventh or ninth grade in the school setting. This later introduction to the sport for boys may help keep the fire of desire burning bright and thus circumvent some of the burnout that can come with other sports that are introduced in elementary school.

By about 12 years of age, most kids are mature enough in motor development and body strength to handle the basic volleyball skills. Still, even at this age, coaches should not be surprised to see their players' ball control skills change almost daily. For this reason, my staff and I liked to lengthen the selection period for team members of this age group to more than two weeks so we could get a clear idea of each player's abilities.

The Learning Environment

It is up to coaches to develop the appropriate environment for learning and to decide what elements are needed for effective instruction based on the skill level of the participants. A good learning environment permits players to try newly acquired skills or tactical knowledge without fear of failure or initial reprimand. Volleyball is a game of errors; this is due in large part to the need to control a ball without actually catching it. These errors can be caused by incorrect court position, poor body position, the incomplete or faulty employment of a skill or technique, lack of focus, lack of discipline, or the prowess of opponents that control the speed of the game. But players are expected to learn from their mistakes and not repeat them over and over again. When a rally is terminated either by a great play from one player or an error by another, players should adjust and move forward.

The first step a coach should take in creating a good learning environment is to have a clear sense of the capabilities of each player. How can players demonstrate their understanding or skill in meeting the objective of a particular drill, and by what standard will they be measured? Coaches need to decide what degree of learning they expect. A good goal is to have each player learn a skill well the first time it is taught so that he or she will "own" it after numerous repetitions and continue to employ it correctly. A player won't benefit from practicing a skill incorrectly.

Coaches can use the following steps to help players learn a skill well. I have taken these steps from Madeline Hunter's "Direct Instruction Model: Elements of Effective Instruction."

1. The first step is for coaches to **get the players' attention** by putting them into the frame of mind they need in order to understand what is expected of them. Players should also measure their success by their personal improvement, with the idea that they should be comfortable but not necessarily satisfied with their daily accomplishments.

2. Now the coach must **provide the information players need** to gain the knowledge and skill to perform. The information can be provided using several mediums to accommodate the players' various learning styles. Coaches should make sure to focus on only one or two aspects at a time that are critical to performance success.

3. Once this information has been presented, the **players watch as the coach or other players model the skill.** It is important that players understand what is expected of them in terms of technique, movement, position, and ball control.

4. Coaches then **give directions** that break the process into parts, keeping the steps simple, manageable, and in the correct sequence. Coaches can use teaching tactics that involve mirror instruction, footwork drills, slow-motion movements, and phantom contacts (that is, contacts without a ball) before finally putting the skill together with a ball.

5. Next comes **guided practice,** in which coaches do the steps with the players, observe the players' actions, and provide feedback.

6. Now players are asked to **do it alone.** Coaches continually check for understanding by either asking questions or requesting that players model the desired skill.

7. The coach brings closure to the training sequence by **reinforcing the major points** that the players just learned so that they can apply these skills when exposed to a similar situation in a game.

8. Finally, players need to be given the opportunity for **independent practice** to reinforce what they have learned. These practices should be repeated on a preplanned schedule in enough different contexts so that players can apply the skill to any relevant situation. Players must be able to apply the knowledge and skill in contexts other than the one in which it was learned.

Coaches need to work to reinforce players' strengths and continually repeat skill sequences to correct any weaknesses. When drilling a new skill, it is always best to keep the number of players involved to a minimum so that each player can receive maximum contacts with minimum downtime. Once the players' muscle memory has taken hold with respect to a skill, it is time to increase court area and ball speed to simulate game speed.

There are numerous drills that can be used to teach the skills and teamwork necessary to play volleyball well. Coaches need to avoid too much repetition by employing several drills that meet the same goal. I include some drill ideas in subsequent chapters; others can be found in other volleyball coaching resources at your local library or online. When a coach is exposed to new drills, either from books or attending a clinic, he or she must realistically determine which of them can be used with his or her players. This determination depends on the specific level of skill of the players.

It's important for both coaches and players to be positive, as this helps facilitate a good learning environment. Coaches can see and respond to each player's improvement by specifically commenting on what he or she has done well, while at the same time giving tips for further positive development. For example, a coach might say, "Your prejump back arm swing was great, but you need to elevate the height of your front arm swing as you lift off the ground for your maximum jump. Let's see if we can get you to jump even higher next time when you are attacking."

Coaches should communicate one on one with players, being as specific and positive as possible. When providing feedback, coaches need to make sure that what they are illustrating and what the player is hearing are the same. On many occasions, I would ask players to tell me what they thought they did well and what adjustments they could make to perform a skill even better.

© Mary Langenfeld

An outside attack versus a double block.

Coaches must also incorporate into their practices drills that permit players to excel under new interpretations of the rules of the game. Some of the most recent trends that affect the way the game is played include rally scoring, playing on when a serve hits the net, and using open-handed or overhead passing for contact on the first ball. Additional factors that are changing the game are players at each position who are taller than in the past and those who have increased athleticism, speed, and power. The game is more technically and tactically demanding than ever before with more attacking options, the addition of the libero position, and varied blocking schemes. In addition, players must continue to develop strong mental skills as well as the ability to interact well with others. The ability to see what is happening on the court and communicate quickly with teammates can provide an edge in the rapid execution of movement necessary for team success.

Learning Body Positions and Movements

Teaching players how to position themselves and react on the court is centered on reducing the number of errors they make. In learning how to react on the court, players need to focus first on seeing the ball. If a player can't see the ball, he or she is slower to react. Players must also anticipate the ball coming to them, even wanting it come to them. Wanting the ball to be hit to you increases your focus and readiness to handle it. This makes a player proactive about getting into position to do the right thing. Some specific drills that help players anticipate the ball coming to them are described in chapter 5.

For players to maximize their ability to see, move, and control the ball, they must develop solid fundamentals. This includes being in the correct body position for their court responsibilities. Whether serving or receiving, all players need to focus on their own body position and their court position in relationship to the boundaries, antennas, and their teammates. Players must give themselves and their teammates every opportunity to successfully play the ball. A player's ability to recognize where the opponent's setter is located, communicate that information quickly to teammates, track the moving ball, and anticipate what will happen greatly enhances positive ball contacts and successful team play.

It is also important that players know how to move without changing levels (that is, without bobbing up and down). Players may go lower or run "downhill" to intercept a ball inches off the ground. Those in the back row must be in a low, balanced defensive position to prepare for digging the ball, and those in the front row must be in an upright and balanced blocking position ready to jump or move each time the opponent touches the ball.

Players must know their relationship to the boundary and the antenna and how many steps it takes to use the antenna and the boundary to play the ball. Front-row players need to know how the antenna can assist the block. Back-row players need to understand how the antenna changes their area of coverage, since it reduces the court size in relationship to where the ball must now cross the net.

They must also know their area of responsibility for the defense their team is playing and where they must move based on the opponent's set. It is important for players to stop and balance each time their opponent prepares to contact the ball, even if they haven't reached their assigned area. This prevents moving the wrong way when a ball is contacted.

It is important for players to be aware of the options available to their opponent based on the direction, height, and speed of the first pass. Higher passes indicate a slower *starting* offense and provide more time to be prepared. Passes toward the sideline or away from the net reduce the opponent's ability to run a quick, middle, or combination attack.

Volleyball incorporates play above the net as well as play just inches off the floor. Players must develop the ability to control their body with balance in both the vertical and horizontal plane while moving diagonally, laterally, and vertically.

Due to differences in player height or quickness, various patterns can work, and each player can choose the movement pattern that suits his or her talents best and provides him or her with the greatest opportunity for success. Coaches should work to eliminate incorrect player movements and those that do not enhance a player's ability to be successful. Players' movements specific to their offensive and defensive role on the floor are covered in more detail in chapters 4 and 5, respectively.

The critical components of ball tracking, movement, and balance ultimately determine the level of competence a team can attain, since it is these components that control a team's ability to consistently pass the opponent's serve. Without great movement and ball control, a team cannot neutralize the opponent's serve and has difficulty defeating an equal or better team due to their inability to side-out. In all of the movement drills I provide, I advocate using three or more steps in *every* movement to ensure that no player stands flat-footed or takes one long lunge step to play the ball.

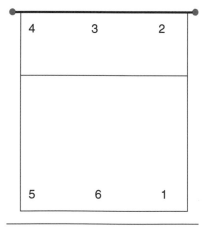

Figure 2.1 Universal court zones.

A major key is to develop players' court awareness so that they can read their opponent and anticipate what is about to happen. The best way for them to develop this awareness to is to play the game.

The numbering systems for offense vary, but the six court zones, based on the clockwise service rotation, are universal and never vary: the right-back area is 1; the middle-back position is 6; the left-back position is 5. These are shown in figure 2.1.

• **Lateral movement.** A lateral movement is a general move made horizontally to the right or left, parallel to the net. Players can use lateral movements to get into position to block, receive a serve, or cover an attack. When moving laterally, players should keep the shoulders and hips square to the net. They can rotate the shoulders and hips toward their target just before contacting the ball if they are in position early or, when necessary, while passing the ball.

• **Diagonal movement**. Diagonal movements permit players to move toward or away from the net while heading either to the right or left. This allows them to keep their vision on the ball and the upper body rotated toward the target. These movements can be used when receiving a serve, playing defense, and moving off the net in preparation to execute an attack approach.

- **Forward movement.** In forward movements, players simply lead with the right foot, even if they are left-foot dominant, as it is more difficult to turn a ball to the right when leading with the left foot. Some coaches even have their players open their hips to the right so that they always lead with the right foot. They then follow with the left foot in a walking fashion and finish with a step to the target as they pass a ball directly in front of them. The speed of the steps is dictated by the speed and trajectory of the ball. Players can use this footwork to get to a short serve or while facing the target to handle softer balls when playing defense.

Learning to Compete

Volleyball is a sport in which a loss of mastery or confident play is only a bad pass away. The rhythmic flow of a rally can change several times as the ball crosses the net. The final result of that one rally can ultimately disrupt momentum. But when a pass, set, and attack take place in the predetermined sequence, the result makes the game look almost too easy. An observer can replay the contacts in his or her mind without putting any significance on the incredible amount of training it took for the individual players to work together in controlling the ball in order to score that one point.

Being both physically and mentally ready to compete means that inexperienced participants are prepared to meet challenges as part of a cohesive team. This preparation includes developing basic physical conditioning, consistent ball-control skills, visual tracking, and court awareness through effective practice. Players must then be able to use their individual skills consistently with others when in team training sessions. Most players will be comfortable with their skills during a small, coach-directed drill. But some players may hesitate and be more robotic when trying to use the same skills at game speed and with a full squad on the floor. In a competitive situation, there are so many variables to consider. Coaches must be able to identify players whose game-time skills need improvement, as well as those whose skills are not as apparent in training but who shine during competition. The challenge is to blend players who are ready to be on the floor during games into a cohesive team and to identify situations in which uncomfortable players can achieve success.

Learning to compete also involves players preparing for their next competitive match. The ability to compete as part of a team is the result of guided, sequential training sessions. Daily drills in individual, group, and team practice sessions provide players with the repetitions necessary to improve play. A player must first establish a strong foundation of skills and then drill these skills during pressure situations, such as under game conditions at game speed.

Many of the drills throughout this book help players apply their skills under such conditions.

Skill Training

Ensuring that players are ready to compete requires that they be exposed to the correct, most proficient muscle movements and body positions for each specific technique they learn. This exposure needs to be introduced with demonstrations or videos and followed by a step-by-step sequence of instruction. As Rich Schall, boys' coach at Derry Area High School in Derry, Pennsylvania, wisely notes, "The instructor in the early stages of learning should provide knowledge of results when the player has not yet developed the internal standard of correct performance." Not only should players be able to see how to perform skills correctly, but they must also continually strive to duplicate the exact body movements necessary for consistent play. Coaches need to take into account individual adjustments that players may need to make due to differences in body type, size, arm span, or flexibility.

The body position and the movements of each skill should be taught in stop-action—each phase of the skill is held still temporarily so that feedback can be provided—and should gradually progress to one fluid movement at game speed in order to compete successfully against the top opponents. Correct movement also means using the correct technique for the ball being played. For example, players who use a lateral extension when a sprawl is called for display the ability to use defensive skills but an inability to understand which technique is most effective for that particular ball situation.

Coaches must also pay attention to each player's body position, making sure it is correct and that he or she is comfortable, and his or her individual readiness to handle the sequence of the opponent's contacts. Coaches must teach the skills necessary to meet the demands of today's style of play, but it would be irresponsible for them to fail to teach players techniques that are time- and result-tested. For example, a coach wouldn't want to consider reducing the amount of forearm-pass contacts that players receive during practices just because they are permitted to use open hands for the first contact. Great player anticipation, court awareness, positioning, and use of correct body position provide for the most controlled movements. Quick, concise movements allow players to intercept the ball within their centerline and offer the greatest opportunity to control the ball. This creates the best chance for success.

Players may correctly demonstrate a skill but do so with their own quirks. Even if those quirks don't seem to limit their play, coaches should work to change them if they prevent players from improving in the early teaching stages. Players need to understand that being taught a skill again to help break a bad habit may temporarily result in a reduction in perceived effectiveness. But in the long run the new and improved skill proficiency will raise their play to a higher level than they achieved before.

Many players have natural abilities and have developed the necessary game skills. Coaches should put such players into positions where they can control a ball using the abilities and skills that they are most comfortable with in pressure situations. For example, the best natural serve-receive passer should be responsible for the most court space so that he or she receives more of the opponent's serves.

To prepare themselves for competition, coaches must find the time to enhance their own learning and abilities. This includes improving their observation and feedback skills; their ball-control skills such as their ability to place a serve or attack a ball in a defense drill; and their capacity to make good court adjustments, player substitutions, and time-out decisions with confidence. Coaches can enhance their skills by going to clinics, asking questions of other coaches, watching other teams practice, watching videos, reading books, and observing camp training. I constantly videotaped camp training sessions for later use when teaching individuals and teams. The tapes not only show correct techniques but also provide an illustration of how the techniques can be used at greater speed.

It can also be beneficial to attend other matches as an observing coach. In 1982 I went to the NCAA semifinals held at Penn State University and charted the serve-receive patterns of the UCLA men's team. It took almost two complete games before I could understand what I had written down. I have also relied on a men's Olympic match I taped from television to see how Team USA was able to isolate their two best passers in such a way that they were responsible for the serve-receive coverage of the entire court. I then incorporated into my program things I learned from these observations, tailored to what my players could handle. Don't be afraid to challenge players and the team as a whole to raise their level of play.

Mental Training

Developing mental readiness in players is harder to do than developing their physical skills. For some athletes, mental toughness is fleeting. They may exude mental toughness when things are going their way, but they lose this confidence and begin to hesitate as soon as they make a mistake or are losing. Being mentally tough means competing intelligently, aggressively, with passion, and with a desire for the ball even when things are not going well for either the individual player or the team.

Players' psyches can be fragile. This may sound like an overstatement, but the difference in their rate of success may begin more with their toughness or competitiveness than with their mastery of skills on the court. For this reason, I recommend that coaches work into their drills and practice sessions situations that mimic the pressure of the game. This way, athletes can learn to perform and stay mentally tough even when they are losing.

Basketball coaches try to duplicate the pressure of a player shooting a foul shot to tie or win a game with no time left on the clock in practice sessions. Volleyball players must do the same by aiming a serve with accuracy to a certain zone or opposing player or trying to score with a kill from the next set. Money Ball and the scoring drills that I discuss on pages 13 and 96, respectively, are good examples of the sorts of drills that sharpen athletes' mental toughness.

The scoring system in volleyball means that it is a game of mistakes. Forced and unforced errors in today's game are worth a point for the opposite team. This is a major change from when an error by the serving team resulted only in a side-out. The mental strength of players and coaches can make the difference when playing in tight games and crucial rallies. To prepare mentally, players must be able to visualize themselves performing a skill correctly, and when a skill is performed incorrectly they must effectively adjust based upon their own observations or feedback from their coach. Should a player falter during a drill, this being evident through body language or another observable response, coaches must know the cue word or gesture that can enable that player to refocus and move forward. Players must be able to evaluate the situation in which they find themselves and, if necessary, use a relaxation technique to continue on in a positive manner. Players can learn to embrace the very essence of the game and relish the opportunity to test their skills and mental toughness against that elusive ball.

The outcome of a person's participation in any endeavor can be directly linked to one critical element—his or her attitude. Attitude is more important than failures, successes, or even what other people think, say, or do. It is more important than being gifted or skilled. Most important, we have a *choice* about the attitude that we embrace each day. I think Charles Swindoll, author of the article "Attitude," is correct when he says, "life is 10% what happens to me and 90% how I react to it." We are in charge of our attitudes. Players may enhance or retard their development by the way they react and respond to what happens to them or their team. A player's taking ownership of his or her own development can be the key to moving forward.

CHAPTER 3

Team Selection and Cohesion

How do coaches and players create that team-first philosophy and get everyone on the same page: reaching for the individual and team goals that have, up to this point, been only dreams? One way is to replace the *ifs* with *whens.* That is, coaches and players need to see their goals as truly attainable.

There are many ways that both coaches and players can create a team-first philosophy for the program. My staff and I used a few approaches to emphasize training focus, team play, and cohesiveness during the season. For example, before each day's practice we would post in the locker room the daily practice plan and a motto for the day. Each player knew that at some point during the practice one of them would be required to quote the motto and interpret it for the team. Another tactic some of our teams have employed is to use the word "family" near the end of each team discussion or huddle. My recent players really enjoyed ending each workout by saying three letters, each letter signifying a word that summarized my perception of how the practice went. Some examples are NST (no support today), GCT (good communication today), FIT (fantastic intensity today), GFT (great focus today), GTP (great target passes), and so on. I would not tell the athletes what my three letters stood for so that they would have to formulate their own phrase. Before leaving the gymnasium, the players would come individually or in groups to see if their phrase was the same as mine or an even better reflection of the day's work. I'd also get some pretty funny responses.

There are ways to help build team cohesion off the court, most of which involve teammates simply getting together for such activities as regular pasta dinners, bowling, going to the movies, and so on. Teammates can also bond by attending training camps during the summer or holding a tie-dying event to create team warm-up shirts. The idea is to get together off the court and to do so regularly, at least once a month, even during the off-season.

I cannot say enough about the importance of team chemistry and having supportive contributors make up your team. My staff and I preferred to refer to all our team members as contributors rather than using terms like starter, seventh person, or role player. We looked for competitors who could finish and who wanted the ball when the game or match point was on the line. Coaches can see team support develop spontaneously just by watching how players react to a play that has just been completed. Those players who aren't in the game but who are cheering for their teammates provide the perfect model of the kind of continuous support that leads to solid team cohesion.

Forming a Team

Forming a cohesive team begins with selecting competitive athletes who show a strong work ethic. Yet, it is even more important to select good kids who attempt to make positive decisions on and off the court. At the developmental (middle school to junior varsity) level, athletes don't have to possess great skill, but they should show receptivity by listening, trying, and putting energy into their efforts. Good players rather than great players tend to make up the bulk of the squad. Such players—who focus on doing the little things correctly—are successful because they develop good skills, attempt to use the correct techniques for the situation, and work to achieve good movement to the ball so that they play the ball and the ball doesn't play them.

After several practice sessions early in the season, my coaching staff and I looked for players who attempted to make smart decisions, displayed court awareness, showed a competitive spirit, and were willing to support and encourage their teammates. It is important to identify the players who relish the opportunity to pass the serve or take a swing at the ball when the other team is serving the game or match point. The toughest situation facing a coach is to be able to identify those young players who are resistant to pressure and have strong finishing power.

There are several factors that affect player selection. Coaches need to determine how many players they need or would like to have move through their program. For example, the program I worked with pulled seventh and eighth graders from three middle schools as well as the parochial schools in the area. So I started with 30 or so young athletes, aware that not all of them would stick with volleyball over the next five years. We would end up with 15 or 16 ninth-grade players, 12 to 15 tenth-grade players, and 8 to 10 each of junior and senior players.

The size of a squad also depends on what positions a coach needs to fill, space considerations (that is, how many courts are available or how much gym space the team will have for practices), how many coaches are available for the team, and how much playing time would be realistic for each player. Coaches need to figure out how to choose players who will complement their program through the years, based on who is graduating, what positions will be vacated, and how many players at each position are currently working their way to the varsity level. It is important to determine how to test and evaluate players at tryouts and foster a positive atmosphere during this stressful selection process. The way these considerations are addressed may differ depending on whether the program is a club team or a scholastic team.

Determining Player Needs

Club programs may have several teams in each age group that are grouped according to the players' abilities. This format allows each program the option of entering several of their teams in different tournaments. The selection of players for club programs depends on the desired squad size and how much playing time each player can expect to receive. Athletes pay a nominal fee to try out, which may go to gymnasium rental time or be applied to the overall club fees once the athlete plays for the club. After tryouts a letter is sent to each player's home explaining to him or her where he or she would fit into the program. Players and parents then decide whether they will accept their option. The top club teams generally limit their squad size to eight or nine players. This reduces the number of specialist substitutions a team can make and, with the exception of the libero, may even prevent the coach from selecting back-row specialists. The smaller squad size also provides each player with more opportunities for technical and tactical training, as well as more time on the court during match play. In this format, the top players can be showcased at large tournaments in front of numerous college recruiters.

A club squad of eight or nine players may choose to keep two setters, two or three swing hitters, two middle hitters (who could be replaced by a libero), and two back-row specialists (or two players who can sub in to the front or back row). When coaches are evaluating players' talent, they should look for certain characteristics that may help them visualize the player in a specific position or with a specific role. The following is a list of positions and brief profiles for each:

- **Setter**. A setter gets to the ball for the second contact to deliver it effectively to a teammate for the attack. To play this position, a player must have the physical ability to get to every ball and to use his or her hands. The setter must also be able to put a ball in a location where a teammate can get a positive touch on it. The ability to get his or her hands above the net when in the front row and to dig balls in the back is also a good prerequisite. A player with strong will power, a confident personality, big shoulders, poise, and leadership skills does well in the setter role.

- **Swing hitter.** Swing hitters control the first and the third balls. This position requires a player to accept the responsibility and handle the pressure of passing the opponent's serve as well as attacking the third ball for a real point. The swing hitter should be able to block and be a good or even great defensive player. If you are lucky enough to have three swing hitters on your team, the third can be a player who is able to play on both the right and left sides or possibly in the middle.

- **Middle hitter.** This position is also often called middle attacker. A taller player with good horizontal and diagonal footwork normally fills this position. It requires the ability to block as well as the ability to transition off the net to attack various sets. A hard-working player, the middle hitter often doesn't get the recognition from spectators that other players do. Good middle hitters get satisfaction from setting the offensive tempo of the game as they attempt to keep the opposing middle occupied.

- **Back-row specialist.** This player should be comfortable with his or her serving and passing skills and be an aggressive defensive player. The back-row specialist accepts the challenge to not let the ball hit the floor.

- **Libero.** This is a newer position for a player who enters and plays back row as a passer and defensive player. A collegiate female libero can go in for both of the middle hitters but can only serve in one rotation during each game and cannot set in front of the 10-foot (3-meter) line. The male libero cannot serve according to current rules of play.

Squad size can be adjusted by adding a player to fill any position as well as identifying a couple of players that could be the libero. It is beneficial on larger teams to consider having as many players of different age levels as possible represented in each position. This allows the program to continue to develop. When squads have 15 or more players over the course of the season, it is not unusual for players to improve to the point that they force the coach to find a way to get them some added playing time. Situations also arise in which a player becomes injured or is not available for a particular tournament. Adjustments must be made by either moving a player from another squad or playing with one less player.

Scholastic programs may be required to follow the squad size guidelines set forth by their school district and its athletic department. Some districts mandate a no-cut policy, which states that every player who comes out must be given a place on the team. Other policies may dictate how big a squad should be (for example, a minimum of 15 players) rather than letting the coach make this determination. Both situations can cause problems for coaches who may have inadequate space and, as a result, have to limit the number of contacts that each player gets in order to ensure that all players get equal playing time. This limits the flexibility of the game strategy as well. It is very difficult to demonstrate consistent success or have a positive record of wins and losses when such policies are in place.

Other coaches may encounter problems with getting potential players to come out for the team and, for this reason, keep everyone who tries out. When this occurs, a player may be put into a court position out of necessity rather than because it best suits his or her abilities. This can happen, moreover, regardless of the player's readiness to compete. Smaller schools do not have the number of students that

As players improve their ability to contribute on the court, the coach will find a way to increase their playing time.

large schools do from which to draw players. All the sports compete for the same small pool of student-athletes.

For scholastic teams, keeping a squad of at least 12 players enables all players to be on the court during team drills and therefore provides each player with more repetitions than he or she might get on a larger team. But having just 12 players may not provide enough competition within the team or give it enough flexibility if any players become injured, ill, or academically ineligible. So this number should be considered a bare minimum.

I was fortunate as a coach in that I was never told how many players to keep or how much playing time each should have. Rather, my coaching staff and I independently decided each year what our squad size would be at the middle school, junior varsity, and varsity levels, and we would make these determinations based on a five-year plan. We kept at least 15 players on our middle school and junior varsity squads. Our varsity squad size was closer to 20, with a goal each year of having at least eight seniors and eight juniors. We wanted each group of eight to include two left-side hitters, two middle hitters, two setters (or a setter and a right-side hitter), and two back-row specialists—one being trained to play the middle-back, or 6, position and the other trained to play the left-side, or 5, position.

When selecting players, we would consider whether an individual athlete could contribute to the team, even if that contribution was made mostly during practice. We would also make sure both the athlete and his or her parents were comfortable with that situation. Larger squads permitted us to continue to have good competitors when players moved, decided to concentrate on another sport, or were injured. For many years, the substitute entry rules permitted each player three entries with no team total. As a result, more players were able to contribute during games. Now the National Federation of State High School Association rules provide for unlimited individual substitutions while regulating team totals, so coaches must be more careful with the entries. Under the new rules, we found success by alternating players over complete games rather than during a game.

Our five-year plan demanded that we take a long-term view of the squad makeup. At the middle school level, when we were not able to distinguish between the playing ability of two players, we kept both players. We also kept an additional player when we anticipated that a conflict might arise with a two-sport player once he or she reached the junior varsity level in two sports that overlapped.

Occasionally, however, we would have a varsity team on which a portion of the starters were freshmen or sophomores, even though we had a large school. If the freshmen and sophomores couldn't start for the varsity squad, they would play junior varsity. Some young players would be in uniform for the varsity match in case they might be given the opportunity to play. Our first girl's state championship team was made up of 12 seniors, four of whom alternated games. That year we had our smallest junior class ever with five members. Our starting setter and other contributing players were sophomores. The five juniors had the luxury of competing daily against the seniors in practice. The following year, these five confident new seniors started and provided leadership for the returning sophomores, two starting freshmen, and other newcomers. They won the state championship again, and the following year the blend of players won again.

Selecting Players With Tryouts

Coaches and those who assist in team tryouts must learn how to evaluate the tangible skills and identify the intangibles that can make candidates good team members. A varsity coach who is coordinating a tryout for middle school or junior high players also needs to take into consideration how he or she envisions younger players fitting into the program five years down the road.

Players can contribute to a program in many ways, and coaches need to consider these ways as they make selections. For some players, being a member of the team and program may do more for them personally than for the team, in the traditional sense of actually contributing on the court. One female player that I selected in eighth grade was diagnosed with Hodgkin's lymphoma between her sophomore and junior years. A spot was saved for her on the squad, and she attended practices and matches as often as her treatment and stamina allowed. She might participate for an hour twice a week or stay for an entire session once a week. She attended all the home games, participated in warm-ups, cheered from the bench, and occasionally entered a match and played. Her teammates drew strength from her determined attitude, and she inspired all to play harder.

When possible, coaches should attempt to select left-handed players for the team. I've always considered this a plus. During tryouts I'd set up most of the initial court drills from the right side of the court to provide left-handed players with better vision and timing in the initial learning stages. Teams with left-handed setters and opposites (right-side hitters) change opponents' blocking angles and give them additional coverage concerns.

Answering the following list of questions helped me and the coaches with whom I worked to prepare for effective team tryouts and squad selection.

1. How much time (if any) is available to hold skills clinics before tryouts in order to introduce the skills that will be evaluated?
2. How many people can assist in evaluating players' skills during tryouts?
3. How many courts or how much space is available for testing?
4. How many balls are available to provide players with as many touches as possible?
5. How many teams compete at each grade level, or are grade levels mixed together to form a school team?
6. Does the school have a no-cut policy or a minimum squad size to which coaches must adhere?
7. How many players can you realistically get into matches?
8. With rally scoring and 18 entries, will you have enough players to substitute at more than two positions?
9. Does your district or state have the libero position?

Skills Testing

Using a series of tests (such as height and reach measurements; vertical jumps; kneeling ball throws; quickness tests; and evaluation of passing, setting, and serving) helps coaches to see some of the genetic gifts potential players may have. Don't overlook a tall player whose athleticism may still be catching up with his or her body. As coaches often joke, "You can't teach height." Coaches will want to evaluate whether taller players show good footwork and jumping ability such that their height is even more of an asset. (Note that many girls have reached their full height by grades eight or nine, whereas boys often do not reach their full height until they are in grades 11, 12, or even later).

It is also important for coaches to test players' ability to throw a ball and jump vertically. Both of these skills lend themselves to being strong in the front row. With normal daily repetitive jumping in practice and additional strength training, players can increase their overall jump height, but genetics will still be a primary factor in their jumping ability. Tall players with long arms may be able to contribute at the net, and with extensive training, just might become dominant players. Coaches may also want to test for tracking vision and passing form. With mental toughness and an ability to handle an opponent's serve, these athletes can keep a team in every game.

In some form or other, my staff and I used the following physical skills testing to identify players with potential in the sport.

- Standing reach.
- Standing vertical jump (best of three attempts). No steps are permitted but players use a prelift back arm swing and sequential front-lift arm swing.
- Approach jump (best of three attempts). Players use steps to develop a takeoff.
- Ball throw (best of three attempts). Players perform from a kneeling position and then standing, using correct throwing form.
- Standing long jump (best of three attempts).
- Four-line agility run. Coaches time this run. Players run from the end line to the 10-foot (3-meter) line and back, from the end line to the center line and back, from the end line to the far 10-foot (3-meter) line (ducking the net) and back, and finally from the end line to the far end line and back. If there is concern about the players ducking the net safely or if there are time constraints, you can modify this test by making it a two-line agility run. This keeps the players on one side of the net for two sprints, and it becomes a test of quickness rather than conditioning.
- Athletic catch. Players (one to catch and one to toss) start at positions on the court that the coach designates. The player designated as the leader moves the ball as the athlete being tested either opens his or her hip accordingly or steps back to the side to which the ball is being moved. The leader tosses the ball to see if the candidate can close the distance to the ball and catch it over his or her shoulder.

Technique Evaluation

My program had our older junior varsity and varsity players in the district demonstrate to newer players correct techniques and form. This works in tryouts as well. It allows the older players to be role models and later in the season to possibly act as mentors to the players with whom they have worked. This also provides the older players with some ownership of the program and a tangible sense of carrying on a tradition.

Older players teaching younger players benefits the experienced squad members because they are asked to do more than demonstrate a skill and break it down for the newer players. They must also observe and analyze the techniques of the younger players. This reinforces correct form in their own play. We also asked the older players to provide the coaches with information on what they saw, such as the younger players' listening skills, attitude, ability to cooperate, willingness to show effort, and energy level. The younger players were given numbers to put on their backs so that they were evaluated as anonymously as possible. This avoided built-in biases when evaluating their play.

Players should be evaluated with respect to their form; ball control; and the consistency of their techniques for the forearm pass, overhead pass, attack, and serve. For the forearm pass, overhead pass, and attack, two to four players form lines and work with their evaluators. When possible, coaches should put two experienced players together. One such player is designated the leader and tosses or passes a ball back and forth with a player who is trying out while the other experienced player records the candidate's technique and success based on a 0 to 3 point scale, with 3 being a perfect pass to target and 0 being an error. For the serve, each candidate uses an underhand or overhand technique to complete nine total serves, with three serves each into the three different court zones—the right third of the court (zones 1 and 2), the middle third of the court (zones 3 and 6), and the left third of the court (zones 4 and 5).

Next, coaches need to evaluate movement and play under gamelike conditions. Two older players are part of a six-person team. These two players are positioned in the front and back middle. The most important rule for play is that the front middle player sets the second ball. A candidate will later replace him or her so that the candidate sets the second ball. One older player remains in the back middle to vocally help coordinate and be available to touch the first or third ball. This drill permits coaches to evaluate how much a candidate understands about the sport and how a play flows from the action taking place around him or her. The drill is important to separate the candidate's playing ability from his or her skill-repetition ability.

Once the candidate's level of ability and understanding has been established, the planning of sequential learning sessions can begin (see chapter 10). The goal is to establish solid, consistent fundamentals that translate into positive player development. Take care to progress at a rate that all players can handle.

Gamelike Scenarios

While testing is one facet of tryouts, I recommend that tryouts provide players with as many gamelike situations as possible. Testing really only identifies those players who seem to have the most going for them in terms of volleyball-specific skills and genetic athleticism, whereas watching players in gamelike action gives a coach a better reference for what a player's potential is. Drill sessions also do not give the full picture of the sorts of qualities players might have that would benefit the squad. Players who are average when doing drills may shine during actual play because they have the ability to see and understand the flow of the game and anticipate what should be done. By the same token, players who demonstrate exceptional skill during drill sessions may freeze up during continuous action or may be conservative in their play, as they are unaccustomed to making a mistake and don't respond well to pressure. Playing in gamelike situations provides some athletes the chance to shine and gives coaches a sense of those extra intangibles they need to make a sound evaluation of a player.

During tryouts, coaches can create some scrimmage situations that help players work through rally points. Even though the scrimmages are controlled, players feel the pressure of being watched and trying to make the team. By watching them play, coaches can also identify players who react selfishly or negatively, exhibit poor listening skills, or are not receptive to constructive criticism. These players could be disruptive to the team and program. Some athletes may also demonstrate that they can be verbal leaders who can quickly communicate with others whose court awareness is not as well developed. Scrimmaging also allows a coach to identify how different combinations of players might affect team chemistry and to differentiate players according to their ability to react and positively handle balls that trap an attack swing on the net or other unusual shots and deflections.

On many occasions, the tryout process is pressure-filled for young athletes. If tryouts are held over just one day, a coach may not see an athlete at his or her best. I therefore recommend providing at least four days of tryouts to make the initial cuts and up to six more days to determine the final squad. This allows coaches to get a better feel for players. If a coach is unable to separate between two players, keep them both and let them differentiate themselves from one another in skill and talents over the course of the season. If a coach has to limit his or her squad size and can elect only one of the players, select the one that seems more competitive. Although team chemistry is part of the equation, the more competitive athlete will not only be successful individually but will improve the play of those around him or her.

Playing As a Team

Once a group of players has been selected, daily training together will further encourage each player to use his or her assets in a way that best helps the team. Players will begin to understand their role is on the team as well.

A player's attitude carries over to how he or she perceives and reacts to his or her role on the team. There is a special skill in putting together a successful team. Most teams have one or more players who can always be counted on to fill in for an injured, sick, or struggling player. These contributors may have one great talent but otherwise may be average players. I once coached a middle hitter who possessed great blocking hands and pretty good timing, but he was not quick enough to pass or transition as the team needed. Still, he fulfilled a valuable role in the third game of the state quarterfinals when we faced a team with a great right-side hitter. We inserted him into the lineup to replace our outside hitter and now had two middle hitters. His role was to block from the middle while our other middle hitter played left side to make the best use of his attacking skills. We not only were able to block the opponent's great right-side hitter, but the opposing team, in turn, was not able to block our "new" left-side hitter. This role player was a vital cog in the success of our team in this situation and others like it.

Players and coaches alike need to know what it means to be a contributor. In a perfect world, it would be advantageous for athletes to play two sports—one as a starter and one as a role player for the team. This would allow players to understand what other players on their team experience.

Many high school players who play on average teams choose the club route in order to have the opportunity to play with more talented players and against more competitive teams. But *how* a team plays really is more important than *who* that team plays. The challenge that players or coaches confront and the subsequent satisfaction they derive from helping to raise the team's level of play to the point that the team achieves greater success than expected is what makes competing such a natural high.

A team can accomplish many things if it is made up of a cohesive group of players who are willing to fight the odds. Individual players working together to keep the ball from hitting the floor in their court while making the other team react to their own play is what teamwork is all about. Donna Pfeifer, a coaching colleague of mine from a neighboring school, has said many times, "We can be successful if we have three dedicated, hard-working, pretty talented teammates from every class." Combine those players with players who want to help raise the level of play and go for it!

Learning individually and as a team to develop a work ethic, raise each member's level of play, and overcome adversity and disappointments is very challenging day to day, but it is also what makes the sport and being a part of a team so rewarding in the end. By learning to work together, filling various roles depending on team needs, earning respect and trust, being leaders, and being resilient and supportive of each, players begin to appreciate the importance of team cohesion. As I discussed in chapter 1, it takes time and work for coaches to help players buy into the importance of a team-first philosophy as opposed to a me-first philosophy. Coaches must work hard to blend the varied personalities within the team—quiet and boisterous players, calm and nervous ones, as well as flamboyant and modest personalities. Many players will buy into the team-first philosophy early, some will join later, and others may never get it. But it's important for a coach to keep trying. Teaching players how to be team members will not only help the volleyball program, it will also help players throughout their lives.

Teamwork in volleyball means that players learn to improve the flow of the ball during play. Each player's goal is to *better* the ball, so that no matter what kind of ball contact a player receives from a teammate, his or her efforts should be oriented toward improving the situation. This is what teamwork is all about.

CHAPTER 4

Offensive Skills

Volleyball, like many sports, is kinder to those who have good movement skills, body control, and balance and who consistently use correct techniques. Yet, unlike other sports, volleyball leaves little room for error since its rules permit only one rebounding contact. Players with excellent depth perception and natural tracking skills are likely to have a good feel for where the ball is going and to get themselves into position for a positive contact. Repetition, repetition, and more repetition—with emphasis on perfect form—is what enables any player to enhance his or her skills. The naturally gifted athlete should be able to make better last-second adjustments for a positive contact, but he or she should not get into the habit of merely relying on his or her athleticism.

There are several offensive skills that all volleyball players must perfect to play at their best. The serve may be a more critical component of the offense than previously thought due to the error to ace ratio. Therefore both effective serving and the passing of an opponent's tough, controlled serve are vital skills necessary to score points. In addition, players must have the ability to consistently transition from any kind of pass to an offensive strategy. Subsequent to the controlled serve-receive pass, offensive play depends on the setting and attacking aspects which I cover in later sections of the chapter.

Serving

The serve, although somewhat neutralized by the legal double-contact by an opponent's hands, is still among the most important ways that individual players can contribute to the team effort. Players who develop an accurate, tough serve enhance their team's chances for success in volleyball. A service error in today's game not only gives the ball back to the opponent (that is, causes a side-out) but also results in a point for the other team. Players must develop confidence in being able to serve consistently and effectively to a specific player or a weak area in the opponent's receiving pattern. By serving in a way that challenges the opposing team, a player gives his or her team a greater chance of directly scoring a point, limiting the opponent's offensive options, or getting a free ball.

The two basic types of serves are categorized by the ball's movement and rotation. These are the classic floater serve and the standing or jumping topspin serve. A floater serve results in unpredictable ball movement for the receiving team's players. Because solid contact on the ball in one spot produces erratic ball movement and the toss and contact are a little more natural, the floater serve is a good first option for most players. Younger players begin with an underhand swing, and as they become stronger they progress to using their natural throwing motion and contact the ball with an overhand swing. However, more players are experimenting with a standing or jumping topspin serve as an alternative threat to challenge opponents. With the additional use of the back-row attack, today's players are more comfortable with their toss, steps, and ball contact from the 30-foot (9-meter) service distance.

The server starts in a vertical upright position. When using an overhand throwing motion, he or she remains upright throughout the serve. But when using an underhand serve, he or she leans forward from the waist until after the ball has been contacted.

Players need to develop their own rhythm and sequence for initiating a serve. This routine, similar to a basketball player preparing to shoot a freethrow, permits them to clear the mind and visualize a successful serve. Players first select the area behind the end line from which to begin the process. The next step is to determine the distance behind the line from which to serve. Players who use a jump serve or need to develop more forward body momentum start further behind the end line.

Some players start with their feet balanced and shoulder-width apart and then step forward as they toss the ball. Other players find that a heel-to-toe postion, with the toe of the back foot aligned with the heel of the front foot, is a comfortable stance from which to begin the serve. Players must also determine whether they wish to take a full step forward, a partial step forward, or no step at all. The lead foot (left foot for a right-handed server) should point or step to the player or area to which the serve is directed. The server is not trying to beat opposing players by surprising or faking them out but relies, rather, on the speed and movement of the served ball. Placing the lead foot in the correct position helps the server square the hips and shoulders toward that intended target, which improves the chances for a successful serve. A jump serve involves a step-toss-jump sequence in which the player elevates off the ground as he or she stretches to attack the ball.

The Toss

Once the server has established a comfortable foot position, he or she prepares to toss the ball with both hands, with the serving hand or with the non-serving hand. The straight nonserving hand lowers with the ball, then, as one non-bending unit, the arm lifts up from the shoulder to toss the ball to the reach height of the server (figure 4.1). The serve is similar to a tee shot in golf in that players need to focus on the ball, even though they often want to see where the ball is going and thus make the mistake of shifting their head before ball contact. This can result in a mis-hit on the hand contact surface or a ball driven out of bounds. It is ideal to practice the step-toss without actually contacting the ball. This allows for repetition of sequential movements without the concern associated with making positive contact.

For a floater serve, the ball needs to be above and slightly in front of the striking shoulder, just high enough to bring the serving arm and hand forward with the arm at full extension on ball contact. The server wants to contact a nonmoving ball—one that has stopped going up and is about to start coming down, so that the ball is not traveling down through the striking zone when contacted. He or she should contact the ball slightly below its center to make its initial movement forward and slightly upward.

Before the toss, the server must decide if he or she will hold the serving arm and hand above and behind the shoulder and head

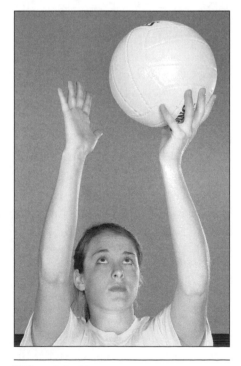

Figure 4.1 The toss.

(this is called the bow-and-arrow position) or whether he or she will move the arm up and behind as the ball is tossed. A server having difficulty timing the toss should consider holding the contact arm up and in position to move forward.

A toss above the shoulder results in the ball taking a more arched trajectory, whereas contact in front of the shoulder produces a flatter serve. A ball tossed behind the shoulder initially makes it a little easier to create a standing topspin serve. To perform such a serve, contact the ball low on its back side with an open hand and fingers wrapping around and over it. This wrapping motion generates the topspin. A player tossing for a jump serve starts further behind the end line so he or she can take two or more approach steps. The toss needs to be higher and further in front of the server, and the ball may have overspin due to the wrist action of the toss.

Hand Positions at Contact

The theory behind a floater serve is to have one surface of the hand contact one centered spot on the ball with no subsequent movement of the hand or the wrist. The topspin serve requires more hand surface on the ball and a different follow-through to impart more ball rotation. Floater servers need to experiment by using various hand surfaces to make contact with the ball to determine the one that is the most comfortable and therefore will result in more consistent serves.

For the **cupped hand**, a player places the fingers tightly against each other and the thumb tightly against the index finger (figure 4.2a). There should be a slight flexion at the knuckles closest to the palm area. As a result, the heel of the hand, the side of the thumb, and the tight fingers form a concave contact surface. It is a solid surface and one that some use to make an attack contact, but it is not the largest possible surface.

For the **solid-flat hand,** the server spreads the fingers and thumb apart. He or she can also tilt the fingers back slightly. The surface is wide and solid, with contact on the palm of the hand. A server forms the **three-quarter fist** by bending the first knuckle of each finger down and placing the thumb alongside the index finger. The contact surface is the fingernails and the heel of the hand.

The **full fist** is formed by folding the first and second knuckles down toward the heel of the hand and placing the thumb alongside the index finger (figure 4.2b). This provides the smallest surface for ball contact, but it can also offer servers what they may consider to be a more natural feel. This gives them more confidence that they will make solid contact. This technique can prove problematic, however, in that servers may strike the ball slightly off-center or only contact the ball with a portion of the fist. I have seen players generate more power on contact with this hand position, but I have also seen it produce many service errors.

Arm Action

Once the throwing motion has been initiated and the ball has been contacted, what does the server do with his or her arm? For a floater serve, the arm can continue in the same direction as the line of flight of the ball and finish along

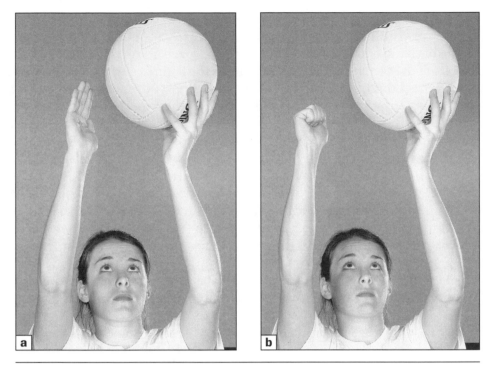

Figure 4.2 The cupped-hand serve (*a*) and the full-fist serve (*b*).

the serving-side hip. If the serving arm continues to follow through on a path across the body or outside the line of the shoulder, the resulting serve goes off course. The arm can also stop once contact has been made, if the server bends the elbow slightly and pulls the hand back toward the body. The impact of the hand contact and the speed of the arm swing direct the ball. As the hand contacts the ball for a floater serve, there should be absolutely no movement in the wrist or with the fingers. With a topspin serve, on the other hand, the wrist should snap and there should be maximum hand and finger rotation over the top of the ball to generate spin. Some players, contacting the ball at 2 o'clock, are not only able to impart topspin but also can add cross-spin to produce a ball that curves downward and toward the sideline.

I mentioned previously that there are two basic kinds of arm swings, underhand and overhand. The underhand arm swing involves a pendulum motion that generates the arm speed necessary to have the power to serve the ball at least 30 feet (9 meters) so as to clear the net. The arm is held straight through the movement, and the hand position used is a matter of individual choice. The shoulder and arm muscles control the entire motion. The most common mistake that servers make with the underhand arm swing is tossing the ball into the air before contact. This forces the player to contact the ball as it is moving downward, which increases the chance of an error. Instead, the ball should be held in the hand of the nonswinging arm as if on a platform. Just before the hand of the swinging arm comes into contact with the ball, the server removes the platform hand to permit contact. Another common mistake made with this serve is using a closed fist turned vertical. This reduces the size of the contact surface and pulls the arm across the body on contact, which results in the serve going out of bounds to the side opposite the serving arm. With any serve, the contact surface (the palm if the hand is open) should face the ball and the direction of the subsequent serve.

More experienced players or those with a natural sense of the arm swing movement use the overhand arm swing for serving. This requires shoulder and hip rotation prior to the hand contact as well as a sense of the arm speed needed to propel the ball the minimum distance to cross the net into the opponent's court. For an overhand serve, the arm's natural throwing motion is used with the arm initially bent and straightening on contact. Servers must decide whether they want the contact to produce topspin or a floater. I like to alternate during all warm-up drills between a serve with topspin and a stiff-wrist floater to force servers to learn how to control their hands in order to provide the proper contact surface to produce the desired effect.

The plane through which the arm travels has a definite effect on the contact and ensuing follow-through. Many younger players, in my experience, are unable to control their arm swing through the entire process of serving. At some point in the swing, either before or after contact, the elbow drops down and inward toward the body or the hand flies out away to the side. Both of these movements cause erratic ball flight and service errors.

The speed of the arm swing determines the distance of the serve, as well as the time it takes the ball to get to the receiver. A player serving a floater can get more movement on the ball by speeding up his or her arm and striking the ball harder when serving from a greater distance behind the end line. To increase the velocity and rotation on a topspin serve, a server should increase his or her arm speed and the quickness of the hand snap over the ball. Increased speed and rotation produces a tighter spin and causes the ball to drop more rapidly. Many serve receivers try to read the arm swing and the movement on the ball, so the server should try to make every serve arm swing identical. The change in serving distance should come from the acceleration or deceleration of the serving arm and should provide an advantage to the server as it is more difficult to read by the passers than a distinct change in arm motion. Several of the drills I use to improve serve control involve a partner, a net, a call for correct ball contact for the type of serve used, and an emphasis on controlling arm speed.

Serving Strategy

Players need to develop the ability to make tough, playable serves that force the opponent to move. I have seen many hard floaters or vicious topspin serves that, because of their initial trajectory, are easily seen by the opponent to be traveling out of bounds. Therefore, the opponent knows that these serves do not have to be played. Developing a good serve requires recognizing and attacking an opponent's weakness by directing a serve to a receiver who has committed an error on a pass or has just come into the game. In addition, each reception pattern

Jump Serve

Players have long shown a keen interest in attempting the jump serve. It has become even more popular now that net contact on a serve does not end play and more players are comfortable attacking from the back row. The critical elements of an effective jump serve are the toss, the footwork required to jump properly, and the ability to coordinate the arm swing and hand contact to the proper spot on the ball (figure 4.3a).

When teaching the jump serve, my staff and I began by having players work on tossing and taking a two-step approach to jumping. Instead of hitting the ball, however, they just caught it at first. Once they developed proper timing when jumping and catching, we added the arm swing with ball contact to propel the ball to a partner who was also 15 feet (4.5 meters) from the net but on the other side. The distance from the partner was increased once the player served consistently at that distance.

A jump-floater serve should have a flatter trajectory due to the increased hand height from the jump (figure 4.3b). The ball should be contacted at a three o'clock position on the ball, as opposed to the four or five o'clock position that is used for a topspin serve.

Figure 4.3   Tosses for the jump serve (*a*) and the jump-floater serve (*b*).

has inherent soft areas that can be exploited. A good serving option in today's game is a serve that is played inside the 5-foot (1.5-meter) line, by someone other than the opponent's middle hitter. This short serve can disrupt the hitters' attack angles and force the opponent to use more a standard type of offense.

Coaches also must consider several variables when deciding what serving strategy to teach. These variables include

- whether or not they have the option of entering serving specialists at least once a game. These serving specialists count toward the 18 total entries for a game. Coaches using serving specialists should also strive to have the best players on the court at the end of the game without having reached the maximum entries. This strategy also involves saving one entry so that a critical player can be entered in a tight game.

- whether or not coaches can set up the initial team rotation so that the first three serving spots are filled by the team's best three servers. This ensures that the best servers get the most opportunities to serve in each game.

- whether or not they are going to signal the service zones on each play. This takes the pressure of making this decision off the server. It does, however, put pressure on the server to serve where the coach indicates. A server who demonstrates his or her own awareness of where to serve shows an understanding of game strategy.

- whether or not the team has received instructions about a receiver to whom the server should or should not serve. Servers knowing to whom they should not serve show good listening skills and the ability to respond effectively to the opponent's receiving pattern.

- whether or not there are servers who can serve to weak receiving areas. A server can also take receivers out of their intended offensive pattern by serving to a weak area. This may force a less capable player to receive the serve or interrupt the intended attack angles of the opponent's hitters.

- whether or not they would prefer to have each server use his or her best serve and direct it to the area he or she can hit most consistently. When a server serves to this area, it forces the opponent to field the ball instead of letting the ball go out of bounds—which can happen when the server is trying to serve to an area with which he or she has had little or no success. Basically players and coaches must decide if it is better to force opponents to play the ball or try to surprise or ace them.

- what to tell the server who is serving directly after a time-out. One time-out strategy that may be used by the opponent is to disrupt the rhythm of a server who has been successful on his or her previous two or three serves. Coaches should ask the server to start the rhythm over and concentrate on forcing the opponent to play the ball. I've heard a coach joke that if he had a nickel for every serve missed coming out of a time-out, he could take his family on a vacation.

Serving is one aspect of volleyball in which players can strive for consistency without a partner. Players can serve against a wall, or serve 20 consecutive balls taken from a carrier over the net and then retrieve the balls and start the drill again. The following are good, basic drills to help improve players' serves.

CATCH-BOUNCE

FOCUS

Players should avoid changing their motion when serving to different receivers (who are at varying depths), as this gives away the intent of the serve. The motion should remain the same; the speed of the server's arm and subsequent contact allows the ball to travel short or deep.

PROCEDURE

Partners face one another across the net; three other sets of partners can share the court and net at the same time.

1. Two players face one another across the net with 20 feet (6 meters) between them; each player starts on his or her own 10-foot (3-meter) line.

2. One player serves a flat serve, a floater or topspin, that crosses the net no higher than midway up the antenna. Preferably, the ball crosses within 6 inches (15 centimeters) of the net or lower. The receiving partner should be able to catch the ball at face height while in a setting position.

3. The partner who first receives the ball returns the serve by duplicating the initial serve.

4. The second serve taken by each player should look exactly the same, except that the arm swing should decelerate before contact. The ball should cross the net with reduced speed, land inside the 5-foot (1.5-meter) line, and bounce one time to the partner.

5. Each player takes six serves at this distance.

6. Next, each player moves back 3 to 5 feet (1 to 1.5 meters) and repeats steps 1 through 5, aiming to get the second serve of each pair inside the 10-foot (3-meter) line.

7. The players then move back 5 more feet (1.5 meters) and repeat steps 1 through 5. If players have moved 5 feet (1.5 meters) each time, they end up serving from the 20-foot (6-meter) line for a total serving distance of 40 feet (12 meters). The goal for the second serve of each pair would be to land the ball inside the 10-foot (3-meter) line, preferably even closer to the net.

8. The players now remain at the 20-foot (6-meter) line and repeat steps 1 through 5 but with the goal of having the first three serves caught and the last three bounce. The last three serves should be short enough that they bounce at least two times before reaching the partner.

9. The players now move behind the end line. The first player to serve aims to put the ball within the last 3 feet (1 meter) of the court. The partner no longer catches the first serve but allows it to land deep and determines its distance from the end line. The next serve should be short and bounce three times before reaching the partner.

BUTTERFLY DRILL

FOCUS

This drill, named for the path the players create as they rotate, not only helps them control their serves but also permits each player to work on his or her individual serve-receive techniques.

PROCEDURE

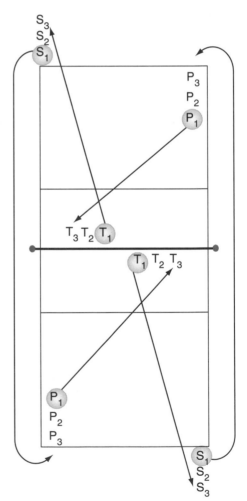

When working with groups of 12 players or fewer per court, players set themselves up in three columns: servers, passers, and receivers (see diagram). When using both sides of the net, place additional players in the passing column and try to maintain three servers and no more than three targets. When you have more than three in the target area, the players tend to move forward out of the target zone. Each player waits until he or she is at the head of one of the three columns to be part of the action. When a larger squad is training, this drill can accommodate all players by using both sides of the court.

1. Players on both sides of the net rotate through the different stations of serving, targeting, and passing. Servers can start in the right back 20 feet (6 meters) from the net and can move to 25 and 30 feet (7.5 to 9 meters) from the net and then behind the end line once they are warmed up. Receivers can start in the left back and as a group can be switched to middle back, right back, left front, middle front, and right front throughout the drill so that the serves are made at different depths and into different zones. Using the left-back first passer as an example, the player passes the serve directed to his or her area, rotates to the net and waits in

a short line before receiving a ball from the corresponding passer. The player takes that ball back to the service area to serve to a receiver across the net.

2. After the serve, the player jogs around one of the net poles to the end of the opposite receiving line.

3. Players count the number of perfect target passes, and the drill is not over until the players have reached a goal set by the coach (either reaching a time limit or a certain number of perfect passes).

Passing

The two main offensive passes are the forearm pass and, for more experienced players, the overhand pass. The forearm pass is used to contact and control the first ball sent over the net by the opponent. It is performed by bringing the two forearms together to work as one surface. I refer to this technique as a pass to emphasize ball control, as opposed to a bump, which implies less control over the trajectory of the ball.

The rules used throughout the world today also permit the use of hands in the overhead pass position for this first contact. But younger, less experienced players should concentrate on the forearm pass so that they learn to track balls better and move quicker to be in the best passing position. I also minimized the time I spent teaching the serve-receive overhand pass to younger players because they lack strength in the hand, wrist, and forearm areas. Moreover, using this technique results in less movement and encourages players to become too stationary. It can create a situation in which they try to reach for the ball rather than moving to be in the proper position to receive it.

Forearm Pass

Historically, the forearm platform has been the most commonly used surface for controlling the first ball sent over the net by an opponent on a serve or attack. The goal of the forearm pass is to effectively and consistently place the ball along the net where your designated setter can comfortably set it. All players on the team should have the ability to control the ball's height and direction with their forearms. Keeping this in mind, the players who perform this skill most consistently should be assigned the most responsibility to control the first ball.

Players start in a relaxed stance—with the legs slightly flexed—to receive serve, ready to move comfortably in any direction to intercept and control the ball. To perform the forearm pass, a player leans forward so that his or her arms hang toward the floor and are naturally straight. The player then uses one of the following methods to create the passing surface:

• **Fist wrap.** Fold one hand into a loose fist. Players should practice this "loose fist" grip with both hands to determine which hand wrap feels most comfortable and is the quickest and easiest to put into this position. Wrap the other hand around the fist, making sure that the thumbs are parallel. Next, press both thumbs down toward the ground. This helps produce hyperextended elbows that lock the arms straight. The radial bone on the thumb side of each forearm is part of the contact area (figure 4.4a).

• **Cupped hands.** Put the sides of the hands opposite the thumbs together. Make sure the heels of the hands and the wrists are at the same level. Rotate the backs of the fingers of one hand onto the front of the fingers of the other hand, making a cup. Put the thumbs together so that they are parallel to each other (figure 4.4b). This technique may expose more of the soft tissue on the inside of the forearms. The surface produced from this grip is a little wider and aids ball control. Since this area is softer, it reddens easily and tends to hurt more at the beginning. Players may want to wear long-sleeved shirts during training to help

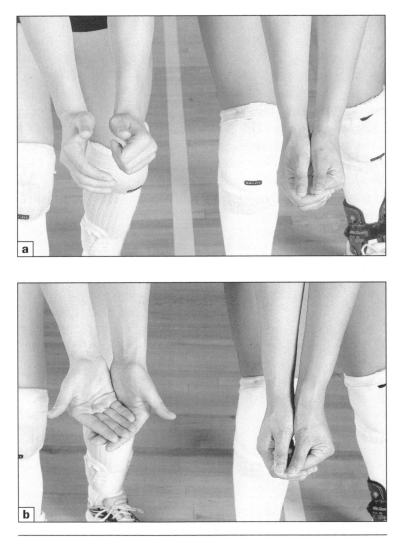

Figure 4.4 Forearm pass hand positions: fist wrap (*a*) and cupped hands (*b*).

cushion the impact. This area hardens in time and the impact is not as bother-some. Female players with more flexibility at the elbow can make their forearms come together from the wrist all the way to the elbow. Most male players can only make the forearms come together for several inches above the wrists and therefore have a separation of up to 3 inches (7.5 centimeters) at the elbows.

Players should not create the forearm platform before or while moving. Instead, they should move naturally and then let the arms hang straight in anticipation of bringing them together before contacting the ball. The platform should be formed while in a balanced position and with the hands facing the ground. This helps to keep the chest down and prevents players from bending their arms at the elbow, or "praying," as they form the platform. The hands are then put together while keeping the elbows away from the body. The shoulders should be squared to the target, as the player reaches out to make contact with the ball and drives the ball toward the target. The optimal height of ball contact with the arms is between the knees and waist.

Passing from the centerline of the body helps to ensure that the hips and shoulders are facing the target. When balls are played outside the centerline, players are forced to angle the arms to the target. Angled arms that are parallel to the ground rather than slightly vertical may produce balls that skip off the arms and away from the court.

The release angle of the ball coming off the forearms should be between 45 and 90 degrees. A release angle of less than 45 degrees occurs when the hands are pointing almost straight down and results in the ball moving forward and toward the floor. An angle of 90 degrees or more may result from a player unintentionally getting too close to the ball and raising his or her chest up as contact is made. When playing behind the 10-foot (3-meter) line, the chest should be pointing toward the floor. A ball played with the forearms close to the net, inside the 10-foot (3-meter) line, has the player intentionally keeping his or her chest and forearms high, as there is no room to diagonally pass the ball. Players must also be cognizant of the location from which the setter is releasing. Any setter release from the back row or from the left side of the court justifies a higher pass to permit the setter to get to the target in a balanced position before the ball reaches the target area.

Overhand Pass

Since the rules of play governing the first contact permit the use of hands to receive a served ball, I will briefly cover the overhand pass here. The hands are used primarily for digging, as a defensive technique on the first contact , however, and this is dis-cussed in more detail in chapter 5. On the first contact, the player may double-contact the ball but may not lift or carry it. Therefore, coaches must design and implement drills to develop players' ability to handle this served first ball with their hands.

In preparation for the 1984 Olympics, the US Olympic program headed by coach Doug Beal and his staff incorporated a two-person passing system into their game (see page 123). The two passers involved were Karch Kiraly and Aldis Berzins. Not only did Kiraly and Berzins receive most of the serves, but they also demonstrated the technical and tactical use of swing hitting—which allows the passer to receive the serve and move, or swing, to any attack zone. When using the two-passer or three-passer formation, front-row players not designated as primary passers must assume passing roles when a short serve is received. On many occasions, they will use the overhand pass to keep the ball out of the net and immediately transition to their offensive attack pattern.

KNEELING AND STANDING FOREARM PASS

FOCUS

Pass the ball in the body's centerline with emphasis on the forearm contact and follow-through.

PROCEDURE

Each player pairs up with a partner. One player, the passer, kneels on kneepads or a cushioned mat at the 10-foot (3-meter) line facing the net. Facing the net is critical for the passer to get a feel for ball height and distance. The tossing partner stands with his or her back to the net and repeatedly makes underhand tosses to the passer. Once a passer has developed passing proficiency, the tossing partner can use a two-handed push or chest pass to the passer, which adds speed and a different ball trajectory. Then follow these steps.

1. When the passer is kneeling on one knee, the lead foot can be slightly to the outside of the corresponding shoulder. He or she lowers the chest and rolls the shoulders slightly forward.

2. As the ball is released from the tossing partner, the passer prepares the forearm surface and extends it away from the body to contact the ball.

3. Immediately after the release of the tossed ball, the tossing partner places a setter's target hand above his or her head into which the passing player is to drop the ball. This provides immediate visual feedback to the passer regarding the accuracy of the pass.

4. The passing player may need to adjust his or her arm angle to permit the passed ball to drop into the target hand. Should the ball be too low, the passing hands are angled too much toward the ground. If the pass goes straight up into the air, the passing platform is more parallel to the ground.

5. After several passes, look at the forearms for a red area. The red area should be 2 to 4 inches (5 to 10 centimeters) above the wrist with similar distribution on both forearms. Redness at the elbow area indicates the ball is being played too close to the body, whereas redness on the thumbs or hands indicates the ball is too far away from the passer on contact. This could be a result of a bad toss from the partner or the passer's inability to track and play the ball at the proper distance in front of the body.

6. The passer passes 10 balls before alternating with the partner. Increase the distance from the target each time the partners rotate.

This kneeling position also provides the opportunity to work on the left-to-right passing follow-through. A ball should be tossed outside the receiver's left side between the ankle and knee. The left-to-right follow-through is critical to making sure that balls passed from the left sideline are going to the target, especially when the player cannot get his or her hips and shoulders in a position to face the target.

Next the player repeats the steps, but with the passer starting in a standing position approximately 10 to 15 feet (3 to 4.5 meters) from and facing the net. The passer should assume a balanced position with the chest down and feet balanced to begin a weight shift to the target. I recommend that the passer make a short step to the target with the right foot while shifting his or her weight forward. When the passer does this, the hips must come forward. Coaches should watch and provide feedback to any player who is passing the ball forward with the arms while the hips move back. A player who shifts the hips back is pulling the ball away from the target when passing and is disrupting his or her follow-through.

MOVING FOREARM PASS

FOCUS

Players learn to move quickly to a point where they can intercept the ball along the centerline of their body, building on the kneeling and standing forearm pass drills.

PROCEDURE

Coaches start by demonstrating the three footwork movements that players use in this drill—the I pattern, the X pattern, and either a right or left lateral movement—or having an experienced player do so. Players mirror the movement. Then they follow these steps, working in groups of two:

1. The tossing partner makes an underhand toss in front of the passer that requires the passer to take three short steps to intercept the ball. The direction of the steps varies depending on the footwork required.

2. The passer starts with the right foot, brings the left foot forward to balance the feet, and steps with the right as he or she shifts his or her hips through the pass. How far the ball is in front of the passer determines the length of the passer's steps. Note that the passer should not take one long step forward to the ball. This lowers the center of gravity and changes the passing angle. This also puts the stepping foot in line with the back foot and inhibits lateral balance. Should the ball float or move to the side at the last second, the passer may not be able to adjust to the flight of the ball.

3. Following the pass, the passer opens a hip and uses lead and crossover steps to return to his or her initial starting place.

4. Players rotate and repeat for five sets of 10 repetitions.

As players become more familiar with the X pattern, change it so that the first pass is right front, the second is left back, the third is left front, and the fourth is right back. The next phase of this drill is to incorporate the steps and subsequent pass with receiving preliminary serves coming over the net (serves designed to force the player to move but not to ace the player). The server can continually move his or her position back to simulate a normal serve with increased power.

Setting

Setting involves the simultaneous use of both hands to direct a ball to a location where a hitter (also called an attacker) can hit it over the net using his or her maximum vertical jump and a full arm swing. Setting occurs during the second contact in a team's transition to offense. The setter, a specialist, is trained for the purpose of quarterbacking the offense. Should the ball need to be set on the second contact by a nonsetter, then this person is called a help setter.

The physical and mental ability of one or more players to handle the second ball, control its height and speed, and consistently direct it to a particular location is essential for a team to compete at a high level. Quickness to the ball, receiving it in a vertical or jumping position, and setting it accurately to various locations are necessary elements of both a basic and advanced offense. Setters must be able to play the ball above and in front of the forehead and release it without its coming to rest or spinning.

Setting Technique

The first step to learning how to set is establishing a pocket with the hands in which the ball will fit. The coach should personally fit the ball into each player's hands and make manual adjustments so that he or she can create the best pocket possible. This means making certain that the player's hands are wide open and rounded to mold to the shape of the ball. The player's index fingers should be spread 2 to 3 inches (5 to 7.5 centimeters) apart with the thumbs facing each other or back toward the setter. The thumbs should never face forward as they then would touch the ball first and cause it to spin (sometimes even backwards over the setter's hands). The ball should rest on the pads of the fingers. The player's fingers should be vertical and the hands turned slightly toward each other with the index fingers and thumbs forming an enlarged triangle (figure 4.5a).

The ball should completely rest on the three pads of the index fingers, on two or three pads of the middle fingers, and on one pad of the ring finger as the little finger touches the ball. The player's hands should be held up in a

Figure 4.5a   Forming the pocket.

ready position 2 to 4 inches (5 to 10 centimeters) above the forehead with the elbows at a 45-degree angle away from the middle of the chest.

Once the coach has helped the player fit the ball, the coach can place one hand on the front of the ball (the part farthest from the player) and ask the player to push it against the coach's hand as the player extends his or her arms forward and presses behind the ball to full extension. The player does not release the ball; the coach keeps pressure on it as it is returned to the starting position. Repeat this at least 10 times or until the player is comfortable with the position. After each player has been fit, he or she should pair up with a partner (preferably a varsity player) and continue with repetitions of this setting motion. The coach can walk around and provide feedback.

After players have established a pocket and done the required setting reps, it's time to work on footwork and body position. To prepare for the set, players must always have the right foot, the foot closest to the net, forward in a heel-to-toe position in front of the left foot. The width of the feet should be slightly narrower than the shoulders. Having the right foot forward permits a rotation from the waist up to the shoulders and allows the setter to track the ball without twisting the lower body. The setter then rotates the shoulders back to a 90-degree angle to the net. The right foot points to the 3-foot (1-meter) line to assist in keeping the ball a full arm swing away from the net. The last three steps the setter takes are shorter and quicker to help him or her get under the ball and remain in a tall, vertical position (figure 4.5b). Taking a long last step with the right foot lowers the center of gravity, forcing the setter off-balance. This requires a higher set to compensate for the lower position. A setter should always stand as tall as possible or jump vertically when releasing the ball. This permits earlier contact of the ball and allows for speeding up the set and the time and distance to teammate contact. By jumping, the setter can hold or delay the reaction time of the blockers.

Figure 4.5b Getting into a tall, open position.

The setter presses the right foot down into the floor as he or she extends the arms and legs on ball contact. The left (back) foot moves forward as the ball is released to finish in front of the right foot. This forces the setter to continue his or her body movement in the direction of the set. Should the set be made to the left front (often called a 4 ball when the outside hitter is available for a high outside set), the setter continues to move forward to form the cup around the hitter.

Younger players should start with the hands closer to the forehead or in a flexed position. This permits greater extension of the arms to push the ball farther. Younger players also tend to need more extension from the legs and hips. Stronger, more experienced players should keep the hands further from the forehead to produce a quicker release of the ball from a higher point (figure 4.5c). They need less leg and hip extension as well. The hands should finish closer together on release to ensure that the force stays behind the ball.

One final note on the setting technique: generally young players do not set high enough when pushing a ball to the left front or back to the right front. For players 14 and under, the ball is normally set 8 to 10 feet (2.4 to 3 meters) above the net to provide the hitter with time for the approach and takeoff (see "Evaluating the Setting Technique").

Figure 4.5c Extending the arms while making contact.

Types of Sets

Setters must be able to set the ball from antenna to antenna. Setting balls forward or backward from the left to the right antenna forces the opponent to block the 30-foot (9-meter) distance and to read and cover attacks coming from different angles. Setters must receive thousands of repetitions that permit them to develop the confidence and timing to set balls in front of and behind them at different heights and speeds.

In the previous section, I covered the general technique for the front set. However there are other types of sets that come into play during most matches, including the back set, back-row set, and jump set.

Evaluating the Setting Technique

The following list includes some of the most common examples of incorrect setting technique and how to correct them.

- The hands are not open to span the surface of the ball. Coaches should ask the player to spread the fingers apart or refit the ball into his or her hands.

- The hands are too close together and interfere with each other. As a result, the hands are not evenly distributed on the ball. Coaches should either ask the player to separate the hands or refit the ball.

- The fingers of each hand face each other, which raises the elbows to an awkward angle. Coaches should ask the player to drop the elbows closer to the side to force the hands into a more vertical position. Coaches can also stand behind the player and keep pressure on the elbows so that they don't fly away from the body.

- The tips rather than the pads of the fingers make first contact. The player should reform the pocket to force the ball onto the finger pads.

- The thumbs face the ball and contact it first, causing it to spin off the hands and backward over the player's head. Coaches should have the player catch the ball with the proper pocket to illustrate the position of the thumbs.

- One hand is dominant (usually the basketball-shooting hand), resulting in the ball sitting on the palm of that hand and the corresponding elbow dropping down and in closer to the player's body. Coaches should toss the ball to the player so that he or she catches it with both hands balanced.

- The player's hands do not finish behind the ball but instead go outward and away from the body. As a result, he or she does not generate enough power to set the ball far enough. To correct, the player should push against a ball that the coach continues to hold.

- The angle of release is low, resulting in a flat set that is difficult for a teammate to play successfully. Check the finish position of the arms and hands to determine why the set did not go far or high enough. Rehearse the finish position with a soft toss drill in which the player sets a ball that is tossed from a distance of less than a foot (30.5 centimeters) into the player's hand.

- The ball is contacted in the correct position above the forehead but is lowered and then lifted up before release. This is an illegal lift and will be called by the official. Coaches should have the player catch and hold the ball in a higher position before permitting the continuation of the set.

- When setting the ball backward, the player makes contact with the ball behind the head instead of in front. Players also may contact the ball on the fingertips, resulting in the ball spinning off the hands flat and low. It is not uncommon for younger players to finish with the hands and arms straight upward so that the set goes upward but not backward. Using the step-hip or arm-only action, the arms and hands must finish behind them. The left or back foot hip action is done simultaneously with the arm action to force the hips and shoulders in front of the arms. This automatically brings the setter's body in front of the hands, ensuring that the ball will go back instead of up. The arm-only action begins with the setter almost catching the ball and moving or carrying the ball to a position above the head before releasing the ball. Begin teaching the setting technique again with the player catching and holding the ball. Proceed to the step-and-hand-push motion. Culminate with an exaggerated follow-through.

Back Set

With the back set, the ball is set to the right front or right back of the court to be attacked by a teammate. The set must be done from the exact same hand and body position as a front set so that an opponent cannot read the direction of the set before the release of the ball. One necessary difference from the front setting technique is the direction the right foot is pointing. Should the right foot point to the 3-foot (1-meter) line, as it does for the left front (4-ball) set, the result is a ball that goes backward and hits the right antenna or goes over the net into the opponent's court. Rather, in this set, the player's hips must be at a 90-degree angle to the net so that the right foot is either parallel to the net or the toe is pointed slightly toward the net. This keeps the player's hips turned toward the 3-foot (1-meter) line on the right side of the court.

As mentioned previously, a younger player needs to use more leg and hip extension than a more experienced player. With the ball being contacted in front of the forehead, the player steps and moves his or her weight onto the right foot as he or she pushes the arms upward vertically. As the arms are moving upward the left foot moves forward, essentially bringing the hips in front of the arms. This causes the arms to go behind the head before the release. The player should turn his or her head toward the net to track the flight of the ball while simultaneously rotating the right foot and hip back and away from the net to cover the hitter.

Stronger players can move the hands and arms toward the back without using the left foot and hip-forward movement. They should also rotate the right foot and hip back and away to get into a coverage position. Players can do this from a standing or jumping release.

Back-Row Set

For a back-row set to be effective, once again the opponent should not be able to determine whether the ball is going forward or backward or toward the front or back row until the ball has been released. For younger or novice hitters, the ball is set so that it comes down approximately 9 feet (2.7 meters) from the net. This permits a hitter to take off behind the 10-foot (3-meter) line and eliminates a line violation. For more experienced hitters with strong vertical and long-jump abilities, the back-row set can be to within 5 or 6 feet (1.5 or 1.8 meters) of the net. The setter releases the ball above the left shoulder rather than directly over the head. This changes the trajectory of the ball, sending it away from the net. The most common mistake is for a player to want to face the back row before the set, giving the opponent the opportunity to read the direction of the set before the release.

Jump Set

Younger players may be uncomfortable using this set if they haven't practiced it enough in training or if they lack confidence in their jumping ability. Experienced players should consider using it as their primary setting option as it forces the opponent to honor their front- or back-row starting position as well as their ability to now initiate a quicker release, especially on quick sets.

The setter can jump using one of the following takeoff techniques:

1. If the player's hands are up in the ball-receiving position early, then they can do a butt jump or a leg and hip extension to go up and catch and eventually set the ball at the apex of their jump.

2. They can also perform a short arm swing by keeping the elbows flexed and driving the elbows back behind the hips so that the hands are even with the sides of the body. Simultaneously with the forward arm swing, the player extends the legs and drives the elbows and forearms above the head to create additional lift.

3. The third technique is a straight, long arm swing behind the body with the hands reaching further behind than the elbows to create a longer lever-type lift. This technique must be done earlier to get the setter into the air to correctly time when to contact the ball. The hips and shoulders must be at a 90-degree angle to the net to prevent the hands from contacting the net.

Players can learn each of these techniques by working on them without a ball to help them get comfortable with the takeoff, balancing, and generating power in the air before landing under control. Next, a partner can toss the ball so the player jumps and catches the ball in the correct hand-to-forehead relationship. Then the partner, standing in front and facing the setter, can give a shorter toss so that the setter can work on making a quicker jump. Finally, the partner can toss from a 90-degree angle to the setter. This forces the setter to rotate the upper body to follow the flight of the ball and rotate back before contacting the ball at the highest point possible before the ball release.

When handling a tight pass—one that is right on top of or within inches of the net—one of the most common jump-set mistakes is that the resulting set is too tight for the hitter to swing his or her arm, or the ball goes over the net to the opponent. The setter's goal is to "better" the ball. Just because he or she is trapped along the top of the net does not mean that the set should trap the hitter too. The goal is to provide the hitter with the opportunity to make a full arm swing.

Two techniques can help the setter compensate for a tight pass and release the set to begin an attack. Both techniques depend on how early the setter gets to the ball. If the setter is early, he or she should rotate the right elbow in toward the center of her chest, which in turn rotates the hip toward the 3-foot (1-meter) line and the back toward the net. The setter's chest faces toward the back left corner of the court (figure 4.6) and permits the resulting set to be off the net. This also has the setter landing with the right heel on the centerline and prevents a parallel foot that could result in a foot fault. Having the setter assume the correct position and then tossing the ball into the pocket he or she has already created can help the setter practice this technique.

The second technique is useful when the setter is late to the ball and has the chest parallel to the net as he or she faces it. This forces the setter's arms wider or makes him or her pull the elbows back to not hit the net. It also forces the setter to side-set the ball over the left or right shoulder, depending on the direction of the set. The setter is actually setting a blind ball, meaning that he or she cannot see the hitter before or during the release of the ball.

To duplicate a jump set and work on the release and follow-through at the top of a jump, the hitter can stand on a box between 18 to 30 inches (45 and 75 centimeters) high. The relationship of the two players should be such that the setter releases the ball in front of the hitter to provide him or her with a reaching full arm swing. The hitter can be open to the setter with the right shoulder and approximately 3 feet (1 meter) away at a 45-degree angle. A coach or player tosses a ball to the setter to initiate the jump set.

Figure 4.6 If the setter gets to the ball early, he or she can rotate to compensate for a tight pass.

A quick 1-ball set (that is, a set that forces a full arm extension from the hitter and is 1 to 3 feet , or 30 centimeters to 1 meter, above the net) is based upon the jumping ability of the attacker. Balls less than 1 foot (30 centimeters) above the net must be attacked extremely quickly because the low height makes it easier for the opponent to get his or her hands over the net to block the ball. How to work on timing is described in the attacking section later in this chapter, but it is important to keep in mind that the ball should be set in front of the hitter's hitting shoulder so that he or she can see the ball, net, and opponent as he or she attacks.

A 1-ball set that travels 2 to 5 feet (60 centimeters to 1.5 meters) from the setter's releasing hands is called a 21 set; this increased distance is crucial to keeping the opposing middle blocker off balance. A 31 set has the same 1-foot height and trajectory of the ball, but the distance of the resulting set is 5 or more feet (1.5 meters) from the setter's hands. Some coaches and players refer to the 21 and 31 as shoot sets. Should the offense design this set for the left-front hitter, it is then called a 41 set. Accuracy and timing make this a more difficult play to execute.

A similar set but one that is slower and probably more conducive to younger players, is a 2-ball set, or similarly a 22, 32, or 42 set. In each case, the ball is set between 2 and 4 feet (60 and 120 centimeters) above the net. The hitter does not have to be in the air as early as for the 1-ball set and the timing is easier. The 2-ball set can also be used for the second hitter in a combination play or second tempo play (see chapter 5). One of the two hitters running the combination goes to her correct position with respect to the setter, expecting a 1-ball set, while the second hitter drives into his or her correct position expecting a 2-ball set.

Sets that are quick and behind the setter can be the same height as the front sets but they provide some different approach angles for the hitters. These different attack angles also force the defensive blockers to make adjustments. When the blocker cannot make the appropriate footwork adjustments, the advantage goes to the offensive player. Hitters can start in front of the setter and end up swinging at a ball set behind the setter, such as a tight or wide slide (see page 76 for more on these). Or the hitter can start behind the setter and attack the ball there. The only difference is that the height of the set and the distance from the setter to the hitter are predetermined and known by both. If the pass to the setter is bad, the hitter calls off the predetermined set with a vocal cue that indicates that the hitter is available for a set of a different height. Once again, the setter should release the ball to a hitter standing on a box to provide the correct relationship and duplicate the height of the set as much as possible. It is difficult for a setter to be able to turn the head quickly enough to determine the height and angle of the set, so this is where a coach's feedback can be very helpful and videotaping the session even better.

Quick 1-ball back sets are at the same height as a front quick set, but the distance from the setter depends on the attacking arm swing. If the back set is to a right-handed hitter, the hitting arm is further from the setter so that the ball must cross his or her body to get to the hitting arm. A left-handed hitter receives a ball closer to the back of the setter since the hitting arm is closer to the setter. A wide slide set is similar in height and distance to a front 32 set, but it is a back set. The attacker goes behind the setter and takes off from one foot to attack the ball that is close to the right antenna. Figure 4.7 illustrates the many different sets.

Figure 4.7 Basic sets.

SETTING PROGRESSION

FOCUS

Set with the correct hand positions, then slowly work up to quicker releases.

PROCEDURE

Two players pair up: one player tosses the ball as the partner prepares to catch-set, and then during the progression, set the ball. The players stand parallel to the net to simulate a game-type set, or one player can stand 10 to 12 feet (3 to 3.7 meters) from the net facing the partner, whose back is to the net. Players then proceed with the following steps.

1. One partner tosses the ball to the setter, who catches it and checks to determine if he or she needs to make any changes in hand position.

2. Once the setter has inspected his or her hand position, he or she push-sets the ball back to the tosser.

3. The tosser continues tossing the ball to the setter with tosses that require the setter to use quick footwork to catch the ball in a vertical position with the ball directly in front of the forehead.

4. Partners switch roles after 10 repetitions.

5. Once both are comfortable with steps 1 through 4, they repeat the steps but keep the ball moving by setting instead of tossing and then catching. Each player sets the ball even higher and slightly in front of his or her partner to allow time to use the correct steps to catch the ball. Remember, the ball should be set with the right foot slightly forward.

6. Once players are confident with this setting and catching routine, they can eliminate the catching phase. The ball should be released in a manner that an official would not call a carry or lift. Players continue until the ball is released from the setting pocket without any hesitation. They can adjust the distance between them to permit longer and shorter sets. One option is to have one player set a ball and the second player try to duplicate the height of the set (from a standing or jump set).

Many younger players initially contact the ball in the proper hand-to-forehead relationship but then lower the ball below the chin or down toward the chest. These players are attempting to generate more power, but they end up carrying or lifting the ball back to the starting position before release. Should the player not have enough upper-body or arm strength, he or she should increase flexion and generate more power from the legs and hips.

More advanced players can double-set (set to himself or herself and then to a partner) or add a jump set or back set.

GAME-SITUATION SETS

FOCUS

This drill provides continual ball movement in a sequence similar to game situations. The setter has to fine-tune his or her footwork such that the feet and hands are in perfect position to set to the outside.

PROCEDURE

Game-situation sets can be executed with three players and two ball carts. Eventually the players only need one ball. Players start by forming groups of three: a setter, tosser, and receiver. The tosser stands 2 feet (61 centimeters) directly in front of the setter, who is located in the target zone along the net. The receiver stands 20 feet (6 meters) from the setter on the left sideline 3 feet (1 meter) from and facing the net. Players then follow these steps:

1. The setter stands tall with the right foot in a heel-to-toe position in front of the left foot and the width of the feet slightly narrower than shoulder-width. The hands should be ready to accept a ball and should not be forced to move by the direction of the tossed ball.

2. The tosser softly underhand tosses a ball into the setter's hands.

3. The setter extends the arms and pushes the ball 20 feet (6 meters) to the receiver. The receiver catches the set ball and places it in the second ball cart.

4. The setting player continues until every ball in the first ball cart has been used.

5. The three players rotate until each one has had the opportunity to set at least one cartful of balls.

6. The receiver can stand on the right sideline so that the setter sets the ball backward from a short toss.

7. The drill can be made more advanced by continuing with a toss that requires the setter to move three small steps forward before the set. The steps should be right, left, and right. The setter pushes the last right step down on the court as he or she extends the slightly bent knees, hips, and arms simultaneously. The tosser stands 5 to 10 feet (1.5 to 3 meters) from the net and tosses the ball to the setter to simulate a forearm pass.

Once you've mastered this drill, try it with five players and two balls. This makes things happen quickly as the setter alternates between a front and back set. The two balls come from two different players and the setter must get to the ball, set it, and immediately look for the second ball and set that one. If the timing of the balls coming to the setter is off, the player off the net double-sets to himself or herself until the ball can be released to the setter. While the first ball is going to the receiver, the second ball is initiated by the second helper off the net.

Attacking

A successful volley is the culmination of the three sequential ball contacts. The third contact is a spike for a point or side-out. The two preliminary contacts are designed to set up the third contact—the attack—by giving a hitter a full, high swing at the ball. An effective attack depends on the ability of one of the eligible front-row hitters to take a full swing at the ball with the purpose of terminating the play. A team that is able to determine the area of the set and the speed of the attack can keep the opponent off-balance. A team's inability to attack the third ball, by the same token, reduces the effectiveness of the play and provides no guarantee that the offense will succeed on that particular swing. Attack errors result in immediate points for the opponent.

This section breaks down the attack into the phases that precede the actual contact of the ball—the prejump arm swings, player throwing motion, hand position, and some basics for timing the moving ball. Hitters (those attacking the ball) should incorporate their maximum jump and reach into each attempt. Players must be disciplined to know when to begin moving forward and when to leave the ground to attack the various sets. Finally and most important is to hit intelligently in order to achieve the best results.

In the preliminary evaluation of young athletes, a coach can watch the throwing motion and objectively measure shoulder power by using a kneeling and standing throw test. Most coaches mentally evaluate at a higher level those athletes who naturally have a high-reaching throwing motion. Some athletes throw a ball well but have difficulty timing their swing above the net to hit the ball from a high reach. For this reason, an athlete with good timing, a good throwing motion, and a strong jump is immediately slated as a potential candidate for the front row.

Attacking Technique

Most of the sports that require a throwing technique rely on the athlete's ability to throw the ball by pushing off the back foot. The feet are on the ground even though preparation steps have been taken before the release of the ball. During an attack in volleyball, players must simulate the body position and movement of a stationary player while in the air at the top of their jump. The bio-motor fundamentals necessary for an effective attack are a throwing motion that involves the arm opposite the hitting arm reaching forward and pulling down to the outside to initiate the proper hip and shoulder rotation, a high arm reach, the body in a position to pike at the waist at ball contact (that is, to bend forward while keeping the legs straight), and a proper follow-through.

I present the following technique elements in the order in which my coaching colleagues and I taught them to our players.

Throwing Motion

Many players and coaches call arm swing what I refer to here as throwing motion. I call it throwing motion to help coaches and players visualize the correct motion, since it bears a strong similarity to throwing. Beginners often find it best when learning to use a ball that they can comfortably hold with spread fingers so that it doesn't fall out of the hand before the throw; often a volleyball is too big and results in an athlete dropping the elbow to prevent the ball from falling from the hand. Using a smaller basketball has the advantage of weight overload for more experienced players, but many younger players are not comfortable trying to hold such a ball while using a natural throwing motion. We have found that a 16-inch (40.6-centimeter) mush ball, or Chicago softball, is best for beginners.

When practicing the throwing motion with a smaller ball, players can use softball gloves for catching their partner's throw so that there is no fear of hurting a hand. As the players practice, they gradually can increase the distance of the throw. The throwing motion should be similar to that of a person throwing the ball from center field while playing softball or baseball. The arm should reach high with the hand leading; this is quickly followed by a wrist snapping motion. The arm and hand should finish along the throwing side of the body. Performing this motion from a kneeling position can help isolate hip rotation and place emphasis on shoulder rotation, reach, and follow-through. Once the player is comfortable with these movements, he or she is ready to practice using a volleyball.

To progress in their proficiency with this skill, players can find a partner and throw back and forth. Each thrower releases the volleyball slightly in front of the shoulder with the target being the face of the teammate. The teammate catches the ball in a setting position with strong, firm hands to simulate the first ball contact of a serve-receive or defensive dig. Alternate this throw with a release that would have the ball hit the floor halfway between you and your partner. This ball may bounce high, depending on the force of the throw, and should be played by the partner with one open hand tilted back to simulate a reaction to the ball. The coach should make sure that the throw into the ground is done from a high release with a slight abdominal pike. Some players try to get power from bending from the waist instead of using arm acceleration.

Hand Position and Ball Contact

To help players get a feel for hand position on the ball during an attacking motion, each coach should practice fitting the ball into a solid palm with the fingers spread as he or she holds the hand above the head. Think of the ball as a clock face, with the contact area at one or two o'clock. The player's elbow should be bent and behind and above the shoulder. This creates an open position to the ball, permits the elbow to be free of the side of the body, and allows the hand to lead as the player reaches for the ball. Contact on the fingers produces a paintbrush swing or, in effect, the hand pulling down behind the ball instead of going through it.

Should a player contact the ball with the heel of the hand, even if the heel is solid, the result will be a ball contacted at a lower point that has very little topspin. This occurs since the heel is lower than the palm. These few inches lower may cause the ball to go into the net or a block. The player and coach should listen for a smacking sound, which indicates a solid palm contact on the ball. Immediately on contact, the loose wrist and hand should snap over the top and around the ball to impart spin.

Spin is a critical element to the attack, since it rotates the ball down into the court. Once the player has learned how to establish spin on the ball, he or she can then focus on how to accelerate the arm. Players who have developed a feel for the attack swing should learn how to attack to various areas of the court. The ball should be hit deep into the court rather than down close to the 10-foot (3-meter) line. This will force defensive opponents to react to balls directed to any zone or that go in any direction when ricocheting off an opponent's blocking hands. Hitting down on the ball can result in a ball being hit into a block, or worse yet, into the net.

One of the best ways to work on attacking ball contact and control is to stand on a box that is 18 to 36 inches (45 to 90 centimeters) high or on a chair seat and work on attack swings by hitting a ball tossed over or along the net by the coach or a partner. Listen for the sound of the contact and look to see if there is rotation on the ball. Once you have mastered these skills, it's time to work in the jump.

Prejump Arm Swing

The backward arm reach before the jump needs to be high enough that the palms of each hand (facing up) are above the shoulders. Players should flex the knees and hips as they swing the arms back. Having full forward movement of both arms provides maximum lift. Players should swing the arms back so that the palms face the ceiling. They should then bring both arms forward simultaneously and lift them high enough in front of them that both elbows go above the shoulders. At the same time, players should rise up on the toes with the hips and knees extended. Players should repeat this motion without jumping in order to get a feel for the lifting action of the arm swing.

Once the players are comfortable with the lift and extension, they can rotate the hitting arm back. In doing this, the elbow should already be above the shoulder and the attack hand open. The opposite hand and arm pull forward and downward with the elbow leading. This initiates the hip and shoulder rotation of the hitting arm toward the ball.

Jump

The next step is to use the arm swing plus hip and leg extension to lift off the ground. After numerous repetitions to establish elevation and arm preparation, players pull with the non-hitting arm, rotate at the hip, and take a fully reaching arm swing while in the air. The hitter finishes by landing in a cushioned and balanced position.

At this point, players can add a two-step approach, starting with the back foot (right foot for right-handed players and left foot for left-handed players). As the correct leg starts to go forward, the player leans the shoulders slightly forward and swings both arms back to shoulder level with the palms facing the ceiling. The second leg follows and the second foot is placed in front of the lead foot in a balanced heel-to-toe position. The feet are turned toward the set. This keeps the hip and shoulder open to the ball. The player then lifts and extends off the ground to a height that can be obtained from a two-step approach. Once a hitter explodes into the air, his or her body stretches vertically as he or she reaches to contact the ball at the highest point possible.

To provide players with a visual reference to their jumping reach, we now move them a little more than two steps from an antenna and at a 90-degree angle to the net while facing one of the antennas. Using the two-step approach, players can individually compare their jumps and reaches to the antenna. After they have driven off the ground and both elbows have cleared the shoulders, they extend the hitting arm and hand as high as possible and touch the antenna with the fingertips. Players must understand that because they contact the ball with the palm that the hitting height will be one red or white section below their maximum touch. When players are comfortable with the correct forward movement, foot placement, and arm lift, they are ready to move to the three- and four-step approaches to help them generate more power going into the final takeoff and thus achieve a higher touch.

How Many Steps on the Approach?

- **No steps.** A hitter is one arm length from the net when a ball comes directly over the net from the opponent. The hitter uses his or her arms without taking a step to jump about the net to attack the ball back to the opponent.

- **One step.** A player goes off one foot to attack a ball that has been unintentionally passed over the net. This is similar to the slide, discussed in great detail in the following section.

- **Two steps.** The hitter uses two steps when he or she is close to the net from a receiving position or block landing and has time to take the last two plant steps as he or she calls for the ball.

- **Three steps.** The hitter uses three steps when he or she has come from a double block and has had the opportunity to get depth from the net. The steps are left, right, and left as he or she calls for the ball.

- **Four steps.** The hitter uses this option when he or she is releasing from a deeper serve-receive position or a free ball call that requires four steps to get into the proper position in relation to the setter.

- **More than four steps.** A hitter uses several steps when he or she is swing hitting from a passing position with the three-passer formation or running off the net from a right-side block and transitioning to an attack.

Timing a Moving Ball

Once players understand the basic technique for attacking, they can work on how to time their attack to a moving ball. Hitters should realize that the height and location of the set varies until the setter is able to establish a consistent location. The two variables of the attack that the hitter can control are having a maximum jump on each attempt and contacting the ball from a high reach that is slightly in front of the attack shoulder.

Hitters should give themselves enough room for a three- or four-step approach, and they should not begin the approach until after the ball has left the setter's hands. This can be drilled in practices by having hitters catch the ball at the top of their jump. It is better to be late and still have the ability to take a ball over the net than to go early and have the ball travel over or behind the body. In other words, hitters need to stay behind the ball.

Another progression drill that can help develop timing is to "attack-catch" the ball. This involves using a maximum jump and throwing the attack hand forward to contact the ball. At the same time, the pull arm hand stops the ball. Players then land in a balanced, cushioned position.

Off-Speed Attacking Shots

Off-speed shots are shots a player propels over the net with an unexpected ball speed, angle of attack, or spin. Front-row players must learn to control these shots.

The **tip shot** is also called a dink. To tip, players use their open attack hand to direct the ball to a specific spot on the opponent's court. The hitter should use a maximum jump and full arm swing so that an opponent cannot read the intention of the shot. The ball is contacted by the first pad of each open finger of the tipping hand (figure 4.8a).

If a front-row hitter is forced, due to a bad set, to direct a ball to the opponent without power, he or she should tip the ball to the other team's setter or to the center of the court inside the 10-foot (3-meter) line. This forces the opponent to run the offense with the help setter. A setter can also use the tip as an offensive attack but should be aware of where the ball is in relation to his or her own face and where he or she is in relation to the net. A ball away from the setter's face and net is directed downward or deep by tipping with the left hand. A ball closer to the face or net is tipped down with the right hand. The setter may also reverse the right hand so that the palm is up and the thumb is closer to the net to execute a **back tip** (see figure 4.8b). This hand position directs the ball behind the setter into the short 4 zone closest to the opponent's left antenna. A ball a little farther off the net that allows the setter to slightly rotate or open the right shoulder to the net can be pushed first to the deep 5 corner or deep to the 1 corner (see figure 2.1, page 26). The player should slow down the speed of the attack arm and push or press just under the middle of the ball over the block into an open area or the area of a slower moving defensive player.

The **roll shot** is a camouflaged attack shot. The player decelerates the arm motion and the hand comes up slightly under the ball, contacting it at the five o'clock position. This change of ball contact area causes the ball to travel in a slight upward arc over the block to land in an open zone. Which zone is open depends on the type of defense the opponent is using.

The **wipe shot** is a more advanced technique that can be used when the attacking player is trapped with a tight set. In this situation, young players commonly use the outside hand (for example, the left hand when on the left side of the court) and push the ball inside. But this goes directly to the opponent's middle blocker and ends up on the floor on the hitter's side. Instead, for an effective wipe shot, the attacking player should square the shoulders to the net and use the right hand. The only difference is that the hitter places his or her hand behind instead of under the ball to intentionally push the ball into the blocker's hands (figure 4.8c). Once the hitter feels pressure from the opponent's hands on the ball, he or she throws the ball-controlling hand to the outside so that the ball goes off the defender's hands and out of bounds. Advanced players can use a full attack swing and change the arm angle to hit a ball off the outside hand of the opponent's right-side blocker. It is said, in this situation, that the hitter used the opponent's hand to the advantage of the offense.

Figure 4.8 The tip shot (*a*), the back tip (*b*), and the wipe shot (*c*).

Attacking Special Sets

All front-row players should be able to attack a quick (1-ball) set even though tradition has this attack predominantly coming from a middle hitter. The footwork and timing of the attack may be slightly different, depending on the skill level of the passers and the setter. It helps the setter when he or she hears the voice and feels the energy of the middle hitter on every play to get a feel for the hitter's timing. The middle hitter must make himself or herself available and be a threat whether he or she approaches from the left, middle, or right—as well as whether he or she takes off from a no-step, one-step, two-step, three-step, or four-step approach. The hitter opens to the pass and releases forward when the ball passes the shoulder to initiate the approach needed to time the pass and set.

The height of the pass determines the closing speed of the hitter, so a low and fast pass results in a quicker approach. The hitter should take off 3 feet (1 meter) from the setter's left shoulder so that the set is between the setter and the net. This permits a full arm swing and keeps the ball further away from the blocker's hands while permitting a larger angle of attack. The most common mistake young or inexperienced middle hitters make is that they only call for the ball and push hard when they think they will receive the set. As such, they essentially indicate to the opposing blockers also when they will *not* be getting the set.

When, therefore, should the hitter take off? This usually depends on his or her experience. The following list describes the different takeoff times used by different levels of players:

- Fast-collegiate or advanced high school or club: The hitter is already in the air when the ball is in the setter's hands, reaching to hit it at maximum height. A jump set permits a slightly flatter set but speeds up the ball delivery and the quickness of the attack.

- High school or club: The hitter is planted in the proper relationship to the setter and lifts the arms to jump, so in reality the hitter is on the way up.

- Junior varsity: The hitter has the feet in position to jump and is starting the forward arm-swing lift to jump off the ground after the ball has been set.

- Middle school or 14-and-under club: The takeoff is similar to the junior varsity attack, but the ball is usually set a little slower and sometimes referred to as a 1 and 1/2 set.

Shoot sets (21s, 31s, and 41s) are designed to force the middle blocker to track the approach line of the middle hitter rather than having the middle hitter always come to the middle of the net to hit. It also forces the right-front blocker to decide if he or she can or should get involved. The timing and steps can be similar to those for the 1-ball set, but it is delivered sooner and with a flatter trajectory.

For the slower 22, 32, and 42 shoot sets, the hitter still waits until the ball crosses the shoulder (if coming from the middle) and starts to move forward, adding a slight hesitation before exploding into the last two steps. The distances from the setter are the same. The 42 set is easier to time and usually more successful for the left outside hitter.

The **slide set** evolved from coaches determining that athletic players who had been accustomed to one-foot takeoffs in basketball for lay-ups could attack a volleyball extremely well using the same takeoff technique. The two most common approaches, tight and wide, reflect the philosophies of holding the combination block set by the left front and middle blockers or forcing the opponent to decide which hitter to block.

In the slide set, the attacking middle takes the first two steps (right, then left) toward the front of the setter. This hard front-drive fake is designed to sell to the two blockers that the hitter is going to attack in front of the setter. When the ball touches the setter's hands, the middle hitter pushes off from the left foot toward the antenna at a 45-degree angle and chases the ball. It is critical that the hitter chase the ball, otherwise he or she is in front of the ball and ends up reaching back to try to save the ball behind the non-hitting shoulder. Figure 4.9 illustrates several types of attack.

Figure 4.9 Types of attack: 4 ball (*a*), 31 ball (*b*), 1 ball (*c*), slide set (*d*), and back set (*e*).

A **tight slide** can be hit two ways, depending on the jumping ability of the middle hitter. The second hold step is to the hip of the setter instead of in front. The hitter drives into the air from the left leg immediately and attacks with a 1-ball set directly behind the setter's head. This works best when there are three hitters in the front row and the setter is in the back row. The **wide slide** has the hitter finish the four-step approach or an additional right-and-left takeoff step. A younger player may need six steps to get all the way to the antenna. By using the hold step, the left-front blocker may commit to a block, or the left- and middle-front players may interfere with each other's ability to get back to the outside to block. This step also can isolate the middle hitter on the left-front blocker. The setter can jump or tip to hold the middle blocker. Another option is to run a back-row "pipe" or "B" to use all the zones of the net.

To force the action, the middle hitter or the person running the slide changes the angle of approach to immediately show the slide move. The setter needs to push the ball a little more quickly since the approach begins early. This forces the opponents to decide whether to single or double block the slide.

The middle hitter on the slide must avoid both a centerline violation and hitting the official's stand (a violation would be called if he or she gains an advantage from the contact) when landing. He or she can avoid the centerline violation by stepping out of bounds under the net. Following the attack, the player must determine if he or she can get back to the middle to block or have the setter block middle for that transition (figure 4.10).

The **fade set** involves a middle hitter running either a tight slide or a wide slide behind the setter. The hitter leaves first and forces the two blockers to react to the slide move. The fade is designed for a left-handed right-side player. This player goes second and outside the slide hitter. The player needs to be on the right foot when the ball is in the setter's hands. The setter can set a 22 or 32 in which the right-front hitter chases to the middle. This requires a one-foot takeoff for the right side.

The middle hitter can most easily transition to a slide attack in front of the setter from the left front in serve-receive after a block attempt to the opponent's right-side attack. The hitter starts as though he or she is running a traditional 31 set but changes on the second or left-foot step to come toward the setter. The hitter takes a right-left-elevate step to attack the 31 set. The logic is to pull the opponent's middle blocker to the

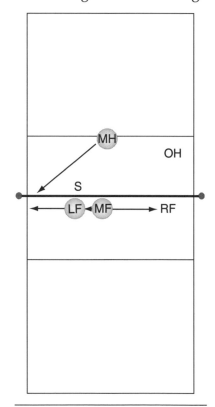

Figure 4.10 The middle hitter must attack quickly and then block, or arrange to have the setter block, the middle.

right to stop the traditional 31 and quickly move back inside the blocker toward the middle of the net. This may be difficult to time for younger players. It may be easier to run a quick 1-ball set in front of the setter while taking off from one foot coming from serve-receive or from a double block left. Figure 4.11 shows the movement from the serve-receive position. The middle hitter starts along the net in the serve-receive position (1) and moves to the 10-foot (3-meter) line (2) before doing a front slide (3).

For drills that help players develop their attacking skills, use the Pepper drills on pages 107 to 111.

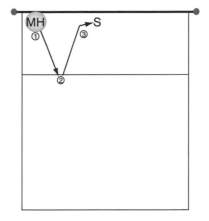

Figure 4.11 The path of the middle hitter executing a front slide.

CHAPTER 5

Defensive Skills

In today's era of rally-score volleyball, one great defensive play can make a big difference in a game's outcome. To be successful, teams must win *real* points in addition to the side-out points. The first way to score a real point is with an ace serve. But probably a more realistic method of achieving success is a team's ability to block or dig an attack and then transition to an offensive strategy.

Kids want and need to be challenged, and developing and using defensive skills is one of the greatest challenges young volleyball players can accept. Back-row specialists can make themselves so indispensable that the coach must find a way to get them into the game. And those players who are training to play all the way around the rotation are challenged to prove that they should remain in the game.

Defense begins with a basic understanding of body and court positioning and develops further through improving spatial awareness and the communication skills needed to mesh with teammates. Players need to recognize and anticipate what can unfold on the court based on scouting reports as well as tracking the ball and the opponent's movements. They should not overlook the importance of communicating to teammates what they see happening. Players must train to identify the ball sequence that their opponent establishes, what their first responsibilities are, and how to pursue a ball. Teaching players how to read their opponents, quickly accelerate to ensure proper court coverage, and use proper defensive techniques is a rewarding aspect of coaching.

This chapter covers the main defensive skills: blocking and digging, including some "emergency" digging skills needed in unique situations. Even though each player has been trained to use floor emergency skills, the goal should be to play every ball possible by getting to it in a balanced position and staying on the feet. Developing strong defensive skills—based as they are on player anticipation, readiness, and commitment—can help create the self-discipline and energy needed for a team to compete at a high level.

Positioning and Awareness Skills

Players must develop the self-discipline necessary to play from a balanced low-body position so as to play defensively from the floor up. Getting comfortable in this position is the result of regularly training in it. Players must move from their medium starting position to the low-body defensive position each time the opposing team contacts the ball, anticipating that it could cross the net with any one of the opponent's contact touches.

To get into the low-body position, players widen their medium base (taller players have a wider base to help them achieve a lower position) and bring the back forward and the chest down so that the back is nearly parallel with the floor. The angle of a player's back is a matter of individual preference. The position that achieves the best results for each player should be emphasized over all players having an identical style, such as a low, flat back. The body weight is transferred to the balls of the feet, allowing the heels to come up slightly. The knees point slightly in and are in front of the feet, and the shoulders are in front of the knees (figure 5.1). In this position, a player can put one hand down and easily touch the ground. This is similar to basketball players on defense or an infielder scooping a ground ball in baseball or softball.

The low-body position permits controlled movements and trained reaction to balls that are knee to waist high and no more than a few inches off the ground. When moving to play a ball inches off the ground, players should be told to "run downhill" and "finish through the ball" by sliding across the hardwood; this lessens the impact of the floor. Should the ball be deflected on its path to the defensive player, discipline in moving to the ball without changing planes is the key.

Figure 5.1 The balanced, low-body position.

Another part of proper defensive body positioning is being in balance, or being ready to move comfortably in any direction. Playing with balance enables an athlete to instantly and comfortably react to the unexpected and to have consistently good ball control when handling routine plays. Let's look at what balance offers to a defensive player in the heat of the contest.

For blockers, being balanced involves being able to assume the following three body positions:

- Players must be balanced in their movements along the net to avoid knocking their blocking partner off-balance or incurring a net violation.
- Being balanced in the air permits players to use their hands in conjunction with their developed shoulder strength to intercept a ball and direct it into the opponent's court.
- Being balanced upon landing means blockers land under control without incurring a line or net violation. This allows them to push away from the net to begin taking on their next responsibility.

For the digger, being in balance allows him or her to absorb the attacked ball and control its ricochet back to the setter. It also permits him or her to react to a ball that changes direction when it is tipped, rolled, or deflected off the block.

Players also need to know their position with regard to the court boundaries. Each player has two silent partners that never vary: the boundary lines and the antenna. The sidelines and the end line are a defensive player's best friends if he or she knows exactly how far he or she is positioned from them. Players should also know how many steps it takes to place a foot on a boundary line before either the opponent touches the ball or the served or attacked ball reaches that particular line. A ball must cross the net inside the antenna to be legal. This reduces the floor space defensive players must cover. As figure 5.2 shows, the defensive player is positioned so as to cover only the floor space in which the opponent's attack could pass inside the antenna and legally land.

Players must react to the opponent's attack to protect their primary and secondary coverage areas. Thus, they must develop the discipline to be in the correct position at all times. If a player is in the process of moving to a designated area and the opponent is contacting the ball, the player should stop and balance no matter where he or she is on the floor. This prevents the player from moving in a wrong direction. Players may need to slightly adjust their starting position when being screened by one or more opponents. When making this adjustment, they must be attentive to the space left uncovered and compensate by taking additional steps to cover a ball directed to that area.

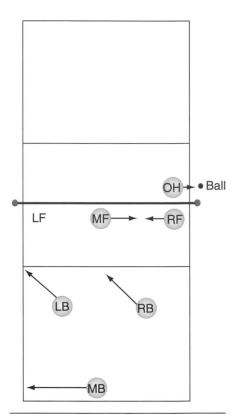

Figure 5.2 Defenders position themselves to cover every inch of legal floor space on an angle call.

Being unable to see the ball puts a player at a disadvantage when quick reactions to an attack may be the difference between a controlled dig and an error. The back-middle defensive player must be more disciplined when behind the double block and must anticipate that balls will come over or off the blocker's hands. They should think "See the ball, anticipate it coming to you, and move to dig it."

Once players understand their starting and basic defensive body positions, they can hone their awareness skills for effective defense. These skills include the following:

• **Recognizing visual cues.** Each player should start by identifying whether there are two or three front-row players among the opposition who may legally attack above the net. But it's also important to recognize if the opposing setter can attack as well, as this means that there are two front-row players and the setter for whom one must account. With a front-row setter, it is important to determine whether he or she is more interested in attacking or running the offense. Setters may only attack or bring a ball over from above the net if they are in the front row, although they can always bring a ball over if it is below the top of the net. A camouflaged back-row setter improperly identified as a front-row player can cause a front-row defensive player to jump to block this ineligible player, thus reducing the number of his or her team's blockers who are available to block the legal hitters.

- **Tracking the ball.** The location of the first pass from any member of the opposing team generally indicates the speed at which it can attack, whether it can attack from all zones in the front row equally well, and perhaps even which player is most likely to receive the set. A first ball passed away from the net or toward the sideline reduces the ability of an opponent to run a quick middle attack, thus enabling the blockers to focus on the other hitters. But, at the same time, the blockers must recognize that a team's errant first pass can also necessitate the use of a back-row attack.

- **Tracking the opposing hitter.** Each front row player must visually track and verbally communicate the position of the opponent's legal attacking players from his or her initial receiving pattern to his or her attack area. Opposing hitters may line up in a certain area and attack from a completely different area along the net. The opponent may overload one area (this is called a tandem or an X) to draw the attention of two blockers and thereby isolate the opponent's third hitter on one blocker. The opponent may attack three areas using a 4, 31, or back-1 call to isolate one-on-one blocking. The 4-1-5 attack sequence (described in chapter 6) is the most basic of play calls, but it forces the opponent to cover the hitters from antenna to antenna. Players and coaches must realize that a basic attack can be very effective. By the same token, using fancy combinations doesn't always equate with the ability to side-out consistently. The opponent may send one player from the inside out and follow with one player from the outside in (this could be called a front X or a wide slide with a middle 2 ball). These plays are illustrated on pages 117 and 118. Communication from the first teammate who identifies this movement can alert the entire team to these sorts of combination or isolation plays. Defensive back-row players must be able to see the ball as well as the opposing hitter's approach and also call out any second tempo players. A second tempo player is one who might hit the second ball in the sequence of contacts. The first attacker may be in the air for a quick 1 ball while the second player, coming in behind on an X or tandem, looks for the second ball in the sequence (a 2 ball).

- **Communicating.** Communication involves being able to give, listen for, and acknowledge verbal cues. A verbal response from team members on the floor indicates that they know the location and total number of legal attacking players across the net. A cue can be given, such as "red defense" (see chapter 7 for more on this) or "SR" (meaning shift the front row to the right to either double the middle or left-side hitter). In this example, the left- and middle-front blockers shift to the right. The first priority for blocking the quick hitter shifts to the left-front blocker instead of the middle blocker.

Players must call for the ball immediately in a loud, traffic-stopping voice to prevent hesitation or keep another player from reaching in front of them to take the ball. Since two players may call for the ball at the same time, players should train to use a machine-gun-type vocal repetition, such as "mine, mine, mine," or calling and opening the arms out wide at the same time to provide a visual acknowledgement to their teammates. These examples of ownership should help prevent confusion and hesitation not only on defense but on offense as well.

- **Using the correct technique.** Once a player has called the ball, it is important to make crisp and quick movements to get to it. As I have stated previously, *play the ball; don't let the ball play you.* I say this to emphasize how players need to be in the correct position to control the ball. The earlier a player can be in position with good body balance, the better chance he or she has of being successful.

Players must attempt to get to every ball using great quickness while leading and finishing with the correct foot. Once a player goes to his or her knees, unless the ball is right in the lap, he or she has virtually eliminated any opportunity to get to a tipped or off-speed ball successfully, if at all. If one gets caught out of position or if the ball is further away, the emergency skills described at the end of this chapter can be used at the completion of a planned contact.

I have had many players see the ball, take the correct steps to play it, and make contact with it only to dig it out of bounds. This occurs because midway through the technique the player turns his or her body in the wrong direction or adopts the form for another technique. For example, many players take the correct steps to use the lateral extension technique but finish with a sprawl. Instead of turning the hips and platform toward the target, they rotate the hips toward the boundary. This results in the ball going out of bounds instead of toward the setter. So whether players are digging or blocking, it is crucial to effective defense that they be able to competently perform their positioning and finishing techniques.

Blocking

The block in volleyball can be as energizing as a slam dunk is in basketball. Blocks often result in a lot of excitement on the court, so players need to keep in mind that this is only one play and immediately refocus on the next play sequence (unless, of course, that block finishes off a game or match). A block can cover up a weak defense or force the opponent to alter his or her normal swing or to use off-speed shots.

Blocking Technique

Players need to learn to focus their vision on the following sequence for blocking—ball, setter, ball, hitter. Once a player has anticipated where the set ball will reach its apex, his or her focus must immediately move to the hitter's angle of attack, the hitter's distance off the net, and ultimately where the attacked ball will cross the net. Combining these elements, the blocking player can get into the proper position along the net and jump into the air with balance to intercept the ball on the opponent's side of the net. Landing with control, finding the ball off the touch, and transitioning off the net are also integral aspects of a proper block sequence.

I've had players say to me, "I have never touched a ball above the net in a block situation." There can be many reasons for this: perhaps their opponents do not successfully swing at the third ball due to poor ball control or a bad set; perhaps the player has never timed the block correctly to touch the ball above the net; or perhaps the blocker is not able to visualize where the ball will cross the net, has never been able to get his or her hands above the net, flinches, or closes his or her eyes. So how can coaches help players successfully block a ball? There are so many factors that players must process: seeing the ball's movement, seeing the hitter's movements, communicating with teammates, taking off and landing in a balanced manner, and making hand contact with appropriate follow-through on the ball while the hands are on the opponent's side of the net. It was my experience that our best blockers had an innate ability to visualize, move, jump, and time the ball to intercept it on the opponent's side of the net. But coaches can dictate blocking situations and provide repetitions in practice to improve players' vision, movement, and timing.

Hand Position and Contact

To teach blocking, I recommend first that coaches have players feel the ball contacting the hands. Coaches can stand 3 feet (90 centimeters) away, facing a player who has his or her back against a wall to prevent him or her from leaning backwards and to reinforce his or her forward reach. Using an overhand throwing motion, the coach releases the ball, from a distance of no more than two feet, into the player's hands. During this throw the coach observes whether the player does any of the following: closes the eyes, flinches, throws the forearms instead of the hands, or leads with the fingers instead of the palms. The player can then proceed to blocking while using a lowered net so that he or she does not need to jump but gets the feel of pressing the hands across the net. Once players feel the contact, they learn to move their hands simultaneously to deflect the ball into the opponent's half of the court.

Players can start by holding their arms out and up in front of them with the elbows as high as the shoulders and with the hands visible and thumbs at eye height or higher (figure 5.3a). The quicker the opponent's attack, the higher a middle blocker initially should hold the hands. The fingers are spread with the thumbs parallel to the top of the net and 1 inch (2.5 centimeters) apart. For a taller player or one who jumps higher, the thumbs may be rotated upward. This pulls the forearms closer together so that a ball that is missed by the hands does not go through the forearms. The player points the fingers up so that contact is on the palms rather than the ends of the fingers. Players' hands should be on the opponent's side of the net. Shorter players may lay both hands back at the top of the net to soft block, which deflects the ball up and back to teammates instead of toward the opposing team.

Players reaching over a lowered net can also get the feel of effective hand-to-ball contact for blocking without jumping. The arms are extended upward and forward to simulate penetrating the net. The elbows are locked and the shoulders are shrugged and firm (figure 5.3b).

Figure 5.3 Proper hand position before and during contact with the ball sends the ball in the desired direction.

Footwork

Coaches and players alike should experiment with shuffle and crossover steps as well as a rotation stop or jump stop for effective blocking. While the steps are being learned, it is vital that the blocker's eyes are on the opponent's hitter and not his or her own feet or on a teammate with whom he or she is double blocking. The speed, style, and length of the steps the middle blocker takes to double with the outside blocker are directly related to the height and speed of the set. Outside blockers should also learn these various steps so that they can close on blocks or transition to the outside, when necessary, to block a slide or shoot set.

Slower shuffle steps or fast walking crossover steps can suffice for blocking in response to a poor first pass, that is, one that indicates to the blockers where the set must go or a very high 5 or 4 set. Faster running-type or crossover steps are necessary when the opposing setter pushes a fast low set—such as a 32, 42, or 41—or when an approach by the opponent's middle makes the middle blocker hesitate and forces that player to turn and run to the outside.

Blocking players have several footwork options available, depending on the distance they must travel to set up for the block. Players can rehearse these footwork movements and techniques without a ball, on a court, or along a wall. Here is a description of the most common footwork options:

• **One step**—step, close and balance, jump. This footwork puts a player into position to take away the shoulder angle of the approaching hitter.

• **Two shuffle steps**—step, close, step, close and balance. Players can use this if the set is higher than a 1-ball set (about 1 foot, or 30 centimeters, above the net), if the direction the ball is set permits the blocker to leave early, or if the player's team is using a special block sequence. The two-step technique can also be done with the foot and leg furthest away from the direction the player is going crossing in front of the body and the second leg following to square to the net in a balanced position.

• **Three steps.** There are three styles for the three-step technique:

1. *The crossover:* Step first with the lead foot (right foot if going right, left foot if going left). On the second step, make a long, aggressive crossover step with the back leg. Plant the lead foot on the third step. Due to the heel rotation at the end of the second step, the blocker's body is already turned toward the net.

2. *The spin and pivot:* Step with the lead foot, then cross over and spin the toe of the second foot when it contacts the ground to pivot the shoulders squarely and land the third step before the jump. This ensures a balanced, straight-up takeoff for the jump as the toes are now pointing toward the net.

3. *The jump stop:* Step with the lead foot and make a long cross-step push to a jump stop. The player pushes off the second step to jump and land in a position similar to a skier preparing to turn. He or she should land on both feet on this jump with the inside knee bent and the outside knee slightly straighter but facing back toward the middle of the court. This is done so that when the player jumps he or she does not float toward the outside or knock over his or her blocking partner. The middle blocker then jumps to block as he or she reacts to the vocal command of the outside blocker. When moving down the net, the middle blocker must focus on the attack angle of the approaching outside hitter. This enables him or her to know where to stop his or her steps in preparation for the block jump (figure 5.4).

Figure 5.4 The jump-stop, or skier's turn, option for three-step footwork.

- **Turn and run.** The speed of the set or the hesitation caused by a strong opponent's middle attacking approach forces the blocker to open and run to the spot where the ball will cross the net. The blocker can anticipate where to be on the court based on reading the angle of the approach and the shoulder angle of the hitter. The blocker moves quickly and either plants the lead foot or jump-stops with both feet to square the shoulders before the vertical takeoff and rotation in the air. There are times when the middle blocker is only able to get one hand, the lead hand, over the net. Many blockers use a full double-arm swing block approach for this type of block and turn or square the shoulders as they are leaving the ground to penetrate the net. This technique is used a great deal with men's teams to enable the blocker to block at maximum height.

Jumping and Landing

The best blockers have great timing, balance, and strength in the air. This enables the blocker to intercept the ball on the opponent's side of the net. The techniques for contacting and deflecting the ball into the center of the opponent's court are performed with greater stability and consistency. Balanced players also will land more often under control. This enables them to get off the net more easily when transitioning to offense. Keeping the body balanced with the feet shoulder-width apart and the knees flexed is the key to any effective jumping technique. Smaller players who can get their wrists above the net can be great blockers because they block with the hands rather than the forearms.

The butt jump is a primary technique players can use to learn to jump by relying solely on their leg and buttock strength and not on arm swinging. From a flexed position, players explosively extend the legs and ankles to jump and simultaneously penetrate the net with the hands, which are moving upward and forward. I use the term 'penetrate' to illustrate that the player is not reaching or throwing the hands over the net. Smaller players may flex their knees to a greater degree in order to add height to their jump. Players must be aware of the possibility of a net violation on the way up. A player can practice jumps using marks (or tape) on a wall to measure each jump. The player places the hands flat on the wall so that he or she does not lead with the fingers.

Landing is also an important part of jumping. If players do not feel the ball touch the hands, they should immediately pull the hands and arms back and drop the elbows against the side so as not to contact the net on the way down. If they contact the ball, they should follow through with the hands to throw it to the inside middle of the court.

Upon landing, players are responsible for any ball that is still above or in front of them in their immediate area. So any blocker who does not score with the block should turn in a flexed position and find the ball. This is the only time that a player can touch the ball twice consecutively, since a block touch does not count as a contact. The blocker may be able to play a ball that no one else on the team would have the chance to play. When the blocker knows he or she has made contact with the ball but is not sure where the ball has gone, he or she should first look up. If the ball goes down, it will be on the floor before he or she can react. If the ball is above the blocker's head, he or she should tilt the hand closest to the ball to be flat and slightly backward to knock or pop the second contact back to his or her teammates (figure 5.5). The hand surface must be solid so as to not

Figure 5.5 While landing a jump, a player who has not scored on a block must track the ball and and try to send it to his or her teammates.

lift, or double, the ball. If the ball is between the blocker and the net, he or she should turn the inside shoulder away from the net and try to pull the ball to a teammate with one solid hand or two arms.

Blocking Positions

Each blocking position has certain characteristics that coaches must look for and players must work to enhance. Right-side blockers must learn to set a block and call the timing whenever the set is to the opponent's left-side hitter. Many opponents frequently set to the left side, so attentiveness by the right-side blocker is critical to the first steps of defensive play. The left-side blocker should be able to block using the antenna for spacing and to communicate the timing to the middle blocker. In addition, the left-side blocker should be able to block a 5 set as well as the opponent's specialty sets—such as a 1 ball, back 1 ball, or slide. The 5 set is a back set at a height similar to the 4-ball set but to the right front of the opponent's court to a predetermined hitter. The middle blocker must have a tireless work ethic. He or she is expected to not only block any player who attacks from the middle but also to get to the outside to double block with his or her teammate. Sets to the middle blocker can range from low quick sets (such as 1-ball sets) to sets slightly farther away (such as 21s, 31s, back 1s, tight slides, and slides). The middle blocker must also be capable of blocking second tempo sets and back-row attacks.

Training the Middle Blocker

The middle blocker must bring an abundance of energy to each play, whether in training or during a match. The middle blocker's role is to help block opponents along the net from antenna to antenna as well as transitioning and being available, using multiple approaches, to attack a quick set.

As Josh Steinbach, assistant coach at Wright State University, has stated, the specificity of this position dictates that coaches must find time to work with these players one on one. If multiple courts are available, middle blockers can be trained separately using specific drills designed for transitioning from the serve reception patterns or from a block, free ball, down ball, or hitter coverage.

The height of the middle blocker's hands in the initial starting position depends on the speed at which the opponent runs the middle attack. The quicker the attack, the higher the hands must start. The middle blocker may not have to jump as high but must be able to immediately penetrate the net to stop a fast set.

The starting position and ball cut-off angle for the middle blocker are determined by the middle hitter's approach angle and primary arm-swing angle. Most middle hitters approach at an angle to the setter and attack with an easier swing toward the 5 defensive position or their opponent's left back. My team's strategy was to force the opponent's middle hitter to cut the ball back to our three diggers' coverage area or make him or her hit one of his or her weaker shots.

The middle blocker initially should attempt to stop a right-hand attack of the middle hitter by taking away his or her right shoulder by lining up the center of his or her chest with the opponent's attacking shoulder and putting one blocking hand on either side of the opponent's attacking hand. Should the player take a sharper angle than that for which the blocker is prepared, the blocker must use a one-step block movement before jumping to take away the new angle. When the opponent's middle hitter comes straight into the net instead of approaching at an angle, then the blocker should front the hitter and prevent the ball from being hit straight down the middle. If the ball is set to an outside attack, the middle must use the correct two- or three-step footwork to get to his or her blocking partner. Players should make sure that they only watch the ball until it reaches the peak and then immediately refocus on the attacking angle of the opponent's outside hitter. They should not look at their blocking partner but stop where they think the ball will cross the net. They should instead listen to the blocking partner's vocal cues for when to jump. The blocker must attempt to deflect the blocked ball toward the middle of the court. Blocking an opponent's shoot sets, such as the 21 and 31, is easier if one focuses on the correct starting position and relies on his or her tracking skills to move over slightly to get in front of the hitter.

Coaches can incorporate into practices drills that concentrate on the middle blocker receiving help from the right-front teammate when attempting to block wider sets, such as the 31 and 4. When the opponent's setter is in the front row, the blocking assignment changes slightly. The left-front blocker blocks the right shoulder and primary hitting angle of the middle attack, and the middle blocker's responsibility is to take the cutback shot. This also permits him or her to start off-center right to take away the 21 and 31 shoot sets while also making it easier to get to the outside to double the opponent's left-side hitter. When communication from a front-row teammate is received or when his or her own vision dictates, the middle blocker can block the second opponent on a combination play.

Training the Right-Side Blocker

Depending on the predetermined strategy, the right-side blocker either sets up to block a shot down the line, in the seam, or cross court. He or she must use the right antenna for spacing and make sure that the right blocking hand is slightly turned in toward the middle of the opponent's court.

The right-side blocker has a formidable task. He or she is matched up against the opponent's most common set and, on many occasions, the best hitter. This opponent can come from the inside out (swing hitting) or from the outside in (transition hitting). Setters tend to push a bad pass to the outside when the serve-receive pass does not permit a middle attack. Right-side blockers must be able to read the approach of the hitter and set the block. Additionally, it is the responsibility of the right-side blocker to call the jump timing so that he or she and the middle blocker go up together.

Right-side blockers must be aware of the opponent's middle hitter staying or moving toward the outside to run a 31 set. They can assist the middle blocker by helping to block the 31 set. If this is a favorite attack strategy of the opponent, they start closer to the middle blocker. One way for a right-side and middle blockers to position themselves is to stand close enough that, with arms outstretched, they can touch one another's fingertips. The right-side blocker then uses three-step block footwork to get back outside to block the 4 set.

When establishing a starting position to block the outside set, the right antenna can be used to attempt to take away the opponent's line shot. One strategy is to permit the hitter to hit the ball down the line. Such an attack must be especially accurate so as to avoid hitting the antenna or going out of bounds. As I discuss further in chapter 7, the line shot can then be dug by the right back in a black defense or by the middle back rotating to the corner in a red defense.

The most difficult situation for a right-side blocker to stop is a great opponent who hits the ball off his or her hands and directly out of bounds. This shot makes it very difficult to use the blocking hands to direct the ball into the court.

Another blocking strategy is to channel the ball to the team's best digger, who, for example, may be in the left-back or the cross-court angle. Blocking the line shot permits the opponent to hit the cross-court shot. Once the opponent's attack has been made, the right-side blocker must also be ready and able to set the second ball as the help setter when the team transitions off the net. Coaches can set up drills to isolate the right-side blocker against the left-front hitter.

Training the Left-Side Blocker

The left-side blocker must be aware of the two situations that he or she may face: either the opponent's setter is in the back row, making three hitters eligible, or the opponent's setter is in the front row, making the setter an eligible receiver.

The left-side blocker must be able to block the middle hitter and still move outside to the left to block the slide set. This blocker must be able to play defense along the net or rotate off the net, depending on what team defensive strategy is chosen (see chapter 7). The left-side blocker may be asked to read-block the middle, which means seeing the middle set before blocking it. He or she may also be asked to commit-block on the opponent's middle by jumping and penetrating the net, whether the middle gets set or not. The left-side blocker must be able to set the block on the opponent's right-side hitter and call the timing so that the double block with the middle blocker is simultaneous. He or she must also be prepared to block the opposing setter when the setter tips or attacks the ball. This is done when the left side is not the primary blocker on the middle hitter.

The blocking drills for the left-side blocker are similar to other blocking drills, but he or she must also be able to block a left-handed hitter as he or she reads the approach angle of this right-side hitter to time his or her block.

Blocking Drills

A coach can start by designing drills to teach blocking without the use of a ball or jump. Once players have mastered the movements without a ball or jump, a ball can be added without a net. Then the net can be added (first at a lower level than regulation height). Finally, the player will be ready to add the jump. Other factors come into play when a player is working to improve movement, rhythm, jump, and ball contact. These include the opponent's play-set, the height of the set ball, the distance the ball is set off the net, the relationship of the ball to the antenna, the defensive scheme the team is playing, the jumping ability of the opponent, and the speed of the hitter's arm swing.

BLOCKING VARIOUS ATTACKS

FOCUS

Learn to block various attacks.

PROCEDURE

Once the basics of blocking are learned with this drill, coaches may vary it by blocking the slide one day, left-side blocking the middle another day, and so on. This drill requires a box that is 18 to 36 inches (approximately 45 to 90 centimeters) high, a coach, and between two and eight players. The defensive players should be set up so that the right-front blocker can help-set a ball played by his or her setter.

1. A coach stands on the box directly across the net in front of the middle blocker. He or she holds a ball.

2. The coach starts by hitting the ball into the hands of the blocker at various speeds. When the coach smacks the ball with the hand and turns the shoulder one way or the other, the middle blocker makes a one-step adjustment before jumping and penetrating the hands to take away the identified angle.

3. The middle blocker continues blocking, but now the coach sets the ball while a middle hitter approaches, jumps, and attacks the quick set from the coach, using the three attack angles.

4. The coach tosses to a setter who has penetrated from the back row, who sets the middle hitter, and the middle blocker blocks the attack.

5. The coach tosses the ball to the setter who has penetrated from the back row, who sets a 1 ball or 21 set. The coach can add a right-front player to help block when the setter sets a 21 or 4 ball. He or she can also set up the drill so that the back-row setter sets a 1 or 4 ball and forces the middle blocker to use the proper footwork to double block with the right-front teammate.

6. Add a right-front attacking opponent and have the back-row setter run a 1 ball, a 4 ball, and a back 5 set. The middle blocker closes and double blocks with the left-front teammate (see figure a).

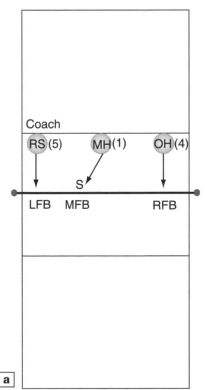

(continued)

7. The opponents run a front X by having the middle hitter come in for a 1-ball set and the right-front hitter coming around the middle to attack a 2 set. The defensive blockers, as well as the back-row players, must communicate when two opponents are running a combination play. The outside hitter is available to attack a 4 set. The left-front blocker should block the 1 ball, while the middle blocker blocks the right-front hitter playing a 2 ball (see figure b).

8. The setter has the middle hitter go first and uses a slide step to hit a back set, and the right-front hitter comes around to the middle for a 2 ball. The outside hitter is available to attack a 4 set. The left-front blocker blocks the slide while the middle blocker blocks the opponent's right-side hitter's 2-ball attack (see figure c)

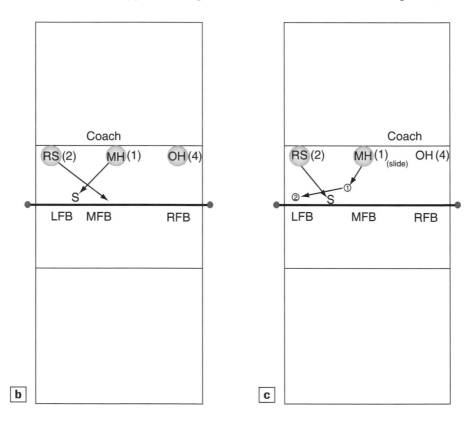

Coaches can continue to vary this drill by attacking the ball from several distances off the net using different arm swings and angles. Coaches can also have a player stand on the box and take a toss for attacking. In this way, the blocker times the player who can hit different angles in order to duplicate game situations. Although not completely gamelike, having a player on a box provides more repetitions without timing mistakes for both the attacker and blocker.

LEFT-SIDE MULTIPLE-BLOCKING MOVEMENT

FOCUS

This drill helps the blocker work on his or her movement from blocking the middle hitter and then getting back outside to block the slide.

PROCEDURE

Six players are fielded on each side of the net. This drill can be done with the coach tossing to a back-row player from the other side of the net and that player passing the ball to the setter (see figure).

1. The left-side blocker starts on the inside shoulder of the opponent's setter.

2. Players begin game-speed play from the first pass.

3. When a pass forces the setter to back up, the left-front blocker remains and reads the middle hitter.

4. When a pass is tight on top of the net, the left-front blocker jumps and penetrates the net with the hands to prevent the hard tip by the setter. On a good pass and set, the left-front blocker must work on three-step crossover footwork to get back to the left to square up and jump to block the slide. The block should take away the cross-court shot first.

5. Players should also work to determine whether they can use a two-step crossover to get back outside. Start with the right (or inside) foot immediately crossing in front of the left foot, step, and square-up with the left foot before the jump.

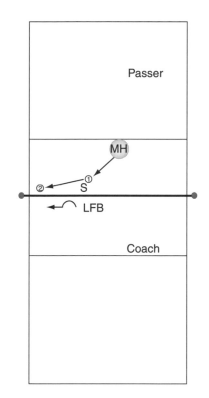

4 VERSUS 5

FOCUS

This is one of my favorite one-on-one attack and block drills because it is played at game speed, it is extremely competitive, it uses two different scoring systems, and the coach can change the make-up of each team. The name comes from the player on one team attacking all 4-ball sets and the player on the other attacking all 5-ball sets.

PROCEDURE

This drill can be played six on six or five on five by eliminating the middle blockers from both teams. Once each team is on the court, follow these procedures.

1. The coach introduces the ball to one court, either with a free ball or a down ball, and alternates sides no matter which team scores. (Coaches can change the dynamics of this drill by giving the ball back to the winning side).

2. The setters are instructed to set every possible ball to the intended hitters, but when this is not possible, the set must go to a back-row player to attack or clear the ball over the net.

3. From here, players play a game using one of the following scoring systems:

   a. Wash scoring. The game is played until one team earns 5 points only from side-outs. If team A earns the first point and is up 1-0 and team B earns the second point, then this washes out team A's first point and returns the score to 0-0.

   b. Rally scoring or point for play. The first player to reach 10 points wins the game for his or her team.

SHIFT RIGHT DRILL

FOCUS

This drill teaches defensive players their coverage responsibilities, which depend on the actions of the opponent's front-row setter and two hitters.

PROCEDURE

A full six-person defensive team is set up versus the opponent's setter, middle hitter, and left-side hitter. Players follow these procedures:

1. The offense runs from a pass or a ball tossed to the setter for a 1 ball, or a slide attack combined with a 4 ball set outside.

2. The left-back defensive player covers the outside setter or middle hitter tip to the right front, or 4 zone.

3. The right side takes the inside tip.

4. The middle-back player covers the deep 5 corner (see figure).

5. The right back, using an overhand dig, takes the attack shot to the right-back corner.

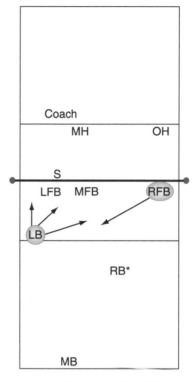

*use hands to take deep #1corner

Digging

Balls that are played from an opponent's standing down-ball swing or jumping attack are referred to as digs. The angle of the ball combined with topspin and increased speed force a player to lower his or her base and play from the floor upward. Balls that are hit high, deep, and inbounds must be played with open hands.

Digging Technique

The forearm platform is a great surface for digging a ball attacked by the opponent. The attacked ball played on the forearms must be *absorbed*, rather than driven. The forearms come back toward the passer on contact to cushion the ball. The angle of the dig to the target depends on where the setter is releasing; it is higher when the setter is playing defense in the back row, and it is angled to the net tape (the white taped area that runs along the top of the net) when the setter is a blocker in the front row. Players who make a second contact on a low errant first dig from a teammate should elevate the ball high and straight up to permit a teammate to get his or her feet into position for the third contact.

An overhand dig of the first ball, using a modification of the setting hands, is popular and necessary at advanced levels. National team players, collegiate men and women, top club team players, beach players, and high school boys all use this technique. Players use their hands to stop and transfer a ball that is coming toward their face or higher back toward the net. Players must have firmer hands that are held closer together to be able to "stop" the ball before redirecting it toward the target.

According to Russ Rose, head women's volleyball coach at Penn State and noted defensive guru, there are four steps to being able to dig and control a ball effectively after a player verbally acknowledges he or she will do so:

1. Make a crisp, balanced movement to intercept the ball. This may be accelerated, depending on the distance of the ball from the primary defender.

2. Touching the ball may be the only thing a player can do, depending on the ball's distance from the player or the speed of the attack. The main point is that a player should not predetermine how much distance he or she can cover and therefore should go for every ball. The concept teaches that at some point he or she will not only get to and touch the ball but also will have success.

3. Using a trained technique, a player will put the best possible ball-controlling surface on the ball. This contact may result in a ball that is stopped and transferred up into the air to be playable by a teammate but that does not reach the target area.

4. Use the correct and most advantageous learned skill to turn the ball up and to the target with control. In this case, the target is the area of the court, usually 8 feet (2.4 meters) in from the right antenna. This is the preferred location for the setter to run the offense. The team now can transition to a multiple offensive-attack phase.

Emergency Skills

Emergency skills are those defensive digging skills that are specifically designed to play difficult balls that have been attacked at varying angles and speeds. Learning these techniques allows a defensive player to accelerate through a ball that appears to be out of reach or unplayable. The first four skills that follow are geared toward attacked balls within arm's reach in various directions from the body. The last seven skills are designed for those balls that require the player to run downhill and accelerate to touch the ball, using the floor as a cushion to spread the body impact when necessary.

- **J-stroke.** This technique, simulating hand-turn control, is used when a player quickly reaches the contact platform under and beyond the ball because he or she cannot get the whole platform in place. The J-stroke can be used to reach to the side, low in front, or when sprinting forward toward the net for a short tip. Players can produce a ball with backspin as they run through the ball instead of trying to stop or going to the floor. Once the connected hands are under and beyond the ball, they rotate backward toward the player's chest immediately following the ball contact at the wrist level (figure 5.6). This follow-through creates a reverse spin on the ball that makes the ball spin backward in the direction of the passer instead of forward toward the net or out of the reach of the next player.

- **Collapse dig.** This technique allows the player to control the ball with the wrist and thumb (hand-control) surface while dropping to a knee, relaxing at the shoulders as the controlling arm surface goes underneath the ball, and reversing the thumbs to move the ball up with backspin (figure 5.7). By dropping to a knee, the player can reach underneath balls that are closer to the floor.

Figure 5.6 The J stroke.

Figure 5.7 The collapse dig.

• **Open-handed dig**. The first technique has a player using the open hands but making them strong, tight, and stiff to stop the ball's forward flight. This dig attempts to push the ball upward and toward the setter in an effort to control the ball back to the target (figure 5.8). The player can also use two open, flat hands tilted slightly upward and backward, contacting the ball with the palms One of the player's thumbs can rest on top of the other, or for those with less hand strength, the thumbs can overlap to provide a more stable surface. This technique is used to stop a ball rather than to try and control the ball back to a teammate.

• **Lateral extension.** The lateral extension is a skill that permits a player to intercept, control, and turn a ball that has been hit hard and at an angle to the body. The ball is hit so hard that the defensive player has no time to do anything but take a reaction

Figure 5.8 The open-handed dig.

step to the side of the attacked ball. The lead step, taken with the foot on the ball side, moves the defensive player from a low starting position to a lower ending position (figure 5.9a). The player's buttocks may be low enough to be "sitting" on the heel of the lead foot. The ball is then contacted, most often on the forearm surface, below the knee and above the ankle—or further away when a player has to extend the arms even further than anticipated (figure 5.9b). The toes of the lead foot are turned to the target, and, if possible, the ball is played inside the lead knee. When played outside the lead knee, the success rate of turning the ball is lower due to the fact that the player's platform is too level and he or she has not dropped the inside shoulder to raise the lead, or outside, arm to form a wall.

As the ball is being contacted, the player continues to turn the lead foot in toward the middle of the body (figure 5.9c). This exposes the outside of the thigh and the side of the buttocks on the side of the step. Once the ball has been contacted, the player should reach out as far as possible with the lead hand and slide it forward so that the armpit is flat on the floor (figure 5.9d). Assuming this is a right extension, the front (right) leg is bent and the back leg is straight and elevated off the ground. The player should scissor the straight back leg down as he or she pulls the lead arm back toward the body. He or she should push off the ground, with the right forearm and left hand and then the right hand, and return to a standing position. Players must be ambidextrous when playing defense and equally able to go right and left. The ability to go in both directions takes time to master since most players are more comfortable going to their dominant side.

Figure 5.9 Lateral extension: the lead step (*a*), contact (*b*), the turn (*c*), and the reach and slide (*d*).

• **Accelerated lateral extension with roll.** This lateral extension is used for balls a great distance away from the player and necessitates using an odd number of steps (three or more, depending on the distance from the ball, but always an odd number). Taking an odd number of steps is done to ensure that the lead foot is also the foot that initiates the last step to contact the ball as the player rotates the hips to the target. The athlete using this technique is pursuing a ball that has been hit away from him or her at an angle, such as a ball directed into a back corner of the court. A player starts with a lead foot in the direction of the play, uses crossover steps, and accelerates to

intercept the ball. Due to the speed the defensive player has generated to contact a ball inches off the floor, a roll can return the player to his or her feet. The initial landing (figure 5.10a) is exactly the same as the lateral extension, but the player converts his or her momentum into a roll (figures 5.10b and c). The lower-bent leg (the right, or lead, leg in this explanation) is pulled up over the top of the left shoulder close to the player's left ear for a tight and compact double bent-knee roll back to the feet.

Figure 5.10 Accelerated lateral extension with roll: crossover steps and acceleration (*a*), landing (*b*), and conversion to a roll (*c*).

Players tend to be more comfortable rolling to one side. Spend additional time on the less comfortable side. My coaching staff and I found that it is easier to start player training using wrestling or gymnastics mats that have a large surface on which players can practice with minimal impact to help develop their confidence.

- **Front extension.** In the front extension, a player goes forward at a 45-degree angle or straight toward the net. The player should lean the shoulders forward and reach with the hands in front of the lead foot. The lead foot has already been turned in to turn the shoulders at a 90-degree angle to the net to permit greater reach. The finish is exactly as shown in the lateral extension. A roll can be used with the front extension, depending on the location of the play. Plays made between the 10-foot (3-meter) line and the net may not permit a roll due to the risk of committing a centerline violation or because of the location of the blockers turning and running off the net to transition to offense from the dig. The blockers must be aware of their teammate digging the ball at the floor level behind them. If the player is close to the net or centerline, instead of rolling he or she should slide and scissor back to the feet, as in the lateral extension (figure 5.11).

Figure 5.11   Front extension.

- **Run-through.** The player runs downhill with the shoulders low and his or her face up to get under the ball. As the player touches the ball, he or she simultaneously turns the platform's connected thumbs back toward the chest to initiate reverse ball spin (figure 5.12). This spin changes the ball direction to upward and backward and provides a teammate with the opportunity to get under the second contact.

Figure 5.12   The run-through.

• **Sprawl.** Defensive players use this technique only for hard-driven spikes that are directly in front of them as they face the target. Many players mistakenly use this technique for balls hit at an angle to the body. This is a problem because the hips and shoulders now face away from the target and toward the sideline. The resulting dig is unplayable by a teammate as the ball goes out of bounds.

A player should balance his or her stance beforehand so as to not be flatfooted. The shoulders should be in front of the knees and the knees in front of the feet with the heels off the ground. Once this balanced, low, precontact defensive position has been initiated, the player takes a comfortable step forward toward the ball, stepping wider than the player's hips. Players usually use the same foot to step forward each time they sprawl, which is fine as long as that step is the quickest and most comfortable for them. The lead foot turns out while the heel turns in on this step. The shoulders should be lower than the hips as the player drives the digging platform under the ball.

Once contact has been made with the ball (the thumbs may be rotated up and back toward the digger's chest), the heels of one or both hands slide forward on the court (figure 5.13a and b). Friction burns on the heels of the hands are common. Sliding works better when there is dust on the floor or a sheen of sweat on the player. Players can train for this by wearing socks on their hands. A commercial product that straps to the hands with protection on the heels of the hands can be worn in training as well as during matches. Since the lead knee has rotated out with the turn of the lead foot, the player's hips can also slide forward. The player extends forward  with the lead leg bent and the inside of the lead knee flat on the floor. The trail leg is straight behind the player. The hip bone of the straight leg is on the ground and can be easily bruised. Players can place padding in this area before training or a match. They can also purchase padded garments to wear under their shorts.

Figure 5.13 The sprawl.

• **Dive.** This is a technique used primarily by male players for softly hit balls that are a great distance in front of the player. After running forward, players executing a dive drive forward from the back foot as they put the opposite knee over the front foot with the shoulders in front of the knee. Players use the same foot to push from each time. They contact the ball on the wrist area and reverse the hands to impart backspin. Contact takes place close to the ground. Once contact has been made, diving players push off with the front leg while simultaneously lifting the back leg (figure 5.14). They catch the dive

Figure 5.14 The dive.

with both hands in a decline push-up position while beginning to lower the trunk. They push off the ground with the hands back toward the hips and slip forward on the chest with the chin turned away from the ground to the side. Note that a common injury using this technique is a split chin; the best way to prevent injury with players who are ready to try the dive is to build upper-body strength so that they are able to catch their body weight in a push-up position.

• **Open-handed scoop save.** Players should pursue a ball that is traveling away from the court by leading with the front foot and running. Taking an odd number of steps is necessary since the player leans over the front foot as he or she reaches out and under the ball. The contact is with the palm, and the simultaneous follow-through comes with the fingers wrapping around the ball as in an upside down spike (figure 5.15). Snapping on the ball with a great follow-through elevates it with reverse spin to a point at which a teammate can play it or direct it back over the net. Female players naturally turn the lead foot in and finish in an extension. Male players land and cushion themselves using the dive technique.

Figure 5.15 The open-handed scoop save.

- **Pancake.** This technique involves sliding the hand forward on the ground so that the ball comes down on top of the back of the hand. Male players have been known to dive first, and females use the front extension first to use this technique. This is not a practiced skill but a reaction from another attempt. Coaches should discourage players from using this technique as a primary skill since they tend to just squat or fall down and reach the lead hand forward. Fast, balanced movement to the ball is still the best option for playing a soft ball in front of a player.

The best way to learn how and when to use each defensive emergency technique and achieve consistency is to play Pepper, a drill that I describe on page 108, immediately following two drills that teach the preliminary skills for Pepper—the Digging Drill and Throwing Skills for Pepper. Playing Pepper with better players helps slower players increase their speed of play. Players can customize Pepper to work on just one technique.

DIGGING DRILL

FOCUS

Teach players how to absorb the ball.

PROCEDURE

For a digging drill to be effective, an accurate ball must be hit or thrown to a digger. The thrown ball may be more accurate, but it probably will not travel as fast or have topspin. Experienced players can be involved in attacking the balls in digging drills. Initially, balls can be hit from in front of the net to a line of diggers, but eventually balls must be hit from a higher trajectory over the net. In order to do this, a box or platform must be used.

1. Players dig from positions such as the following: setters in the right back, middles in the middle back and left side, or outside hitters in the left back.
2. Each player receives one ball from a coach or experienced player. The coach should find a way to determine if the defensive player is flatfooted or has inched in (that is, moved forward) to dig. It is very difficult to watch the player when looking at the ball before contact. Should another person be available to hit, the coach can watch the player's technique. The digger can also start with the toes behind a line and dig the ball with the heels in front of the line. This ensures that the player has in fact moved or balanced the body forward and closer to the attacked ball. This also enables the player to be in a more advantageous lower position because he or she has widened his or her base in the preliminary move and is not flat-footed.
3. After players have had numerous repetitions from one area, coaches should arrange to have balls attacked to diggers from at least three zones along the net: inside the right antenna, at the middle of the net, and inside the left antenna.

THROWING SKILLS FOR PEPPER

FOCUS

This drill teaches players to throw with control so that the ball they deliver to their partner challenges their partner to defend the areas around him or her, such as low in front of the body, beside the right or left knee, or at the face. In order for the Pepper drills to be effective, players also must develop confidence in their ability to hit a controlled topspin ball that makes their partner better.

PROCEDURE

Players pair up with a partner to alternate throwing and catching (then digging) and follow these steps:

1. With his or her back to the net, the thrower throws a ball to the catcher's lowered waist, using hip and shoulder rotation, high reach, proper footwork, and good follow-through.

2. The catching partner works on going from a medium position to a dropped and balanced, low defensive position.

3. Players repeat this sequence, alternating five times each.

4. Players repeat steps 1 through 3, attempting to target the throw to the catcher's knees and ankles, then low in front, outside the right hip, outside the left hip, outside the right knee, outside the left knee, sitting on the right heel (lateral extension), and sitting on the left heel.

5. Players repeat steps 1 through 4, but the thrower takes two quick plant steps, uses a full arm swing at one-half to two-thirds speed, and focuses on an accurate, faster throw.

6. Now the thrower (hitter) hits the ball with control, and instead of catching the ball, the catcher digs the ball with the forearms back to the hitter. The digging partner faces the net so that he or she can get a feel for the height of the ball in relation to the net and the degree of ball control that is needed. Continue with this step until the hitter can contact the defensive pass in the air and direct it back to the partner for another dig. Try for five consecutive hits and digs.

7. It is more difficult to attack the ball outside a partner's hips. Players should practice opening and closing the hitting shoulder before contact in order to direct the ball to the correct hip. Before the hit, the hitter should call the side to which he or she is going to hit. "Right" means to the digger's right hip. The digger may have to use a J-stroke to control the ball back to the hitter.

8. Once full arm-swing control has been improved, it is time for the players to begin playing Pepper.

PEPPER

FOCUS

Pepper is a continuous drill that two to nine players use to warm up or practice vital ball control skills. The basic skills involved are the forearm pass, overhead set, and attacking arm swing. Done correctly, the drill increases players' confidence in their ability to dig a ball to target or attack a ball with control into their opponent's court. Done incorrectly, it magnifies poor skills. The sequence requires the setter to become the next digger, the digger to become the next hitter, and the hitter to become the setter.

PROCEDURE

Divide the squad into several pairs of players. With players who exhibit good ball control, there may be four pairs working on one side of the net. New or inexperienced players will need more space, and there should be no more than three pairs of less experienced players on one side of the net. Once players have their partners, they follow these steps:

1. Players determine their "pepper" area of the court.

2. One player initiates play with an easy, controlled 10-foot (3-meter) serve or an under-hand toss.

3. The player's partner contacts the ball as a first pass, using the forearms, back to the tosser. This pass is a dig back to the tosser, who becomes a setter.

4. The setter sets the digger for an attacking arm swing. This second ball, or the ball that is to be set, is critical. The setter has a good idea that the ball will be dug but isn't exactly sure where that dig will go. Those responsible for the second contact should go for every ball, not just a ball that comes back close to them. They should set the ball higher when the digging partner is coming back to his or her feet from the ground in preparation for his or her full arm swing. The players alternate these skills of digging, setting, and hitting during every sequence of three contacts.

5. The players' goal is to keep the ball in play by not letting it touch the ground (unless there is a question of player safety). Each time the ball hits the ground, players start again with a serve or a toss. When the ball hits the ground far away from the initial pepper area, both players chase and start their pepper drill where they recovered the ball, if possible.

6. Players should have a goal and count the number of successful contacts as they challenge each other to reach that goal. Players can also set a time limit, such as one or two minutes to play Pepper with each partner.

There are several ways to play Pepper. Here are some of the routine types and a few favorite variations.

TWO-PERSON PEPPER

a. **Lap.** Player A (the hitter) hits with control such that player B (the digger) can receive this accurate attack at a height between player B's knees and waist. The hitter then sets and the digger hits. This is warm-up Pepper. The goal is for the ball not to hit the ground, since the ball is moving slowly.

b. **Jump lap.** This is performed the same as the lap version, but the hitter takes a two-step approach and jumps to attack the ball. Add tips and rolls with a full arm swing.

c. **Both jump.** Players jump to set and to attack. Add tips and rolls with a full arm swing.

d. **Angle.** Player A hits the ball outside player B's hip (or knees or ankles). Player B must reach and use a J-stroke to contact the ball on the wrists, immediately curl the thumbs around the ball to impart maximum spin, and control the ball back to player A.

e. **Lateral extension.** This is the same as the angle version, except that player A hits the ball at the shin or ankle area of player B, which forces player B to dig the ball, finish in a lateral extension, and immediately get back to his or her feet.

f. **Sprawl.** Player A hits the ball far enough in front of the partner that it requires a sprawl dig by player B, who goes to the ground and immediately returns to his or her feet to continue the sequence of contacts.

g. **Competitive.** This version combines all of the above two-person control games into one. All available techniques are used, and the ball is attacked with increased speed. Players do not call the side. Instead the defensive player must react to where the ball is hit.

THREE-PERSON PEPPER

a. **One designated setter.** One player, the designated setter, is stationed between and to the side of the other two players (see figure a). These two players, each of whom digs and then attacks, remain the same distance apart while the setter is 2 or 3 feet (about 60 to 90 centimeters) outside their line of attack. The setter touches every second ball as he or she faces the player who just dug the ball to him or her and is now prepared to attack. The setter should stay on one side, as it will encourage the proper follow-through from the digger to the correct side. The setter should then switch sides to help each player practice following through to both sides. When a whistle blows or a call to switch is made, the setter rotates to become a digger and hitter, and another player sets.

A

S

B

a

b. **Set and follow.** Players must concentrate on staying to set following the attacking swing. Coaches need to encourage players to use the correct pattern and discipline themselves to follow the correct sequence. For example, player A hits to player B (who digs) and then stays and sets to player B (who now attacks). Once player A sets player B, player A jogs behind player B. Player B then hits to player C (who digs) and then stays and sets to player C (who now attacks). After the set to player C, player B jogs behind player C, and so on.

c. **Over the net.** Players A and C hit over the net (either by jumping or delivering a standing down ball) while player B sets for both sides by ducking the net. Play for five sequences, starting with a soft floater serve, and then switch setters.

FOUR-PERSON PEPPER

a **Over the net.** Players A and B are teammates with player B doing all the setting to player A and also blocking. Players C and D are partners with player C doing the blocking and setting. Players play for a designated period of time and then switch positions. Another option is to switch the setter and hitter on their side of the net each time the ball goes over the net. Twelve players can be on the court at the same time. Each group gets one-third of the court (see figures b and c).

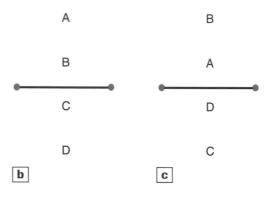

b. **No net.** Players A and B play side by side and face players C and D, who also play side by side. Players A and B have their backs to the net and are inside the 10-foot (3-meter) line. Players C and D face the net and start at the 20-foot (6-meter) line. Players pass and set to each other as one person touches the first and third ball in each rally. Players play a rally-score game to 10 and then switch opponents. Four groups can occupy the court with two Pepper games being played side by side simultaneously on each side of the net.

FIVE-PERSON PEPPER

a. **Over the net.** Players A and B play across the net against partners C and D but a setter sets for both sides by ducking the net. The drill can be increased in difficulty by asking the setter to jump-set each ball. The hitters should attack from between the 5- and 10-foot (1.5- and 3-meter) lines. This drill should also emphasize jumping to make the third contact. Play should take place on one-half of the court so two groups of five players each can play simultaneously.

NINE-PERSON PEPPER

a. **The full court.** All nine players stay on the court until the game's goals have been reached (for example, players have to duck the net five times without the ball hitting the floor). One setter ducks the net and sets for both groups as the two hitters also duck to the same side as the setter. This is a conditioning drill as well as a ball-control drill. Players on defense are working to cover their position responsibilities and defend the sequence of contacts, such as the over-pass, setter tip, and so on. Players emphasize ball control over hitting the ball as hard as possible. Play begins on one court as the left-side hitter calls for a 4-ball set while his or her hitting partner is calling for a 5-ball set. One of the two players will control attack the ball. Both hitters duck the net, whether they receive the set or not. Upon ducking the net, these same players are now available to hit from the opposite call side (see figure). The player who first called for a 4 ball now calls for a 5, while the player who first called for a 5 ball now calls for a 4. If a bad pass occurs or neither hitter is available to hit, the setter sets to players in the back row.

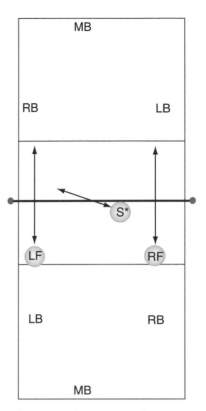

*Setter and hitters duck the net.

CHAPTER 6

Offensive Systems

The first step to establishing any offensive system is to ensure that the team can run an offense from the six serve-receive rotations covered in this chapter. The goal for all teams is to be able to side-out consistently or, at the very least, keep pace with the side-out ability of opponents. Teams must also be able to run an offense as they transition from defense and strive to score the extremely valuable *real* points that can make all the difference in a game. Transition offense is discussed in chapter 8.

There are many factors to consider when training individuals to receive serve. Visualize for a moment the variety of serves, the various areas of the court from which a server can contact the ball, the different speeds at which the ball crosses the net, whether it contacts the net legally, and the six zones into which a served ball can be placed. Coaches can see the task put before an individual and the team. Designing an effective offense depends on knowing how individual players and the team as a whole will react to mistakes and respond to pressure. Once a coach knows how his or her athletes respond to the serve-receive and attacking challenges, he or she can emphasize maintaining player confidence and building positive attitudes on a daily basis.

When designing an offense and serve-receive patterns, a coach must consider how many players are going to pass the served ball and identify these players. It is to a team's advantage to have at least two strong passers. When a team has only one solid passer, smart opponents will serve away from that player. Perfect passes, or those rated a 3, are necessary to run an offense that provides the setter with the choice of setting to any of the three front-row players.

The receiving patterns a coach chooses to use should also reflect player and court coverage roles by providing the best passer with the most area to cover. Still, at some point during a game, a team may have to adjust its receiving pattern because an opponent's server is creating ball-control problems for the offensive players. Most teams have at least one server who serves a very hard floater or topspin serve that handcuffs the offense, and the offensive team's coach may have to maneuver players into different positions to handle the challenge of that particular server. For this reason, daily practice for all players must provide multiple opportunities for them to pass serves that are floating, spinning, placed into corners, or dropped over the net. The previously identified best passers should receive the most repetitions of the really hard, fast serves.

Another vital factor in any offense is the ability of the designated setters. A coach should choose an offense based on the team's setting abilities. For example, in order to run an attack with three front-row hitters, a setter must be confident

© Human Kinetics

Jump-setting for an outside attack or a 4 ball.

in his or her ability to back-set. If a team has younger players, they can avoid the back-set by running a 4-2 offense (which always has a setter in the front row who sets from the front right; see page 121).

Since the setter's role is to run the team's offense, it is necessary to train him or her using specialized sessions that, at least at first, can be held separately from the rest of the team's designated practice. Once setters have experienced thousands of repetitions, they should be integrated into the many daily drills with all of the hitters or a group of specialized ones, such as the middle hitters. There are also training videos and books available that can help players to specialize their training in this area (see chapter 4 for details on the techniques employed in setting and individual drills that can be run to practice them). In particular, I recommend *The Volleyball Coaching Bible*, edited by Don Shondell and Cecile Reynaud (Human Kinetics, 2002). Setters must develop quickness to the ball and balanced footwork. They must also maintain a good vertical body position. Strong technical ability better enables the setter to deliver the ball to a consistent location for each hitter. Accurate ball placement is critical to having a consistent side-out attack.

Which set is used often reflects the quality of the first pass, the talent of the setter, and the athleticism of the hitters. The various types of sets are denoted by the height, location, or speed of the ball being delivered from the setter to the hitter.

Understanding the Types of Attacks

The examples I provide in this chapter are designed either to force the opponent to block all 30 feet (9.1 meters) along the net or to create quicker movements and different approach angles for the hitters. Quicker attacks and the use of different angles force the blockers to either jump more quickly or adjust their blocking steps to get into position above the net in order to take away the hitting angle. The setter's use of tips and the combination of two or more hitters moving into or out of an area are designed to confuse the blockers or make them jump at the wrong time. To run fast attacks or combinations, a team must have a middle hitter whose approach speed and angle as he or she moves toward the setter can set the tempo for the entire offense.

- **High outside set.** The intentionally set high ball goes to either antenna from a setter who stands or jumps to set the ball in front of or behind himself or herself. This is usually a slower set because its height is anywhere from 8 to 22 feet (2.5 to 7 meters) above the net. The distance the ball travels can be anywhere from 5 to 25 feet (1.5 to 7.5 meters), so the opponent usually has the opportunity for two blockers to jump and attempt to neutralize the attack with their hands. Even though the opponent's players may be ready to block against this type of set, it is easier for the hitter to time his or her approach and swing.

With numerous practice repetitions, the hitter can learn how to use the blockers' hands, place the ball into difficult coverage areas, or hit between or around the block.

- **Set for a back-row attack.** There are two kinds of back-row attacks. The first is an attack that is signaled to a back-row teammate before the serve by the setter. It is used in concert with the front-row hitters. This play-set attack forces the opponent to block from antenna to antenna. An example is a signal from a front-row setter to the right-back teammate to hit a C or D at the right antenna. The setter sets a back set with the hitter taking off behind the 10-foot (3-meter) line. At the same time, the setter has the two front-row hitters hitting sets in front of the setter. See the play calling signals on pages 117 and 118. The second kind of set to the back row is a bailout, which is often the result of the first pass being so poor that the setter has no option other than setting to a back-row player.

- **Setter tip or dump.** A player (usually the setter) intentionally places the second contact back over the net to catch the opponent off guard. A tip is directed to a difficult area for the opponent to cover by a front-row player (setter, opposite) using one hand. The difficult areas to cover when the opponent is using a middle-back defense are the deep corners, the short middle, and in the front-court corners directly below the antennas. The tip can be done from a standing position but is most commonly done from a jump. A dump is a ball directed by a back-row setter back over the net on the second ball using two hands in the overhand pass method (see pages 55 to 56).

- **Quick attack.** With a good to great first pass, the setter can have a player (most often the middle hitter) attack a low set from a predetermined area of the court.

- **Combination attack.** Two or more players are available for sets that can be quick or at a slightly slower tempo (at 2-ball height, for instance) in front of or behind the setter. These are sometimes referred to as second-tempo attacks. The objective is to hold a blocker or make him or her commit on the first tempo and follow behind with a second hitter who does not have a blocker ready to jump and block the attack. By holding two blockers with the first two options, the third option has a one-on-one block. Some teams use predetermined combination plays whereby one signal from the setter indicates to all the hitters what their pattern of attack will be. Another way to indicate each player's set is for the setter to signal to each player separately. Hitters will call to the setter a change to their personal attack by using numbers or letters if the pass would prohibit the setter from running the previously planned play. The ability to run combination sets is predicated on the ability of the players to run quick 1-ball sets. The following are examples of combinations with the setter penetrating from the back row with three hitters in the front row:

1. **Front X.** The middle hitter runs a front 1 ball or a back 1 (also sometimes called a 7) as the right-side hitter comes around and hits a 2 ball behind or to the left of the first hitter. The right-side hitter is ready to hit the ball at a slower speed or different height in front of the setter. The left-side hitter is available to hit a 4-ball set (figure 6.1a).

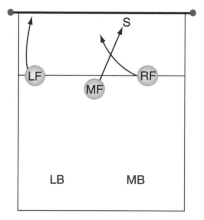

Figure 6.1a   The front X

2. **Back X.** The right-side player receives serve in the right front and hits either a front or back 1 from a blind angle. The middle hitter coming from the middle of the court goes behind the right-side player and receives a back set at the right antenna. The set ball can be of a different height or speed and hit off one foot as in a slide or a back 2 ball. The left-side hitter is available for a 4 ball (figure 6.1b).

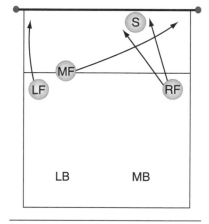

Figure 6.1b   The back X

3. **Double quick.** Both the middle hitter and the right-side hitter push for quick sets. The middle is available for a front 1 and the right side is calling for a back 1. The left-front outside hitter is available for a 4 set (figure 6.1c).

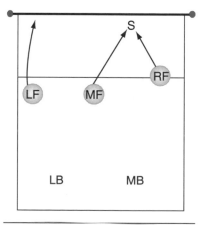

Figure 6.1c   The double quick

4. **Tandem.** The tandem involves the middle and left-side hitters. The middle hitter runs a quick 1 ball while the left-front hitter follows in behind or to the left shoulder of the middle hitter for a 2 ball (figure 6.1d). The right side is available either for a back set 2 ball (sometimes called a 6) or a 5 set.

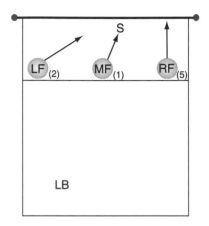

Figure 6.1d The tandem

5. **Front loop.** This combination also involves the middle and left-side hitters. The middle hitter runs a 31 to pull the opponent's right- and middle-front blockers together to block the 31 set. The left-outside hitter sneaks or loops to the inside around and between the middle hitter and the setter for a 2 ball. The right-side hitter calls for a back set (figure 6.1e).

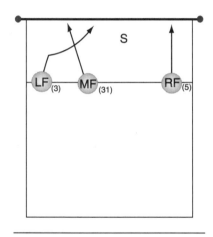

Figure 6.1e The front loop

6. **Left front (31), middle hitter (slide), middle back (pipe).** This combination uses the two front-row hitters plus an attack from the middle back known as the *pipe* (figure 6.1f). The pipe is described on page 120.

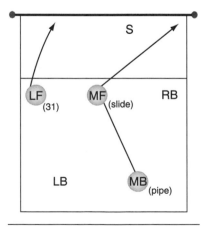
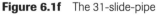

Figure 6.1f The 31-slide-pipe

7. **Slide with a front 2.** The middle hitter runs a slide set to the right antenna to pull two blockers. The left-side hitter comes into the vacated middle and attacks a 2 ball.

Learning to Communicate With Teammates

There are two essential types of communication. The first begins with the setter calling the play-sets using his or her voice, hand signals, or hand and facial signals to indicate which play-set each hitter on the team should be ready to hit. All team members' eyes should be on the setter before the start of each new play. The setter talks to the player standing beside him or her and signals to the rest of the hitters. Hitters verbally indicate any adjustments needed when the first pass is not on target to the setter. For example, if the setter signals a tandem using the left-front and middle hitters but the pass does not permit this set, the left-front hitter calls for a 4 to indicate that he or she is ready for a high outside set.

Offensive attack patterns do not have to be fancy or complex to be successful. It is more important to force the opponent to cover the 30-foot (9.1-meter) distance along the net from antenna to antenna. Combination plays and specialty sets generate a lot of player movement, which forces the opponent to track patterns and verbalize to each other. Such plays and sets also carry a higher risk of the setter misconnecting with the hitter, however. The speed or height of the set may be off, and the hitter may have neither the time nor ability to adjust.

The second type of communication is the critical calling for the served ball by a passer before the ball crosses the net. This prevents hesitation or confusion between the passers and provides the opportunity for the setter to receive a better pass.

Here are examples of the verbal calls my teams used:

- 4.The hitter is available for a left-side attack at the antenna when the ball is played at normal height, usually 5 to 8 feet (1.5 to 2.5 meters) above the net.

- 3. The hitter is between the left side and middle of the net and can attack a 31 or 32.

- 2. The hitter is attacking from the middle as a single attack or as part of a combination.

- 1. The player wants a quick 1 ball that is set in front of the setter

- Tight slide. The middle hitter is approaching from serve-receive or a block transition in front of the setter and will use a one-foot takeoff to attack the ball from behind the setter.

- 7. The player wants a quick 1 ball that is set behind the setter's head.

- 6. The player wants a 2 ball that is set behind the setter's head.

- 5. The player wants a normal set at the right antenna.

- Wide slide. A longer back set at a 2 ball height to the right antenna for a one-foot takeoff.

- Z. A one-foot takeoff with the hitter leaving in front of the setter and hitting the ball behind the setter's head (tight slide).
- 31. A 1 ball in height but 3 to 5 feet (1 to 1.5 meters) in front of the setter.
- Front 1 slide. A set that is about 3 to 5 feet (1 meter) in front of the setter but attacked off one foot.
- 21. A set that is a 1 ball in height but 2 or 3 feet (.6 to 1 meter) in front of the setter.
- A. A back-row attack with the hitter taking off behind the 10-foot (3-meter) line near the left sideline.
- B. A back-row attack performed 8 feet (2.4 meters) in from left sideline.
- Pipe. A back-row attack from the center of the court.
- C. A back-row attack performed 8 feet (2.4 meters) in from right sideline.
- D. A back-row attack from the right or outside-right sideline.

The following are some common hand signals:

- Double fist. One fist placed on top of the other fist to indicate a tandem play.
- Fingers crossed in front of the body and pointing up. A front X play with the middle hitter hitting a 1-ball set and the right-front hitter coming around for the second-tempo ball. The left-front hitter anticipates a 4-ball set.
- Fingers crossed but pointing down. Back X play with the right side hitting a back or front 1-ball set and the middle hitter going behind for a 6 or 5 set.
- The setter with the hands held at the ears and moving back and forth (calling a predetermined play). The middle front runs a 31 shoot while the left front sneaks or loops inside of the 31 for a 2 ball. The right front anticipates a 5-ball set.

In addition to some of the standard calls and signals listed previously, numerous numbering and color systems can signal the various attack zones and play-sets. Some systems use color calls for the back-row attack zones. For example, the left zone could be designated as red, the middle zone white, and the right zone blue. Players on the other side of the net constantly hear letter, number, or color calls, but they still don't know which player will receive the set. Other systems use color calls to designate the quicker attacks at the net. The use of letters can also indicate special sets that would be quicker or more deceptive. For example, your team might call a 1-ball set A, a 31 set B, a tight slide or back-1 set C, and so forth.

Some coaches and players number the areas along the net from 1 to 9. The first number is the zone in which the ball is contacted, and the second number is the height of the set. For example, an 18 call is a high left-outside set. A call of 98 is a high right-outside set. The setter is in his or her target zone at zone 6 or 7.

Special and more advanced calls, such as "hut" and "go," may be made during a transition between the left-side hitter and the setter. "Hut" indicates a ball set at a 2-ball height to the left antenna. Because of the quickness of this type of set, the left-side hitter uses fewer approach steps. "Go" indicates a 1-ball set and a two-step approach for the hitter. Transition offense is covered more fully in chapter 8.

Players can become comfortable acknowledging verbal calls and signals in any system as long as there are plenty of opportunities for learning them through repetition.

Selecting Offensive Systems

The court positioning of the team's players before the serve reflects each member's coverage responsibilities on the court. A player's responsibility depends on how much area he or she can successfully cover, preferably by moving forward. If the player has good court awareness and quickness and can control the height of his or her pass, he or she will likely be given more area to cover. Also involved is the talent level of the adjacent players and the area from which the setter is releasing. A serve-receive player's area may become larger when positioning a setter closer to the net for a more advantageous release to the target.

I've already established in chapter 4 that receiving the serve with a good pass is critical to a team being able to side-out. Coaches need to spend time identifying which players have the movement, balance, technique, and disposition to handle the best servers the opponent has to offer.

Once players have been identified to handle the serve-receive, the coach can make decisions as to the positioning of these players throughout the six serve-receive rotations and the amount of area that each player can realistically cover for that first serve. For example, coaches can ask themselves how these athletes can most effectively divide the court space. If two passers are utilized, for example, they must decide whether one player should cover one-third of the court and the other player two-thirds or whether the players should cover equal halves. If three passers are used, each can take a third of the court.

Coaches should consider designing various receiving patterns that put the best receiver in the middle of the three passers as often as possible. They also need to decide whether the setter will lead the middle hitter or if the setter will lead the outside swing hitter as the team rotates. When the setter leads the outside hitter, especially one who passes well, this setter has to release from up to 26 feet (about 8 meters) of the court to permit the outside hitter to pass a large amount of court space. When the setter leads a middle hitter, the coach can put the middle hitter at the net with the setter standing beside or behind, but not overlapping, him or her. To prevent overlapping a teammate, a player must not be in front or on the other side of an adjacent teammate. Adjacent teammates—or those who

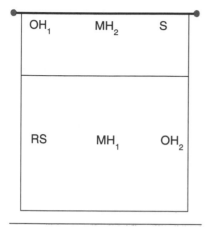

OH₁	MH₂	S
RS	MH₁	OH₂

Figure 6.2 A common receiving pattern.

begin either in front of or beside another player in the six rotations—may have their feet on the floor even with those next to them. Their feet should not be in front of or on the other side of those next to them, though. The official will call an overlap when players violate the designated floor space of an adjacent teammate, which will result in a point for the opponent.

The most common receiving pattern places the two left-side hitters, the two middle hitters, and the setter and right-side hitter opposite each other. This can be set up so that the setter leads the middle or outside hitter through the rotation (figure 6.2).

Another strategy when setting up a rotation pattern is to identify and place the team's best three players into a triangle pattern. For example, a triangle pattern could have the best three players as the right, middle, and outside hitters. The three other players are then flanked by the best and there is also always at least one strong hitter at the net for three of the rotations. A coach could also place both outside hitters and the best middle hitter in a triangle, but this also causes some players not to be able to specialize for all three rotations across the front court. The specializing player most often learns to play defense from one area of the backcourt.

Once the served ball is received, the skill level of the designated setter and hitters ultimately determines the height of the ball and the speed of the offense. Having more than one talented setter provides a team with more options in determining what system of offense to use. There are three basic offensive systems (the 6-0, 5-1, and 4-2 systems) and three hybrid systems (the 6-0 modified, 6-2, and 4-2 European) that a coach can use, depending on the makeup of the team or the opponent the team faces.

- **6-0.** In this offense, the setter comes out of the back row to set for the three front-row hitters. The hitter designated to play primarily on the right side could be the team's other setter, or this hitter could be a left-handed right-side specialist who substitutes into the game in the front row. Coaches choose this offense if they have two good setters who are also accomplished hitters. These two players set from the back row or transition set from a help position when in the right front. They do not leave the game to be replaced by a hitting specialist.

- **6-0 modified.** The previous situation holds true in this offense, but the setters are not opposite each other in the rotation. Rather, they have one player in between them. As a result, one setter sets four of the rotations and the other setter sets two. This is a good choice if one of the setters is also a great hitter.

- **6-2.** A team uses this system when it has two good setters who are not good enough to stay in the game and hit from the front row. They set from the back row and are replaced once they sequentially move to the front row. Many coaches use the 6-2 nomenclature to indicate that there are always two setters, whether they stay in the game or sub out for a better front-row hitter.

- **5-1.** In this offense, one setter sets in all six rotations. When releasing as a setter from the back row, he or she sets for the three front-row hitters. When starting in the front row he or she sets for the other front-row hitters and is eligible to hit also. A team uses this choice when it has one great setter who is able to jump-set and be offensively minded and therefore is also prone to attacking.

- **4-2.** In this system, two setters share the setting duties but always set from the front row. The setter should be able to block; jump-set; and back-set to the right front, back, or C zone. A set to the right front would be a 5 set if the setter stays in the middle front. A more advanced set from the 4-2 system would be a slide set to the middle hitter with the setter starting at least 8 feet (2.4 meters) in from the right antenna. The setter can hit or tip a bad pass over or joust (that is, push the ball into the opponent's hands at the same time the opponent is pushing the ball) with the opponent from his or her front-row position.

- **4-2 European.** In this system, the setter sets from the right front all the time. He or she can see both of the other two hitters and does not have to back-set unless they run a slide set. The slide set may be available for club teams, but it usually is too advanced for junior high and some junior varsity teams (see pages 75 to 76).

Now that I've detailed the offensive-system options, in the next section I detail a few rotation scenarios.

Setter Leads Middle Hitter

This rotation works from a 6-0, 6-2, or 5-1 system. The major effect of this rotation pattern is made clear when the setter must release from the back row. When the setter is in the right-back position, the middle hitter is in the right front. This enables the two players to start close to the net, providing a short release distance for the setter.

In the 5-1 offense, there are several options for covering the floor space. With the W pattern, the setter starts in the right front and leads the middle hitter (figure 6.3a). Five players cover the floor space. They must communicate early, and each player must open like a gate to provide a clear, unobstructed passing lane to the team-mate behind.

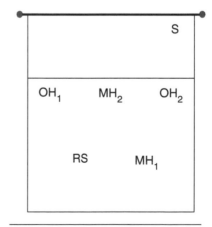

Figure 6.3a W serve-receive pattern.

Coaches will want to devote sessions to the court responsibility of each player, including his or her depth from the net. For example, the outside hitters may be 16 to 20 feet (4.9 to 6.1 meters) off the net if they have the ability to cover that much area forward. Once coaches and players have established the ideal distance, the outside hitters must not move back to pass. Moving back to pass causes confusion for the passer who covers behind and forces the front-row player to pass a ball that is high: near the upper chest, shoulders, or face.

In the U formation, four players are responsible for covering the floor space, but the short-middle area is wide open and vulnerable. Teams can drop back the player in the middle front 6 or 7 feet (1.8 to 2.1 meters) to take short serves with his or her hands. Teams use this formation to prevent an opponent from serving at the head of the middle passer, as in the W formation. Should the middle passer not open fast enough or, worse yet, duck, he or she causes hesitation and confusion on the part of the back-row teammates. The two outside hitters must cover forward toward the net and laterally toward the middle. Early communication from a passer helps to eliminate hesitation and confusion. The two passers in the back, the right-side hitter, and the middle hitter (or a defensive specialist) must cover deeper serves as well as the deep corners. A back-row specialist may also be substituted for a player (such as the DS for MH_1; figure 6.3b).

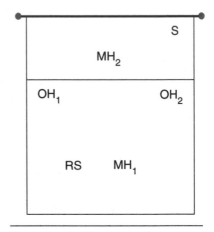

Figure 6.3b U serve-receive pattern.

In the two-passer formation, two players are designated as the primary passers (receivers), and the court coverage is divided between them. The two players can receive serve by splitting the court in half or by having one player take two-thirds of the court and the other one-third. The right-side hitter and the middle hitter in the back are responsible for making "in" or "out" calls. Opposing teams often try to break down the confidence of either the slightly weaker of the two passers or the player who makes an early mistake, so coaches should be ready to make adjustments to this passing pattern if a passing player is struggling.

Many teams use the three-passer formation because it divides the amount of passing coverage on the court into thirds. It also permits a coach to have his or her best passer in the middle more often and therefore forces the opponent to serve to the outside. When the team's best passer or hitter is in the middle, he or she can attack to the left, straight ahead to the middle area, or to the right. This forces the opposing players to track his or her every move. If the opponents don't track this player well, he or she can have open areas along the net from which to attack.

I provide one example of the three-passer formation with the two outside hitters and a right-side passing serve (figure 6.3c). The setter starts in the right front in the first rotation. The advantage of using the right-side player is that he or she can be part of the offense when hitting out of the back row. You could also replace this right-side player with a specialist. The advantage of using a specialist is that this player may be not only a great passer but also a great defensive player. But the specialist may not be as comfortable attacking from the back row.

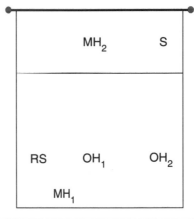

Figure 6.3c   Three-passer formation.

Second Rotation

The setter rotates to the back row and must release from behind the middle hitter (MH_2). Once again, the setter can be even with but not in front of the M2 and cannot be to the left of the outside hitter (OH_2). The W and U formations are shown in figures 6.4a and b, respectively. If the team has two receivers, the right and middle back have to be ready to pass to the short areas (figure 6.4c). When three receivers are used, the formation may look something like that shown in figure 6.4d, or the defensive specialist could drop back so that the right-side front and outside hitters are all in a line. The W formation allows each passer to cover less area of the court, so it is often used for junior high or junior varsity players who are not comfortable covering large areas of the court. The disadvantage comes when a ball is served between two players or at the head of one of the three front-row players. Positive passes are less likely to happen when hesitation or confusion occurs with two or more players.

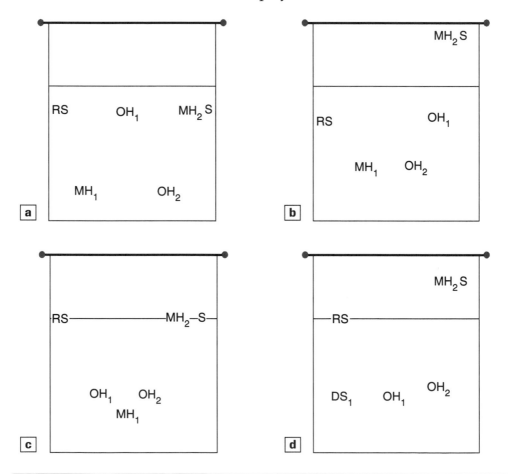

Figure 6.4 Second rotation formations: the W *(a)*, the U *(b)*, two-receiver *(c)*, and three-receiver *(d)* options.

Third Rotation

In the third rotation, the setter rotates to the middle back and releases from behind the middle receiver (figure 6.5a-d). A delayed release by the setter from the W formation can be a distraction to teammates. Teams have been known to serve at the setter on the setter's release path. This forces the setter to either duck or play the ball. In the U formation, the setter can stand at the net behind the front-row player. This position permits a shorter release and can eliminate confusion with the other passers. Whenever a setter has a shorter release, it creates an advantage by permitting him or her to get to the target area more quickly. This allows the setter to be ready to adjust sooner to any type of pass from his or her teammates.

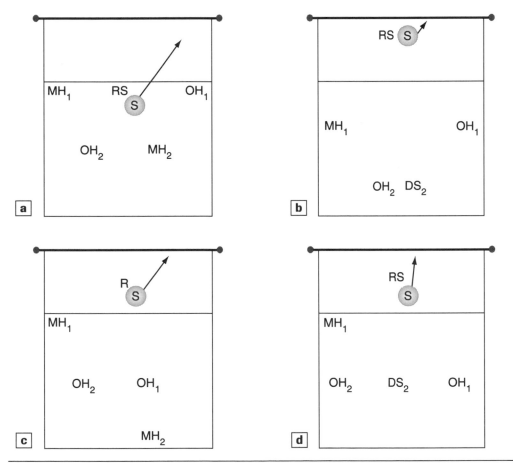

Figure 6.5 Third rotation formations: the W *(a)*, the U *(b)*, two-passer *(c)*, and three-passer *(d)* options.

Fourth Rotation

The setter has rotated to the left back where his or her distance to penetrate to the target is the greatest. He or she can move up to the left corner behind the left-front player to penetrate parallel to the net. Another option is to move the setter forward and toward the center of the court to reduce the distance and angle of the release. Releasing from the left back forces the setter to open quickly so that he or she is able to track the passes from his or her teammates. One way to counter this difficult release is to have the setter stay in the left back to either call the boundaries or pass. Doing this requires the right-front player to set from the serve-receive. The player now in the right front is either the team's other setter or the right-side (opposite) player. Figures 6.6a through d show options for the W, U, two-passer, and three-passer formations, respectively.

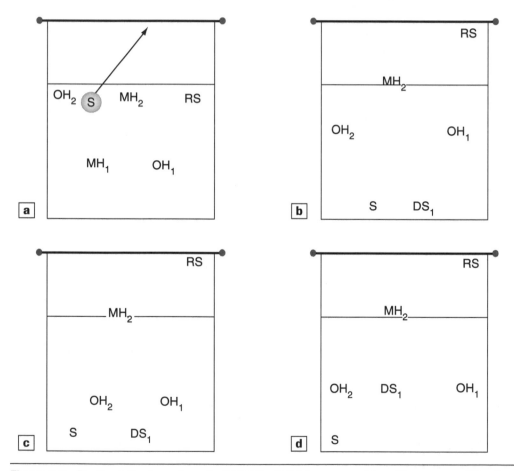

Figure 6.6   Fourth rotation formations: the W *(a)*, the U *(b)*, two-passer *(c)*, and three-passer *(d)* options.

Fifth Rotation

The setter moves to the left front and in the W formation releases across and parallel to the net from the front row (figure 6.7a). The setter may not be to the right of the outside hitter (OH_2)before releasing to the target area. Figures 6.7b, c, and d show the U, two-passer, and three-passer formations.

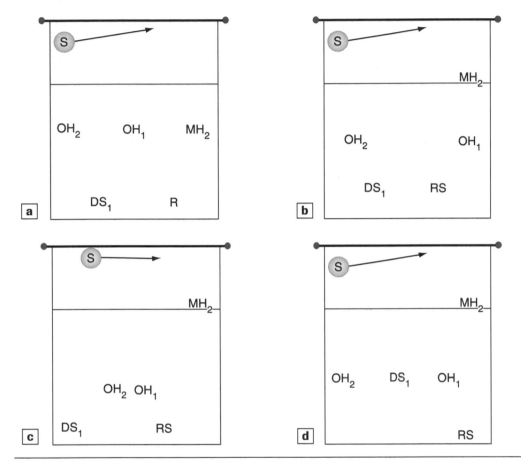

Figure 6.7 Fifth rotation formations: the W *(a)*, the U *(b)*, two-passer *(c)*, and three-passer *(d)* options.

Sixth Rotation

Now the setter is in the front middle. In the W formation, the setter can stay in the front middle or, by switching, offset to the right front (figure 6.8a). The setter stays in the middle to use both front and back sets. He or she switches right to be at the target more quickly and also to front-set to his or her two front-row teammates.

In the U formation, keeping the setter in the middle and setting to the left and right antennas forces the opponent's middle blocker to cover more ground. By having the setter jump to set, the opponent's middle blocker must honor the setter's ability to be an offensive threat by tipping or swinging at the ball. This threat can delay the middle blocker's ability to get to the outside and help double block the outside hitters (figure 6.8b). Figures 6.8c and d show two- and three-passer formations.

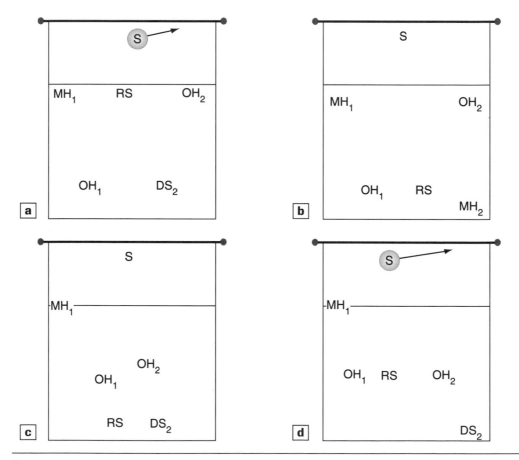

Figure 6.8 Sixth rotation formations: the W (a), the U (b), two-passer (c), and three-passer (d) options.

Setter Leads Outside Hitter

If in a 5-1 offense, the setter leads the outside hitter and (for this example) starts in the back right. When the setter is right back and the outside hitter in the right front is a primary passer, the setter has a greater distance to travel before getting to the target area. This distance can be as much as 25 to 27 feet (7.6 to 8.2 meters) in the two- and three-passer systems.

As the setter moves to the middle-back position in the second rotation, his or her release can be made easier by moving the middle-front player to the net. By doing so, in all but the W formation, the setter is very close to his or her target area and can be ready sooner to handle any pass.

In the third rotation, the setter moves to the left back and has a more difficult approach. The setter should get as close to the net or middle as possible. A team can also use the opposite strategy to set on serve-receive. Every time a setter is in the back left (which occurs in every system except the 4-2), he or she must determine the distance and angle of this difficult release.

In the fourth rotation, the setter rotates to the left front. With the setter now in the front row, the team has only two front-row hitters available. The setter should jump-set as often as possible to make his or her opponents consider him or her an offensive threat.

As the setter rotates to the middle front in the fifth rotation, he or she can split the left- and right-side hitters or go to a strong formation with both hitters coming from the left side. In the sixth rotation, the setter can stay in the right front and keep both hitters in front of him or her or back-set slides that run a hitter to the right antenna.

In the 4-2 offensive system, the two designated setters set from the front row in all rotations. To do this, the two setters must be entered into the game in the front left. Refer to the previous scenarios that cover the 5-1 system for some of the formation options available with the setter in the front row. In the first and fourth rotations, the setter is in the left front. In the second and fifth rotations, the setter is in the middle front. In the third and sixth rotations, the setter is in the right front.

Basic and Advanced Offensive Play-Sets

As the serve-received ball is passed to the setter, the offensive players are in motion; the hitters are either reacting to the setter's previously signaled play or calling for the ball while moving at the speed required for the set. When the ball is passed to the setter target area, the setter has all his or her options available. He or she can set the ball to the player who has been the most consistent, who has the biggest mismatch (for example, a tall hitter over a short blocker), or who faces the fewest blockers. The setter, of course, can also set to the go-to player who has proven to be capable in any situation. The goal is to score either a side-out point or a real point. It does not matter how many fancy or complicated sets are used.

Which offensive sets a team uses depends on the talent of the setter and hitters. Younger players—those in junior high programs or 14-and-under club programs—generally start with higher basic sets. Players and teams can be very successful by hitting a 4-ball set on the left side, a 2-ball set in the middle, and a 5-ball set on the right side. As the setters gain more competence with controlling the height and speed of their sets, they can adjust them when hitters have demonstrated their ability to move quickly into position to attack the special sets. Play-sets that use the quicker 1-ball set and the lower-back sets needed for a slide can be added to the offensive calls when the technical skills to perform them successfully have been developed. The late Jim Coleman, former Sir George Williams University (now Concordia University) and USA national team coach and mentor to Russ Rose, stated, "You can only do tactically what the players are capable of doing technically." Figure 4.7 on page 66 shows some basic sets.

When the first pass is so poor that the setter is fortunate to get the errant ball back into the air, teammates must find a way to clear the ball to their opponent. The following are two situations that are a result of a poor first serve-receive pass. These are not planned in advance as part of the offense but are instead a reaction to the first two contacts:

- **Placing a free ball.** If a team is not able to jump and attack the third contact but, rather, must use the forearms to clear the ball, the resulting contact is called a *free ball.* An offense should try to place the free ball into the deep 1 corner to force the opponent's setter to turn away from his or her teammates to locate the ball. This way, the opponent's setter will not be able to see his or her own hitters early enough to effectively set the ball. Place the ball in the space the setter vacated and force the right-front player to move back quickly enough to try to play the ball.

- **Placing a down ball.** With a controlled third contact (standing with a full arm swing) a hitter needs to place the ball to the opposing setter if he or she is in the back row. This forces another player, the help setter, to run the offense. If the opposing team is playing a middle-back defense (see chapter 7), the offense should direct the ball either to the deep 1 or deep 5 corner. If the opposing team is playing a rotational or middle-in defense, the offense should place the ball into the deep 6 position. These three defensive systems are described in chapter 7.

Back-Row Setter

The following basic offensive play-sets are based on a formation utilizing a back-row setter and three front-row hitters. The objective is to force the opponent's front-row players to have to block from antenna to antenna. The opponent's back-row players must react to the various sets and move to the correct coverage positions.

- **The play called is 4-2-5.** The left-front hitter hits a 4-ball set at the left antenna. The middle hitter is available to run a 2 ball, while the right-side hitter is preparing to hit a 5 set. Because the middle is running a slower set, it is possible for the opponent's blockers to double-team the 2-ball set.

- **The play called is 4-1-5.** The two outside hitters (left and right front) prepare to attack the same type of set, but the middle hitter speeds up his or her attack by hitting a 1 ball. Pushing hard in the middle forces the opponent's middle blocker to focus on stopping the middle attack first before trying to move outside and set up a double block (figure 6.9).

- **The play called is 42-1-6.** The left-outside hitter prepares to hit a faster, lower 4 ball as the right-outside hitter also comes in more quickly to hit a back 2. The middle hitter once again pushes hard to attack a 1 ball.

- **The play called is 42-21-7.** The left-outside hitter again attacks a lower, quick set. The middle hitter is ready to attack a 1 ball, but this set is now 2 or 3 feet (.6 to 1 meter) in front of the setter. The right-side hitter is also running a quick attack by hitting a back 1.

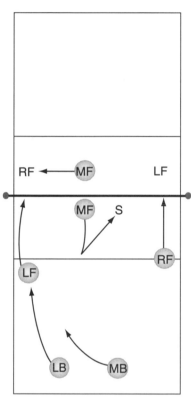

Figure 6.9 The 4-1-5.

Front-Row Setter

The offense has two front-row hitters plus a setter who can go above the net and tip or swing at the ball. The play-sets from a front-row setter can also incorporate a hitter from the back row. The setter should concentrate on jump-setting to hold the opponent's left-front blocker.

• **The play called is 4-1-C.** The left-front hitter is ready to hit a higher outside set as the middle hitter pushes hard for a quick attack. The setter can tip inside or outside (short or long) from the front row. The right-back player can attack from the back row either at the right antenna or up to 8 feet (2.4 meters) inside the right sideline.

• **The play called is 42-slide.** The left-front hitter is ready to attack a lower outside. The middle hitter can either hold or force the blocker's reactions when running a slide (see pages 75 and 76). "Hold" steps force the opposing middle blocker to honor a 1-ball set while pressing the second step outside to run a slide (figure 6.10).

• **The play called is 32 Z.** The left-front hitter pushes inside to run a 2 ball 3 to 5 feet (1 to 1.5 meters) in front of the setter. The middle hitter is attacking a quick set by taking off in front of the setter but attacking the ball 1 foot (30.5 centimeters) behind the setter's head.

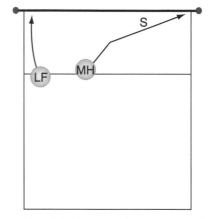

Figure 6.10 The 42-slide.

CHAPTER 7

Defensive Systems

Coaches in all sports believe that strong defense wins games, even championships. Volleyball is no exception. Great defense can shift momentum, increase the amount of team energy and enthusiasm, and generate electricity on the floor. Defense begins with individual players making a commitment to cover their areas of responsibility, pursue every ball, and refuse to let the ball hit the ground. Playing good defense depends on every player understanding the sequence of touches by the opponent, being in the correct court position, seeing the ball, using a low defensive stance, and wanting the ball to come to him or her. Should a coach decide that defense is a priority, he or she must adequately prepare and challenge his or her athletes so that they not only buy into the philosophy but also develop the skills needed to excel on defense.

This chapter identifies the basics of team defense: the positioning of players on the court, their movement to the boundaries, their communication and movement relative to their blocking partners, and how they can help to cover the server's area until the server arrives in his or her proper position after serving. I also cover how a defensive player reads an opposing team's options as that team goes through its three contacts. I discuss the three main defensive systems, or coverages—the middle-back, middle-in, and rotational. Each of these defenses has weaknesses for which coaches must account, but this chapter illustrates how coaches can use the makeup of their team and the players' specific qualities to create the best defense for the situation.

Team Defense Concepts

Defense begins with the front-row players of the serving team preparing to block the opponent's attacked ball before the ball crosses the net. Blocking for a point is the second way to score a *real* point following an ace. Besides a stuff block, blocking strategies include the channeling of the attacked ball to the best defensive player, covering a weaker player or area, and taking away the desired shot of the hitter.

A coach's game preparation should include the development and implementation of a blocking and defensive strategy for his or her team in the practices before matches. The blocking strategy can be communicated to all players from the bench, or the front-row players can signal their back-row partners by using behind-the-back hand signals. A team's base defense should be diagramed on a chalkboard, walked through, practiced on the court, and provided in a handbook for players. Each defense can be color-coded, numbered, or otherwise given a name that is easily understandable to players so that before the serve all players can communicate quickly on the court and react as one unit.

Developing a blocking strategy may not be possible when working with younger age-group players who either cannot realistically block or who have no need to block based on the opponent's inability to attack. In such cases, players should align themselves in a W formation to dig. When a team uses the W formation, a front-row setter stays at the net while the left- and middle-front players stay off the net to help dig. If the setter is in the back row, he or she releases immediately to the front row after his or her team serves. The left-, middle-, and right-front players release back to the W formation to dig.

A team's defensive philosophy must be flexible enough to take advantage of the abilities of the players in the coverage. When a coach chooses and teaches a defense, he or she needs to remember that the defense should not double cover an area or have a player in the shadow of the block (area outside the angle formed by the blocker's hands as they penetrate the net). Defensive players should align themselves where they can see the ball, but upon ball contact they must also pursue a ball that is going into, over, or through the shadow of the block.

The following is the sequence of responsibilities of ball contact for which defensive players must prepare as the opposing team goes through its three permitted contacts. Players must understand that the opposing team is striving for three contacts, but they can intentionally or unintentionally bring the ball back over the net at any time. By concentrating on the opponent's touches, defensive players are ready for the ball to come out of sequence, and thus will not be caught off-guard.

Strong, open hands produce an effective block.

- **Overpass**. The first contacted ball by the opponent that unintentionally comes back over the net is an overpass. The overpass usually results from a strong aggressive serve or attack that is very difficult for the opponent to control.

- **Setter's second contact**. The defensive team must know whether the setter is a front- or back-row player. This determines the legality of the setter being above the net with the ball before the ball crosses the net. The players on the defensive team should know ahead of time whether a front-row teammate will try to block a front-row setter's second attempt or assign back-row players to cover the floor surface. This contact is called a *tip* when a front-row setter takes the ball over from above the net using one hand. When the setter is in the back row, this second ball is called a *dump* and must be released below the top of the net.

- **Middle, or quick attack.** The ball is contacted by a third player in a predetermined play-set along the front of the net. The opponent's skill level determines the height of the set and the quickness of the attack, which for the purpose of this discussion will be from the middle of the net.

- **Second tempo or combination play.** A ball hit by one of the two players running a play. The ball height varies from a quick 1-ball set to a slightly higher 2-ball set, depending on the timing sequence of the play.

- **Outside set.** A ball attacked by a hitter at one of the antennas is an outside set. A right-side set is usually shorter in distance, 8 feet (2.4 meters) or less, and quicker than a left-side attack due to the floor release point of the setter.

- **Back-row attack.** A setter has the option of including a player from the back row in the sequence of the players available to set. If the play is called before receiving the serve, the set can occur with the speed of a combination play. If the serve reception pass is poor, a bailout set may be the only option the setter has available. It is a slower developing play.

There are several player characteristics that are ideal for each defensive position. Coaches can help players develop a defensive specialty by teaching and drilling them in all the responsibilities and techniques necessary to play the right side, left side, or in the middle of the court in both the front and back rows.

- **Right-front blocker.** This may be the setter (in a 5-1 offense) or the right-side (opposite) player. The right-front player should have good block timing, good blocking technique, and strong hands for setting and blocking. This is because the left-side 4-ball set is a common set based on the first pass and the opponent's left-side player is often a go-to person—the player the team wants to hit the ball in crucial situations. When your setter makes the first contact, the right-side blocker becomes the help setter.

- **Left-front blocker.** This player is normally one of the team's best passers and can transition to attack from any zone on serve-receive. This player should be able to help block middle, react to the slide set, and establish the block on the opponent's right-side hitter.

- **Middle-front blocker.** This player should be extremely mobile and athletic in movements that are horizontal and diagonal and must be vertically explosive. He or she must be able to block all zones of the net and transition to be available for a quick attack. This player is asked to block both quick sets and combination attacks. He or she can be a tireless worker who sets the energy and intensity tone for a game and leads by example.

- **Left-back player.** This person should be a great digger and able to attack out of the A and B back-row zones. Depending on a player's quickness, he or she may also be asked to cover additional territory. For example, he or she may be asked to cover 20 of the 30 feet (6 of the approximately 9 meters) from the left to right rather than 15 feet (approximately 4.5 meters) when the setter is also in the back row. This permits the setter to release to the target to set rather than playing a ball in the middle of the court.

- **Middle-back player.** This athlete should be quick enough to cover the court from sideline to sideline in reaction to an attack. Since all of the middle back's teammates are in front of him or her, he or she can be the traffic cop—the coordinator of the defense. The middle back should be a great communicator who speaks loudly and frequently. He or she is respected and trusted for his or her steady, heady play. This player's assignments are to play *splits* (or the gap that appears when two blockers are not shoulder to shoulder), tips that go high and deep off the blocker's hands, and balls hit into the corners of the court. A tall, quick player in this position can be a definite asset to save the high-tipped balls but may not be quick enough to get to the corners unless your team plays a rotational defense. He or she must be able to cover to the right sideline up to the 10-foot (3-meter) line when in hitter coverage. The middle back must not try to help by playing the ball in front of other teammates until his or her own responsibilities are covered.

- **Right-back player.** This player can be a back-row setter, the opposite, or a specialist who enters the game for passing and defensive purposes. He or she should be able to dig hard line and cross-court shots as well as attacks from the middle. This player must also be able to move to dig tips or roll shots close to the net as well as to the middle of the court 14 feet and in. He or she must also be able to play balls off the block that go off the court to the right.

Court Positioning

Being able to frustrate an opponent by digging shots and covering territory can certainly switch momentum in favor of the defensive team. To have this type of defensive success, coaches need to develop base positions for each player. They must also emphasize the need to cover the weaker areas by correctly reading the progression of the play and reacting effectively. A player must understand his or her primary responsibility and trust all of his or her teammates to have the self-discipline to be in the correct floor position as they anticipate a ball coming to their area. As a coach, my focus during each play of the game was on the correct court position of our players before the opponent's ball came over the net. Secondly, I watched to assess each player's body position and balanced anticipation. Just as a tennis player who is receiving serve needs to be in balance with the racket in a ready position before the ball arrives, a volleyball player preparing to play a ball needs to be ready to make the best reaction to the ball.

Front-Row Blockers

The number of eligible front-row hitters the opponent has in each rotation and how those hitters tend to play will determine the positioning of your defense's front-row blockers. The blocking players should initially focus on the starting location of the opponent's setter. When he or she is in the front row, there are two additional eligible front-row hitters. When the setter is starting in the back row, there will be three legal front-row hitters.

If the opponent's setter is a back-row player, he or she is not a legal front-row hitter and may not take a ball that is above the net into the defense's court unless he or she takes off behind the 10-foot (3-meter) line or the ball is below the top of the net. When the setter is in the back row, the left-front blocker has to be aware of the right-side player's ability and set his or her blocker position accordingly. This position generally begins about one arm's length from the left antenna. The middle-front blocker should be one step to the left of center to take away the right-hand hitting angle of a right-handed middle hitter. The right-front blocker should be one arm's length in from the right antenna and adjust from there as the opponent's tendencies dictate. Because the opponent's hitters rotate, the defensive team must know where each hitter is aligned before the serve and track the hitters' angles of approach during each play.

In figure 7.1, the setter is in the front row and the outside hitter has shifted to the outside. The left-front blocker moves in toward the middle to help block on the middle hitter, while the right-front blocker stays to track the outside hitter who is swinging to the outside.

There are, of course, variations to how to run an offense with three front-row hitters. For example, the setter may be in the back row with the hitters stacked to one side (figure 7.2). This may make it appear that there are only two eligible hitters. This highlights the importance of the front-row blockers first identifying

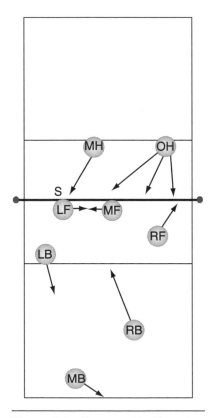

Figure 7.1 Front-row blocking when the setter is in the front row and the outside hitter shifts outside.

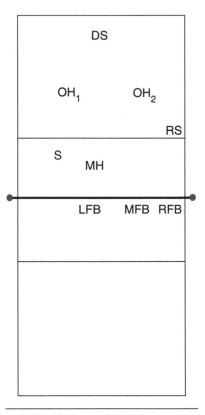

Figure 7.2 Blocking when the setter is in the back row and the hitters are stacked to one side.

the eligible hitters and then communicating their numbers to their teammates. Defensive players must be able to track their opponent's hitters from their serve-receive alignment to the net. The blocking scheme for this situation may start with the left-front blocker moving three arm's lengths in from the left antenna, the middle blocker one step to the right of center, and the right-front blocker one arm's length from the right antenna.

A rotation could also be stacked left with all three hitters positioned from the middle to the left. The left-front blocker then takes a position one arm's length from the left antenna, with the middle blocker one step to the left of center and the right blocker two arm's lengths from the middle blocker.

Blocking positions change if the opponent's setter is in the front row (figure 7.3). In this position, the front-row setter is also a legal hitter and must be accounted for in the defensive scheme. A front-row blocker, across from the target area, may be assigned to block the setter on a great or tight pass. Otherwise the scheme may be to allow the setter to jump and tip or swing at the ball. The defense might then dig the setter's attack with

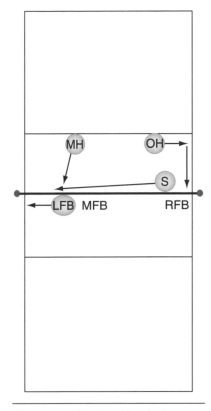

Figure 7.3   Blocking when the front-row setter is a legal hitter

the back-row players. This means the left blocker must single or double block the middle hitter. The left blocker adjusts his or her starting position to the inside of the opponent's target area with the primary responsibility of blocking the opponent's middle hitter. The left blocker prepares to block the quick 1 ball or react to the left to block the slide attack. The middle blocker is one step to the right of center so that he or she can double back on the 1 ball, help on the 31, and double block the outside hitter on a 4. The right blocker is one arm's length in from the right antenna. If the outside hitter is dominating, then the middle blocker starts closer to the right antenna to definitely double the opponent's left-side hitter.

If the opponent's setter is starting in the middle front and splitting the hitters, the most effective blocking scheme is to have the left blocker starting one arm's length in from the left antenna, the middle blocker in the center of the net, and the right blocker one arm's length in from the right antenna. The middle blocker can double left or right but may also be assigned to block the setter's tip. Should the setter jump-set every ball, the middle blocker may be forced to hesitate before moving to the outside. This gives the offense an advantage.

If the setter is starting in the right front and facing both hitters, the hitters can change their approach angles, which necessitates great communication among the blockers. The middle hitter may start in front of the setter and end up behind (as in a slide). The left-front hitter could stay wide, come in for a shoot 31 set, or continue to the center and come in for a quicker set. The blockers need to align themselves as in figure 7.1 (see page 140) with the left blocker blocking the middle hitter, the middle blocker being able to double the middle or the outside hitter, and the right blocker one arm's length in from the right antenna. Our team calls the cue letters "SR" to indicate *shift right*.

Back-Row Defensive Players

Back-row players are a critical component of a team's defense. Coaches must first train their players to be aware of and then handle the sequence of their opponent's touches. Initially, defensive players must be assigned specific floor space to cover. From that original position, each player's coverage area will depend on where the team's setter is located (front or back row), who is currently serving for the team, and the abilities of each teammate. For example, when the middle-back player is serving, the first 20 to 25 feet (6 to 7.6 meters) of floor space from the net can be divided between the right- and left-back defensive players. When the right-back player is serving or is the setter, the left back moves closer to the middle to cover additional space until the setter moves into defensive position (see figure 7.4a). This permits the setter to release to the target and set the second ball instead of playing the first ball and forcing the help setter to run the offense. The distance covered from the net, as indicated earlier, also depends on each player's quickness and ability to read and anticipate the play. When the left-back player is serving, coverage can be assisted by the left front or the middle back (see figure 7.4b) in order to assign the setter less ground to cover so that he or she can effectively run the offense.

Here are some examples of back-row defensive positioning. In figure 7.4a, the setter can dump the ball but cannot jump and tip it down into the defense's court. Also, the defensive team's setter is in the back-right coverage area, so the left back takes an additional 3 to 5 feet (1 to 1.5 meters) of coverage. If the right back is not the setter, this additional coverage may be taken by the right back, who can be the opposite or a defensive specialist. If the server is in the middle-back position, the area of coverage is split evenly—15 feet (4.6 meters) of coverage for each outside-back player from his or her sideline to the middle. If one player is much quicker than the other or anticipates better and gets into position sooner, that player may take 3 to 5 feet (1 to 1.5 meters) more of coverage.

If the opponent's setter is a front-row player, this player is a legal hitter for which the defense must account in the blocking scheme and defensive back-row coverage (figure 7.4b). As a team, the setter's tip coverage is assigned to the left-back and right-back defensive players, with the right-front player covering short tips. The left-front blocker is assigned the responsibility of blocking the opposing middle hitter. In this example, the left-back player starts two steps closer to the left sideline, stands on the 10-foot (3-meter) line, and is responsible for the

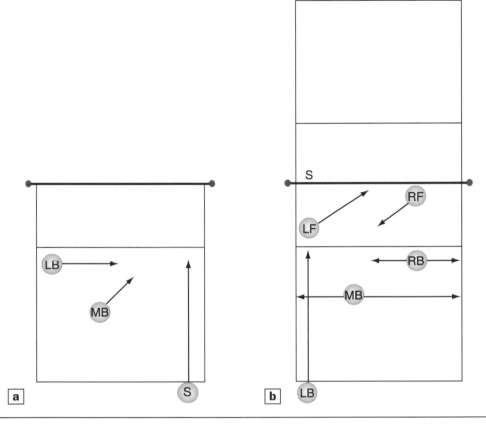

Figure 7.4   Left-back coverage until the setter moves back in defense *(a)*, and middle-back coverage when the left-back player serves.

setter's outside tip from the 10-foot (3-meter) line up the sideline to the net. The right-back defensive player is responsible for covering two-thirds of the court from the middle (his or her first priority) to the right sideline. The middle-back player must be ready to read the setter's intentions and cover the deep tip from sideline to sideline.

Defensive Systems

For the purposes of this chapter, I consider three basic defenses: the middle-back defense, the rotational defense, and the middle-in defense. Adjustments and variations can be added to any of these defensive systems based on the blocking, movement, and defensive ability of a particular team's athletes. The middle-in defense discussed later in the chapter has a different starting base than the other two. I prefer the middle-back defense, and my players' base (or home) position reflected this. The rotational defense is a variation of the middle-back defense, although it ends up almost looking like a middle-in.

I believe that players must have a base position from which they start every play. This base may change slightly, depending on the opponent's rotations and tendencies as well as who is serving for your team. Each player's base position is determined by his or her floor location relative to the boundary lines and antennas. Players must also know who is beside and in front or behind them so that they mesh in movements and communication. Once the players are comfortable and confident in their understanding of their roles and any adjustments they may have to make, decisions can be made to use variations of the base. My decision to use the middle-back was based on my emphasis on player movement. This entailed not only getting to the boundary positions from the base but also moving quickly when the ball was hit to cover the weaker areas inherent within the middle-back defense. I think that a player can be successful playing defense when using at least three steps to get to a boundary, closing and double blocking with a partner, covering the area along the net, rotating off the net or to get to a corner, and running down a ball to the inside or outside of the court. Three or more steps are necessary so that players do not lunge, dive, or reach for balls that should be played from a balanced body position. When players are moving systematically, they communicate better and establish a rhythm to their movement that prevents them from hesitating.

Middle-Back Defense

The middle-back defense can be coded with another name. My team's colors were black and gold, so we called this defense our black (sounds like *back)* defense. The left- and right-back players who start behind the 10-foot (3-meter) line cover the overpass. Each player's distance from the net depends on the area that he or she can cover moving forward. If the right-back player is the setter, then the left-back player can be responsible for two-thirds of the court instead of one-half. If either of these players is the server, then the non-server can cover the server's areas until he or she is able to get into position after the serve. The middle-back, left-front, or right-front player may also be responsible for this coverage.

The left- and right-back players must not permit a back-row setter to dump the ball on the second contact. Should a front-row setter jump and tip, a front-row blocker's strategy may be to block this tip. But this depends on where (that is, in which zone) the setter is when he or she contacts the ball. An alternative strategy would be to assign three players (left back, right back, and right front) to cover floor space. This coverage area can be 30 feet (9.1 meters) wide and up to 20 feet (6 meters) from the net. The left-back player is responsible for the left one-third of the court up to the left antenna from his or her original distance off the net forward. The right back is responsible for the center of the court to the right sideline, but not to the net in the middle and right front. The right front covers the middle of the court to the right antenna from the net to 8 feet (about 2.5 meters) off the net.

In the middle-back defense, the court is covered by four of the six players simultaneously taking at least three steps from the base position to their next assigned area of coverage, such as a middle blocker moving to the outside to assist on a double block against a 4 or 5 ball being set by the opponent's setter. If the opponent sets a 4 ball toward the defense's right antenna, the defense's right-front player sets the block based on the antenna and the hitter's angle of approach and shoulder angle. The right front knows that his or her right-back teammate is taking up the digging responsibility from the right sideline. The middle-front blocker takes three steps to close the block and will jump to block with the right-front teammate (figure 7.5).

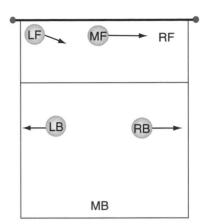

Figure 7.5 Middle-back defensive coverage on a 4-ball set to the right antenna.

The left-front blocker takes his or her first step off the net and two subsequent steps toward the painted center circle on the floor that bisects the middle of the net for both teams. He or she is responsible for balls that ricochet off the net or a block as well as balls that are tipped or rolled into the short middle (inside the 10-foot, or 3-meter, line). The left-back player uses a three-step crossover to place the feet at the left sideline. He or she should align himself or herself outside the left hand of the middle blocker and be able to see the ball at all times. The ball may be channeled to the left back if he or she is the best digger. The left-back player should be able to dig hard attacks in front of him or her—possibly by using a collapse dig, J-stroke, or sprawl—or use a hard extension to the right for a ball angled toward the corner. A left-back player who has the feet at the boundary line should not play balls above the knee or to the left as those balls will go out of bounds. He or she should be able to accelerate to the middle of the court for tips or rolls and to open to the right to sprint for balls that are hit deep cross court into the left-back corner.

Using a crossover step, the right-back player takes three steps to the right sideline. He or she digs attacks down the line using the forearms for low balls and the hands for attacks at the face or above. Any ball hit outside of the right foot will be out of bounds and should not be played unless it is touched by the block. The right-back player must also run to the middle of the court to cover tips or roll shots.

The middle-back player may adjust position slightly if he or she can see or read the hitter. Any hard-hit ball in front of him or her must be played using the sprawl technique. If there is a split in the block, he or she should step forward to be able to dig a ball that comes cleanly through the split or one that may ricochet off a blocker. The middle back must be able to take three or five steps to either corner. This player must be able to accelerate over the last front step and use the lateral extension technique to dig softly placed shots in either corner. He or she must also play a ball that hits off the block and travels behind the end line in any direction.

If the opponent sets a 5 ball to the right front of their court or the left front of the defense's court, this set usually travels 8 feet (about 2.5 meters) or less. This requires the defense and the block to move more quickly. If a defensive player is not ready to play a ball at a boundary in good position before the hitter contacts the ball, the player should stop and balance where he or she is so that momentum does not produce incorrect mechanics. The left-front blocker sets the block, expecting the middle-front blocker to assist on a double block. The right-front blocker takes the first step off the net and two more steps toward the center of the court to get into his or her coverage position. He or she steps off the net at a 45-degree angle, leading with the left foot. The right foot steps toward the middle circle and is followed by the left foot onto the edge of the circle. He or she covers balls off the net or the block as well as tips and rolls. Whether the right-front blocker is also the setter or not, that player should direct any ball he or she plays above and behind the left shoulder. The right-back partner can then set this ball.

The left-back player moves with three steps to the left sideline. This player should turn the feet toward the target as the shoulders face the hitter. He or she is responsible for tips and rolls forward to the antenna as well as to the middle of the court. He or she must be able to dig the hard shot down the line using the forearms for balls below the waist and the hands for those at the face or above. The left-back player should not reach left for a ball outside of the left foot unless it has been touched by a teammate.

The right-back player moves using three steps to the right sideline and takes a position just outside the right arm and hand of the middle blocker. This player must be able to see the ball since he or she needs to be able to run to the center of the court for rolls or tips and dig crosscourt using a J-stroke, collapse dig, or sprawl for balls in front of him or her. Balls to the right above knee height should be out of bounds. The right-back player must be able to use a left extension for balls hit within 3 feet (1 meter) of him or her, or accelerate using three to five steps into the back corner to use a left extension to dig balls. The middle-back player should be positioned to read the attack and dig in front of him or her as well as to run three to five steps to either corner or play balls off the block.

If the opponent sets a quick middle attack (1 ball) and has two additional front-row players available for outside sets, the middle-front blocker blocks the quick set by taking away the hitter's hitting angle. The left- and right-front blockers open their inside shoulders and hips to step off the net as well as preparing to take any additional steps needed to cover the tip. The right-back player must be able to see the attack and dig balls cut back away from the block toward him or her. The middle-back player takes one step to the right to cover the deeper shot toward the 6-1 corner (refer to figure 2.1, page 26). The left-back player is ready to take a ball that hits off the block of the middle blocker and soft shots into the 5 corner.

Rotational Defense

The rotational defense is used when the opposing team sets a 4 ball or sets to the left-outside hitter. In my program, I called this our *red* defense, since both red and rotate begin with R. Any other set results in a normal three-step movement from the middle-back defense. Sometimes teams only rotate when a certain player is hitting from the left front. In other situations, only one person rotates to neutralize an opponent's strength. Some coaches also rotate the team to the left when the opposing team sets a 5 ball or sets to their right-front hitter. There is cause for concern with using this type of rotation for a 5-ball set when the defensive team's setter is right back. He or she then rotates into the deep 1 corner and is not available to get back to the net to set or run the offense. The right-front player then runs the offense as a help setter.

The rotational defense requires four players to make movement adjustments: the left- and middle-front players and the left- and middle-back players. The right-front and right-back players stay in their base positions. The right-front player continues to be responsible for setting the block and calling the jump timing. This defense encourages the opponent's left-front hitter to hit the ball down the line. The main difference between this defense and the middle-back defense is that the middle-back digger rotates to the right to dig in the deep 1 corner. The middle-front player doubles the block to take away the deep middle of the court. The right-back player, who remains in his or her initial base defensive position, is responsible for all tips from the right sideline to the middle of the court. The left-front blocker opens the right shoulder and hip and takes three steps (the second step being a crossover step) to the team's right sideline at a depth of approximately 10 to 12 feet (3 to 3.7 meters). The left-back player also opens the right shoulder and hip and travels with three steps to the deep 5 corner; he or she should be 3 feet (1 meter) from both the left sideline and the backline. The middle-back player, who rotated to the right corner, should dig balls from the knees down or take tips off the block (figure 7.6). The weak areas in this defense are along the net from sideline to sideline up to 8 feet (2.4 meters) off the net and the middle of the court from the 15-foot (4.6-meter) area back to the 30-foot (9.1-meter) area.

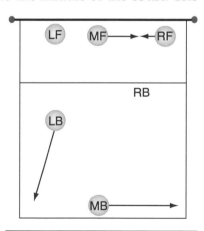

Figure 7.6 Movement adjustments in the rotational defense.

Middle-In Defense

The middle-in defense has a floater, or a player who starts in the middle of the court and follows behind the block to be responsible for the tip or soft roll shot from sideline to sideline. This player starts or switches to the middle of the court anywhere from 12 to 14 feet (3.7 to 4.3 meters) and in, depending on his or her quickness. Should this player be the setter, the team must determine who will be the help setter and how the players can transition to offense. If the defense's setter is in the front row, then the player should be a very quick defensive athlete.

This defense allows a team to cover the corners of the backcourt with the deep middle being the weak area. The offside block can help on crosscourt attacks outside the block or with tip coverage. The back-row player covering the 5 corner and the back-row player covering the 1 corner should be given specific positioning instructions with respect to the sideline and end line. The players need numerous repetitions to determine the distance to the boundary in relation to the height of the ball being played. In the middle-back defense, all back-row players take three steps to move to the boundary lines before the opponent's hit. These players know that the only balls in play are in front of them or to the inside. In the middle-in defense, a player may end up 3 to 5 feet (1 to 1.5 meters) from the boundary. The player has to make a judgment call regarding whether a ball is in or out.

Figures 7.7a through c show several situations in which a middle-in defense can be effective. Figure 7.7a shows the coverage provided against a 4-ball set to the left side of the opponent's court. The setter will start in the middle back at approximately the 12-foot (3.7-meter) line and move behind the block when a 4 ball is set. Figure 7.7b shows the coverage this defense offers against a 1- or 2-ball set in the middle with three hitters, and figure 7.7c shows this coverage with a setter in the front row and two hitters. In this figure, the defense is blocking with a shift-right double block.

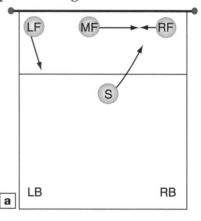

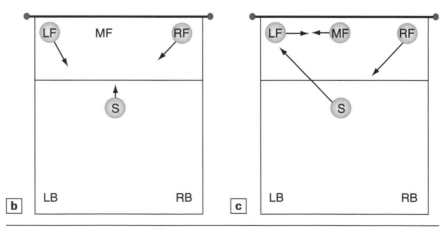

Figure 7.7 Middle-in defense against a 4-ball set (a), a 1- or 2-ball set in the middle (b), and a setter in front and two hitters (c).

Special Blocking Adjustments

The blocking assignments discussed in this section deal with neutralizing the strategy of the opponent's setter and middle hitter. What strategy will you use? Will you single block the opponent's middle hitter and double block the opponent's outside hitter, or will you double block the middle and single block the outside? Does the team try to do both? By moving the defensive middle blocker one step to the right, you give him or her the opportunity to do three things. He or she can help on the 1-ball set, take away the 31 set, and double on the 4-ball set.

I have seen teams preset a double block on the outside hitter even before a 4-ball set has been made to the outside. I have also seen the middle blocker wait and then react to the outside to help block the 4- ball set. In the latter case, the blocker was preparing to help on the cutback as the back side of the middle's 1-ball attack before running to the outside to double block the opponent's left-front hitter. The defensive players who are not involved in the block can be in their middle-back, rotational, or middle-in positions (based on the ball being set to the opponent's left-front hitter). The special adjustments in the back row are used when the opponent sets the middle hitter, who tips or rolls balls to various places on the court as well as hitting hard drives. Once the blockers make their calls and adjustments, the back-row players adjust accordingly—no matter what defense the team is employing.

Shift-Right Blocking Scheme

There are some special considerations for which players must account when the opposing team has its legal attacking setter in the front row with two hitting teammates. The coach can identify this situation from the bench and use a special number, name, or color cue to trigger his or her team's defensive response. Players should also correctly understand and properly communicate how to move defensively before the ball is served. For the purposes of this example of how a team modifies its blocking scheme and defensive responsibilities to account for a front-row setter, I use the cue SR. As mentioned earlier, this stands for *shift right* relative to the beginning defensive position of the left- and middle-front blockers. This defense is a modification of the current base position for the defensive players.

When a team hears "SR," the left-front blocker shifts to the inside shoulder of the opponent's setter while the setter is in the target zone. The left-front player is not responsible for blocking the setter tip. Rather, the left-back player is responsible for covering the setter's outside tip, and the right-back player covers the setter's inside tip from the middle out and at an 8- to 12-foot (2.4- to 3.7-meter) depth. The right-front blocker is responsible for the setter's inside tip from the net to a 7-foot (2.1-meter) depth. The weak areas are the two deep corners, which are covered by the middle-back player. He or she must see, anticipate, and be ready to accelerate to either corner. Or the middle back player can be instructed to cover the 5 corner while the right back player uses open hands to prevent a ball from going into the 1 corner.

The left-front blocker is now responsible for the quick middle attack hit toward the left-back defensive area of the court. He or she is also responsible for the tight or wide slide should the middle hitter of the opposing team use this technique to receive a different set. He or she uses the one-, two-, or three-step movement to get back outside and block the crosscourt hit of the slide attack.

The middle-front blocker can start one step further to the right. He or she can help block the opposing team's middle attack by blocking the cutback shot. This shift to the right permits the middle-front blocker to take away the 21or 31 shoot sets. This shift to the right also enables the middle-front blocker to transition more easily to set a double block with the right-front blocker as they block the outside hitter on the opposing team. The right-front blocker can set his or her block straight up on the outside attack knowing that the middle blocker can get out to help him or her more quickly.

When the ball is set to the opponent's middle hitter, the left-back defensive player, who started at the 10-foot (3-meter) line and two steps from the sideline, takes on responsibility for digging the tip. First, the player must cover a tip over the double block and to the short net area located in the 4 zone. Next, he or she must be ready to cover to the inside and also toward the middle. He or she has no digging responsibility for a hard-hit attack. The right-front player takes three quick steps and covers the middle tip as well as a tip to the side. The right-back player opens and takes three quick steps to the 1 corner to cover the deep roll shot. The middle-back player takes three quick steps to the left to cover the deep roll shot to the left back, or deep 5 zone.

In addition to the blocking and covering tactics of the SR defense, a team can choose to work on two other cued tactics that are variations of the SR: the SRC and SRT. When the left-front blocker cannot time his or her block to the rhythm of the opponent's middle hitter, it may be useful to change to SRC. This call indicates the starting position of the players (SR), and the C tells the left-front blocker that he or she must *commit* to jumping with the middle hitter. The blocker should penetrate the net with the hands before the ball contact by the opposing team's middle hitter. Should the opposing middle hitter run a slide, the defense must rely on digging an unblocked player.

The SRT call is appropriate if the dominating player on the opposing team is the outside hitter. This call indicates that the defense is going to triple block the outside hitter. The left-front player needs to run and form a triple block with the middle and right-side blockers. The three back-row players, no matter what defensive formation is being used, are responsible for covering all tips and balls that go off the block. A coach had better hope there is a block, because the three back-row players are basically covering the entire court.

Based on previous learning, a player should react using the SR adjustments when the opponent's right-front help setter must set the ball. In this defense, the defensive players must employ the SR alignment when the first ball or first contact is played by the opposing team's back-row setter. Once the back-row setter touches the first dig on defense, an alternative setter must handle or help set the second ball for the opponent's offense. The defensive players must see this situation begin to unfold and move to SR.

Blocking the Slide Attack

The slide attack in the women's game has become one of the most predominant attacking weapons. The men's game uses this attack also but currently not to the extent that the women do. Special attention should be given to this attack. Both front-row and back-row defensive players need to drill blocking this attack, playing the ball off the block, playing a tipped ball, and digging an unblocked attack. This forces the opponent to decide how to attack.

Players can drill, setting up a defensive team in a regular blocking scheme or an SR blocking scheme, by tossing the ball to the setter and having a middle hitter run the slide while the outside hitter prepares for a 4-ball set. Coaches can provide numerous repetitions using the following concepts:

- **Single block the slide.** Assign the left-front player to block the slide while the middle blocker stops the setter tip, runs to help double the slide, or runs to double the left-front outside hitter. Since the left back is already on the left sideline, the left front blocker should block the crosscourt angle of the attack.

- **Double block the slide.** Commit both blockers to double the slide since this hitter has been identified as the best side-out hitter and has been very effective in terminating the ball. This leaves the right-front blocker in a one-on-one block with the left-front outside hitter.

- **Double block the left-side attack.** The left-side hitter is deemed the player to double block. The slide is blocked one on one.

While I was coaching, I used a combination of our middle-back defense with some rotational defense movements when we needed to make adjustment calls. These were made against an opponent's left-side hitter when he or she was hitting balls into areas that we couldn't cover from our middle-back defense. Should this hitter have success down the line, a team may instruct its middle- and right-front players to block the line. If this is not successful or if the right-front player is too short to take away the deep-line shot, it is useful to call a *red 6*, in which we only rotated our middle-back player over to cover the deep-line corner. All other players stayed in their basic middle-back coverage. The right-back player stayed in at his or her base for tip coverage rather than moving to the right sideline where he or she might interfere with the vision of the middle-back player (figure 7.8a).

When an opposing team's left-side hitter continued to hit deep crosscourt shots into our uncovered 5 corner, I would indicate to our left-back player that he or she must rotate to a 5 coverage, to neutralize this situation (figure 7.8b). At times, I called for a rotate 4-5 so that both the left-side players moved for crosscourt and deep crosscourt coverage. The middle-back player would adjust a couple

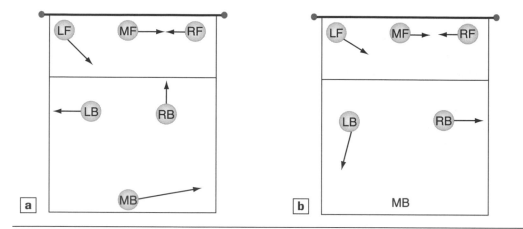

Figure 7.8   Rotational defense to cover the deep line corner *(a)* and to cover the 5 zone *(b)*.

of steps to the right to be ready not only to react to tips and splits but also to get to the 1 corner faster.

Angle Defense

No matter what defense is being used, all defensive players on the court must react immediately when they hear the call, "angle." The antenna becomes the focal point as the blockers anticipate where the ball must legally cross the net. A ball crossing the net outside of the antenna is out of bounds. The off-blocker, front-row player farthest from the antenna who is not involved in the block, and the back-row defenders give up one part of the court to the antenna and focus on covering the smaller portion (figures 7.9) The middle blocker moves down the net to set the block at the spot at which he or she determines it will cross the net. The outside blocker on the antenna side closes the block to the middle blocker. The off-blocker stays right beside the net to take a ball that is tipped or rolled or that ricochets off the net or a blocker's hands. The backcourt sideline player on the antenna side moves into the middle of the court for deeper tips or rolls. The middle-back defensive player rotates to the far corner, while the player on the far sideline moves forward along the line toward the net.

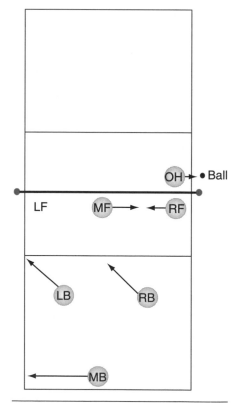

Figure 7.9   Angle defense against a 4-ball set.

Team Defense Drills

The speed and direction of the opposing team's offense correlates to the precision of its first pass. All six players on the serving team—that is, the defense, once the serve has been contacted by the opponent—need to focus on the direction and height of the first pass to prepare to handle the opponent's attack. A passed ball traveling sideways or backwards away from the setter eliminates any need to cover an overpass, setter tip, quick attack, or combination attack. When this happens, defensive players should anticipate blocking a high outside set or a back-row attack. Both of these sets provide ample time for all the players to be in the correct place on the court and in a low, balanced body position.

Players should also anticipate a free ball, which eliminates the block and puts five players into the W serve-receiving position. A good but high pass to the target area permits the opponent to run any sequenced offensive plays but, due to the ball height, allows the defense to position itself without a sense of urgency, using the middle-in, middle back, or rotational positioning. Before a team works on defensive team drills, it should perform some warm-up and reaction drills in order to better understand the need to be disciplined and balanced. Warm-up drills, including Pepper games, can prepare players for digging balls that are hit at various speeds and angles. The following are some good warm-up drills:

- **Partner read-and-react.** This drill helps make sure that each time the opponent touches the ball all of the defensive players are balanced and ready to move. One player tips to himself or herself a number of times before releasing a ball that his or her partner must play by accelerating to keep it from hitting the ground. The number of touches will vary to try to keep the defensive player off-balance. Coaches are looking to see which players lose their discipline and stand up or hesitate.

- **Ball ricochet off the hand.** Coaches can also create teaching sessions in which they ricochet the ball off various surfaces to players; balls then travel to the players at various speeds and angles. This provides the players with the opportunity to develop a good feel for how to handle unusual shots. A coach can ricochet balls to five or fewer players as they rotate through a line. To help a ball ricochet at the last instant, the coach can stop the non-dominant hand in front of a ball coming off his or her attacking hand. Over the years, I perfected this technique so as to be able to put a ball into a preplanned area or at a certain height and distance. Coaches are looking to see whether players stand up and look to see what is happening or react quickly and accelerate to the ball.

- **Digging balls off the net**. The purpose of this drill is to train players to react to a ball that skips off the top of the net, whether from a serve or an attack. (This can only happen on an attack if the ball crosses the net in an area that is not covered by the blockers.) The coach can stand on a chair on one side of the net and work, for example, with the left-back players. The coach should contact the ball so that it hits the top of the net and ricochets over to the defensive players. Missing the net is not a problem because it teaches players to be prepared for the unimpeded shot as well as to react to the ricocheting ball. Players can rotate to the front of the line to get several repetitions of this type of reaction. Should the coach want this to be a six-on-six drill, he or she can move the chair off the court immediately so that normal play continues. The coach should make sure that he or she hits the ball from the opponent's left side, middle, and right side and that the team plays the normal three contacts. Blockers can then be added and the ball can be intentionally hit off their hands or tipped over the block.

SIX-ON-SIX VIRUS DRILL

FOCUS

Read the offense from the first pass so that a proper defense can be established. Both the offensive and defensive teams benefit from this drill.

PROCEDURE

Full teams set up on both sides of the net and follow these steps:

1. A ball is tossed to the "virus" (a coach or an identified player on the offensive side of the net—not one of the six players), who directs where the first ball will go. The virus determines the height, direction, and speed of the ball. The ball may even come directly back across the net to the defensive team as an overpass.

2. The serving (defensive) team's players track the direction of the first pass and determine how to position themselves to respond to it. Here are some possible situations:

   a. A ball has been passed toward the right sideline, the back line, or the left sideline. Can the setter get to the ball? If yes, to whom can he or she set the ball? If he or she cannot get to the ball, who will handle the second ball? Will it be a free ball or a down ball?

   b. The virus can pass a perfect pass to target but at varying speeds or heights. The defensive blockers and back-row players must be able to prepare quickly for what could become a quick attack, outside attack, or combination attack.

3. The coach provides feedback after the play.

Another variation of this drill is for the coach to duplicate a mistake made by the defensive team in order to correct it and reinforce either a better position or technique.

DIGGING BALLS OFF THE BLOCK

FOCUS

The purpose of this drill is for defensive players to learn to react and play a ball that ricochets off blockers' hands.

PROCEDURE

The coach stands on a chair facing the defensive players, who have already moved to their defensive positions in preparation for the opponent's third contact. Two blockers stand across the net from the coach, each holding a linebacker blocking pad. Hitting balls off the pads makes it more difficult for the defensive players to react to them, since their vision is partially blocked by the pads. If pads are not available, blockers can jump and use their hands. From here, players and coaches follow these steps:

1. The coach swings and contacts the ball. As he or she does so, the two blockers raise the pads or jump to block and cause the ball to be deflected back toward the defensive teammates positioned behind them.

2. The blockers immediately hand or toss the pads toward the sideline as they turn and transition off the net for an offensive attack. The defensive dig becomes the first contact as the team transitions for an attack.

3. Immediately after the coach's contact, the chair is removed from the court and play continues uninterrupted until the ball hits the floor. Feedback is given and the drill starts again.

4. The coach continues to work each defensive team from three different angles across the front of the net.

5. The drill then rotates to the next defensive group.

6. The coach provides feedback on the court position of the players (whether the outside feet of the sideline defenders are on the boundary) as well as on their body position before the attacked ball. He or she also observes the reaction of the players to the ball to see if they accelerate without standing up and whether their pursuit angle and steps are correct.

TEAM REBALANCE DRILL

FOCUS

This drill helps players rebalance before each contact.

PROCEDURE

1. The coach stands on a chair across the net from the six players involved in the drill.
2. The coach brings the ball over the net but before doing so may tip it to himself or herself several times.
3. The players must rebalance and keep disciplined until the ball finally comes over the net.
4. The coach takes the chair and immediately gets off the court.
5. Play continues against the team on the coach's side in a full rally until the ball hits the ground.

SIX-ON-SIX SINGLE-BLOCK DRILL

FOCUS

The blocking players work to put up a great one-on-one block against their opponent by reading the approach angle and hitting shoulder. The defensive players must try to dig a ball that has been touched or missed. This is a good drill for emphasizing to those in the defensive back row that if a ball isn't blocked, it must be dug.

PROCEDURE

Players form teams of six on each side of the net and make sure there are no middle blockers at the net. Then they follow these steps:

1. The middle-front player on both teams is a setter who is instructed not to block but is required to set a 4 or 5 ball and cover.
2. Play continues until the ball hits the ground in or out of bounds and a point is awarded to the successful side.
3. Teams play until one team reaches 7 points. At that point coaches can put in new combinations of hitters and back-row players.

FOUR-ON-SIX SERVE-AND-DIG DRILL

FOCUS

This drill teaches four players, one of whom can block, that it is possible to defend the court without a block and successfully transition to offense.

PROCEDURE

Players set up a four-person team with a right-front setter who can only block the opponent's left-side hitter. There is no block in the middle or on the right side. They play against a team of six. Then they follow these steps.

1. The teams of four players serve and play defense. Each player gets only one serve per turn, and servers switch on every play. The three back-row players use the defensive positions according to the team's normal defense (middle-back, rotational, or middle-in).

2. The team can transition to a back-row attack from the three zones or run an outside attack using a 4- or 32-set.

3. A point is awarded for each rally. If the team of six loses the rally, the players must be replaced or change positions. The team of four rotates after each rally whether they earn a point or not.

4. The first team to earn 3 points wins. Each team of four plays three 3-point rally games before a new team is formed.

CHAPTER 8

Transitioning to Score

A team must be able to transition from a defensive or hitter coverage situation to a full attack offense to develop the edge needed to score *real* points. Designing and implementing this phase of the game in practice is, in fact, among any team's priorities. I discussed in chapter 6 the importance of a team being able to pass the opponent's serve and earn a side-out point. Now it's time to cover a team's ability to score points through transition.

The serve-receive is the first opportunity to run a transition to offense and earn a side-out point. Except for a "stuff" block, a rally can be made up of several volleys. Each volley initiates a transition to offense. What offensive options are available depends on a team's ability to cover the floor space and its capacity to get the ball to its own hitters. It is not just one team that is transitioning to offense but rather both teams alternating plays in an attempt to earn real or side-out points each time the ball is in their court.

The ability of a team to transition from the following settings goes a long way toward keeping that team competitive. Chapter 6 discussed the importance of serve-receive transition and the necessity of keeping up or staying even with the side-out ability of an opponent. In this chapter, I discuss and illustrate the transition of teams from the following situations: block and defense, an overpass, a free ball, a down ball, (a tip to the back row) and hitter coverage Each of these situations requires that teammates be in the correct area to fulfill their assigned responsibilities, properly anticipate the ball, and control the dug or passed ball to the target. To earn that real point, the team must provide as many opportunities as possible for its front-row players to jump and take a great arm swing. The transition attack should force the opponent to move faster, cover all of the court, and dig balls that are hit harder and faster at them than their players are used to handling. Giving the opponent free and down balls will not help a team, but it certainly will help the opponent.

Transition From the Block to Offense

Based on their talent and coaching philosophy, teams develop blocking schemes to block their opponent on the left or right sides, in the middle, or from the back row. The block is designed to stuff the ball down on the opponent's side for a point, although it may also work to take away the opposing hitter's most consistent shot or channel the ball to your team's best digger.

Defensive systems are based on the coverage of those team members not involved in the block; a team does not want to block and dig the same area. Perimeter defenses work from the outside (sidelines and end line) by staying wide and running to the ball in the middle or the corners, or by rotating to the corners. Inside defensive coverage (middle-in; see page 145) takes away the short-middle shots with coverage in the corners.

Transitioning from a block attempt can occur from a dug ball directly from the attack or from a ball that ricochets off the net or a block. The transition that takes place will differ depending on the defensive system being used and the direction of the attack.

Middle–Back Defense Versus a Left–Side Attack

The left-back, middle-back, left-front, and right-back players can dig the ball. The left front opens and sprints back to a position outside the left sideline 12 to 15 feet (3.5 to 4.5 meters) from the net to hit a 4 ball. The middle front opens and gets off the net to the 10-foot (3-meter) line and drives forward to hit a 1 ball. The right front opens and sprints to the right sideline 12 to 15 feet from the net to hit a 5 ball. The setter releases and penetrates to the target. Hitting calls can be made by the hitters as they are moving or the setter as he or she penetrates to the net. Teams can have predetermined calls specific to transition, which could include quicker sets to the outside, shoot sets, or combination sets. The fancier combinations are usually attempted when a team receives a ball that is easier to pass, such as a "free ball."

The same situation as that described previously occurs with a dug ball if the setter is in the front row. The setter turns and faces the offense as the left-front and middle-front players get off the net in preparation to attack. The middle-front player can attack in front of the setter or run a slide set behind the setter. The right-back player must be available to attack out of the back row (figure 8.1a).

If the setter is in the back row and digs a ball, he or she must call on a help setter. Figure 8.1b has the right-front player setting. Unless the right-front player is also an accomplished setter, his or her sets will probably be limited to a 4 ball to the left side, a 2 ball to the middle hitter, and a C to the setter.

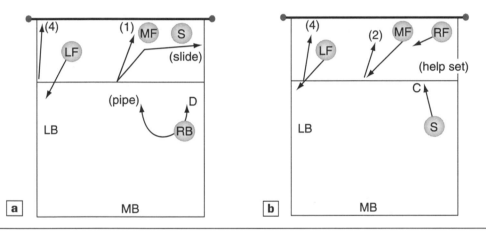

Figure 8.1   The middle-back defense of a left attack with the setter in the front row (*a*) and in the back row (*b*).

Middle-Back Defense Versus a Right-Side Attack

In this scenario, the attack is dug by either the left-back, middle-back, right-front, or right-back player. The left-side hitter accelerates back off the net to hit a 4 ball. After retreating off the net, the middle hitter drives toward the net to hit a 1 ball, and the right front opens and drives back in preparation to hit a 5 ball. The setter releases to the target to run the offense. When the setter is also digging in the back row, the ball must be sent a little bit higher to provide time for the setter to get to the net.

The following two examples are transition reactions when the setter is in the right front. The right-front setter digs the ball; he or she must call for a help set from the right back, who will probably only be able to set a 4 ball to the left front or a 2 ball to the middle hitter or a teammate in the back row. If the ball is dug by anyone else, the setter (who is in the front row) can run the offense. The left side can hit a 4 ball. The middle can hit a 1 ball in front, a 7 behind, a tight slide, or a wide slide.

If the setter is in the back row, the scenario is similar to that for a back-row setter using this defense against a left-side attack.

Middle–Back Defense Versus a Middle Attack

The middle attack can be single blocked by the middle blocker; double blocked by the left- and middle-front players; or triple blocked with the left-, middle- and right-front players.

If the attack is single blocked, the left-front and right-front players cover tips and transition to left-front and right-front positions to call for a 4 and 5 ball, respectively. The left-back and the right-back players dig hard-hit balls angled to the 5 and 1 zones respectively. If the setter in the right back digs the ball, then the right-front player becomes the help setter. The middle-back player off-sets to the right for the hard cutback shot (figure 8.2a).

If the left-front player is in a double block with the middle blocker, he or she has further to go when getting off the net to hit a 4 ball. The setter is also deeper and has further to go to penetrate to the target. The hit can be a 4 to the left side, a 1 to the middle, or a 5 to the right side. Once again, the right-front player will help set when the setter digs the ball (figure 8.2b).

With three blockers, there is the maximum court space to cover. The goal is to block the ball and not let the opponent place it into the middle of the court or the corners. In figure 8.2c, the setter is in the front row and can set in front to the left side or in front or behind to the middle hitter. The right back can also hit a C. If the setter is in the back row, then the right side can transition for a 5 ball. This defense has the worst percentage for making a successful transition.

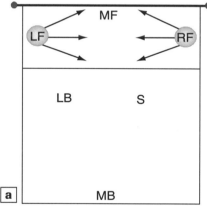

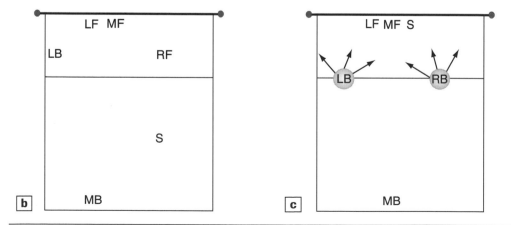

Figure 8.2 Three scenarios for blocking a middle attack using the middle-back defense.

Rotational Defense Versus a Left-Side Attack

The rotational defense covers the corners with the left- and middle-back players. The left-front player covers the crosscourt angle, and the setter or right-back player covers the tip. The middle back player rotates to his or her right to dig the line shots at the intersection of the right sideline and the end line. The transition from the coverage to the attack is easier for the left front because he or she is already playing defense at the 10- to 12-foot (3- to 3.7-meter) line. The setter is inside the line, so the release is easier. The right-side player can open the inside hip and run back to prepare for a 5 attack. If the setter plays the first ball, the right-front player again becomes the help setter.

Here I illustrate the positioning for this defense and the movement necessary for a 4-1-5 offense on transition (figure 8.3). The goal is to permit the left-front player to hit down the line to the corner digger, deep crosscourt to the left-back digger, or sharply crosscourt to the left-front player. The weak areas are crosscourt along the net in front of the 10-foot (3-meter) line and in the middle of the court from the 10-foot (3-meter) line to the end line. The goal of the blockers is to force the hitter away from the middle of the court or to block the ball that would otherwise go to the deep middle of the court.

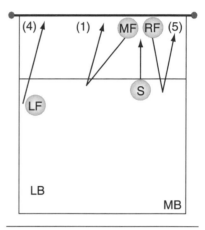

Figure 8.3 The rotational defense against a 4-1-5 attack from the left.

Rotational Defense Versus a Right-Side Attack

Although many teams rotate to the right against a left-side attack, only some teams rotate to the left against a right-side attack. These teams are fewer in number and may only do so when defending a standout hitter from the other team. With this defense, blockers permit the hitter to hit down the line since defensive players are rotating to the corners. One concern with this type of rotation is the release from a back-row setter to run the offense. The setter is now deep in the right corner, 28 to 30 feet (about 9 meters) from the net. It is best to either have an assistant setter take over the offense or to run this rotation only when the setter is in the front row.

Figure 8.4 shows a front-row setter and two hitters. The left-side hitter transitions to a 4 ball and the middle hitter runs either a front quick 1 ball or a back slide. The right-back player is still available to attack a C set. Once again, this

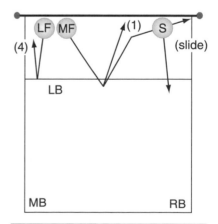

Figure 8.4 Rotational defense against an attack from the right.

defense has an open area in front of the 10-foot (3-meter) line and a big hole in the medium to deep middle of the court.

Middle-In Defense Versus Any Attack

Middle-in defense encompasses the deep-corner defense and left-front movement of the rotation defense. The player in the middle of the defense covers the short areas from the 12- to 14-foot (3.7- to 4.3-meter) line to the net. That player can float along his or her assigned area and cover from antenna to antenna, depending on where the opponent sets the ball. Should this middle-in player be the setter and handle the first ball, then the right-front player does all the transition or help setting. If the middle-in player is in the back row then the setter runs the offense on transition. Figures 8.5a through c show the basic alignments for a left-side, middle, and right-side attack with the setter in the front row. This is mirrored with the setter in the back row. The only difference in transition is whether the help setter can run a quicker offense, including 1-ball and slide sets, or a slower offense using 4- and 2-ball sets. A back-row attack may be an option, but the players need great acceleration to get to the 10-foot (3-meter) line.

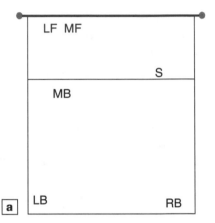

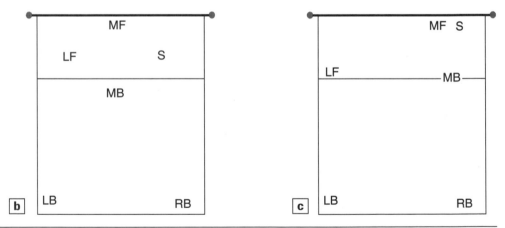

Figure 8.5 The middle-in defense blocking attacks from the left, middle, and right.

Transition From Hitter Coverage

Once the ball has been set, the next team responsibility is for each player to quickly move into coverage. Coaches and players must realize that they are not covering a player as such but the floor space around the hitter where the opponent can block the ball. In the 1960s, 1970s, and early 1980s, a player at the net was called a spiker.

During and after the 1984 Olympics, the player was called an outside or swing hitter. This player is now commonly referred to simply as a hitter or attacker.

All players on the court must release from their court space or approach path once a ball has been set to a teammate. The player's release from his or her serve-receive position may be on the opposite side from which they play defense. A player who specializes in handling the left-back portion of the court, for example, may be on the right side in the serve-receive pattern. There are two theories with respect to where players should move with regard to their coverage. One theory is that back-row players should always cover in the same area, even if they pass a teammate on the way. A second theory is that a player covers the closest area first before switching back to his or her normal side of the court. The coverage position can be regarded as two semicircular layers with the front layer being a *cup* of three players and the deeper layer being made up of two players who fill in the gaps left by the front three players. The focus of each player's vision while in coverage should be on the blockers' hands. The most common mistake made by players in coverage is watching their teammate attack the ball.

How the transition to an offensive attack takes place from a ball blocked back onto a player's side is determined by who plays the ball, who is available to set, and who is available to attack. In the following example, the right-front player may be the setter and the options available to him or her include setting a 4 ball, a 2 ball to the middle, or an A ball to the left back. When drilling, a coach or player can put balls back into the defensive cup coverage as the hitter catches the ball.

The following examples of hitter coverage are determined by the team's defensive and serve-receive positioning.

• **Coverage from a 4-ball set.** When there is a big or tall block from the opposing team, the cup should move closer to the net because the angle of deflection will be sharper and closer to the net. The coverage for the left-back player changes from the 10-foot (3-meter) line, as illustrated in figure 8.6a. Players digging the ball off the block can direct it to the right-back player, who can set a 4 ball to the left front or a 2 ball to the middle or to back-row attack players. Since the back-row setter who came to the front row to set the attackers is now on the left side of the court and in the middle of the cup, his or her ability to run a transition offense is limited to a 4 ball to the left front and a 5 ball to the right front or the back-row attack zone (figure 8.6b). Figure 8.6c shows a team receiving the serve in a U pattern and moving to the cup coverage area. Since the middle hitter has run a 1 ball, he or she will stay at the net while the setter moves around him or her to be in the middle of the cup. The sort of transition used will be similar to that shown in figure 8.7b.

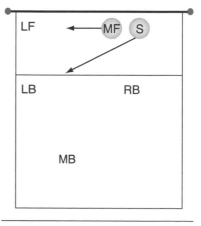

Figure 8.6a Hitter coverage of a 4-ball set.

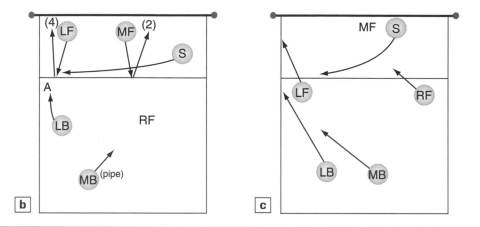

Figure 8.6b and c In cup coverage of a 4-ball set, the middle front player covers along the net.

• **Coverage from a 5-ball set.** The coverage on a right-side, or 5, set makes players rotate to cover. The setter should always turn the head toward the net as he or she checks the accuracy of the set. He or she should step with the right foot back and away from the net as if on a hinge and cover the blockers. Once the middle blocker lands, he or she should go around the setter and become the middle in the first cup. This coverage forces the middle back and the left back to rotate to the 5-set side. The middle-back player sprints to the right sideline to cover his or her new responsibility and works from the 10-foot (3-meter) line in toward the net. The left-back player runs deep to the right to cover the seam between the players forming the inside cup. The left-front hitter rolls off the net to cover the seam between the setter and middle-front player (figure 8.7a).

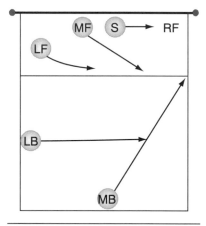

Figure 8.7a Using a cup defense around a set to the right side or a 5 call. In this case the setter stays at the net and the middle front player comes around the setter to form the middle of the cup.

• **Coverage from a free ball.** Transitioning from a free ball should be the easiest and most successful of all transitions. The blockers pull off the net back to the 10- to 12-foot (3- or 3.7-meter) line. The back-row setter releases as soon as the free ball is recognized and gets to the target early. Teams tend to run a quicker or trickier transition when receiving a free ball, going from their defense to the W, or five-person receive pattern. Because the setter is leaving to penetrate and the right front is moving back into coverage, the weak area is the 2 zone. This is especially true since, in my experience, the right front player often reacts or moves back too slowly. A traditional offensive example would have the setter run a 4-1-5 play set (figure 8.7b). A play that would generate more offensive movement is a 4 ball to the left front, a slide to the middle with the right front going second around the middle to hit a 2 ball (figure 8.7c). When transitioning from a block, the same offense can be run as that shown on page 131.

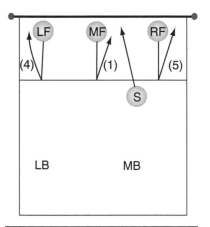

Figure 8.7b Movement at the net showing the 4-1-5 play set for a free ball.

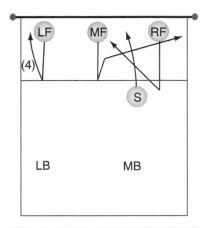

Figure 8.7c A 4-slide-front 2 play set.

CHAPTER 9

Physical Conditioning

Physical conditioning is made up of several connected components that must be addressed together to provide players with complete fitness. Coaches and players must take full account of these components, along with the principles of fitness, as they structure age-appropriate and safe training sessions that include exercises specific to the muscles and skills used in volleyball

Learning to condition the body specifically for volleyball helps athletes prevent injury and produce the strength, explosive power, quickness, and flexibility needed for the game. Proper conditioning also enhances players' aerobic capacity, allowing them to compete at aerobically intense levels while engaging in the multiple volleys and rallies that may last from seconds to minutes during each game. It likewise enables players to recover and compete effectively in tournaments, during which they may have to play multiple consecutive games.

First, I discuss some principles of training and how they apply to volleyball. I also cover how to specialize training to be appropriate for the age of the athlete and his or her physical and mental development. The chapter includes several volleyball-specific conditioning exercises that coaches and players can use to improve their fitness for the sport. Finally, I cover some basics of properly fueling the body for volleyball.

Principles of Exercise

Several principles of exercise can help athletes and coaches organize their conditioning program. Conditioning for volleyball is often a by-product of game-like training sessions, but the better the athlete's base conditioning and fitness the more a coach can emphasize maintaining that fitness while devoting time to technical and tactical training. The principles of training are called the FITT principles and include the following:

• **Frequency.** This refers to how often the athlete trains. It is generally agreed that three to five times per week is a frequency that produces conditioning benefits while also permitting adequate rest and recovery between sessions.

• **Intensity.** This refers to how hard the athlete works for the duration of the exercise to maintain or improve conditioning. For cardiovascular conditioning, this can be related to the percent of maximal effort or percent of maximal heart rate. For strength training, the intensity can be measured by the number of repetitions or amount of weight lifted. The principle of overload also is relevant to intensity. To overload means to work against a greater load than that with which the body is currently fully comfortable in order to make gains in strength and fitness. Athletes do this by gradually and progressively increasing the load or intensity week by week.

• **Time.** This refers to how long a training session lasts. For cardiovascular improvement, 20 minutes of exercise or more is considered necessary. With respect to strength training, time is often measured by the number of sets done for each lift; two or three sets are often adequate.

• **Type.** This refers to what kind of exercise an athlete does. With regard to volleyball, there are four types of conditioning covered in this chapter that I consider to be crucial for properly preparing volleyball players:

1. Flexibility training involves increasing an individual's range of motion using specific stretching exercises. Done properly, flexibility training can prevent injury, increase the range of motion, and reduce soreness.

2. Aerobic or cardiovascular conditioning includes continuous activities, such as running, swimming, and volleyball rallies.

3. Strength training includes such activities as lifting free or machine weights, using stretch tubing, and performing exercises that use body weight as resistance.

4. Sport-specific agility training helps to improve an athlete's quickness in movements with respect to the game he or she plays.

Coaches and players need to consider each of these FITT principles as they develop a conditioning program that is appropriate for a team and its players. Related to the principle of type, as noted previously, is the concept of conditioning specificity. Specificity refers to identifying those components of fitness that enhance volleyball and working on those particular components. It is best to seek leadership and direction from credible professionals and resources, such as trainers and strength coaches, when developing the program for a team.

Volleyball is an extremely dynamic sport when played at the highly competitive high school, club, and collegiate levels. To play the ball while covering the court on each play requires athletes to be constantly moving and responding with agility to situations that require lateral, diagonal, horizontal, and vertical movements. It requires extensive preparation for an athlete to develop the power needed for a vertical jump, using either a one- or two-foot takeoff. It also demands that athletes have the ability to maintain that skill when overloaded with numerous repetitions in a short period of time, such as during a single rally, as well as over a long period of time, such as throughout a match.

Movements that involve lateral and diagonal agility, quickness, and explosive jumping take place numerous times during each individual, group, or team drill. Three or four players on the court, while transitioning both offensively and defensively, can be performing maximum jumps on every given play. The setter positions himself or herself to jump-set a ball at the top of his or her elevation while a middle hitter may already be in the air. If the ball is not set to the middle hitter, two other front-row players can receive the set and jump at their maximum to attack. If the setter is in the front row, additional back-row players can be jumping to attack a set. Across the net, one, two, or even three front-row players try to time their jump to penetrate the net before the ball comes over. In essence, on any given play there could be five or more players from both teams in the air. Back-row players, holding their disciplined low defensive position, must be ready to accelerate using quick steps to get to a ball that has not been blocked. These players may also be going to the floor and immediately getting back up to pursue their next responsibility. After all this, a new play begins.

There is no time limit. Even though rally scoring has eliminated the numerous side-out plays that occurred without a point being scored, the players must deal with these sorts of physical challenges on each point of the match. Playing the best of five games still means training to play up to two and a half to three hours for a match. A volley can be terminated on one swing or block, but a rally can also require one or more players to jump and swing at

Age-Appropriate Conditioning

At what age is it appropriate to begin structured physical conditioning? In my program, during the players' middle school or junior high years (ages 13 to 15), my staff and I started exposing players to drills at more intense paces to stimulate their aerobic conditioning. At the same time, players were provided with the number of repetitions they needed for skill improvement. We would also start players on a strength program but would use exercises that required them to lift or use their own body weight. Using body-weight exercises, such as push-ups, sit-ups, bench dips, and vertical jumps, is a safe way to start younger kids strengthening their bodies without the dangers of balancing free weights or attempting to use machine weights that are too heavy. Players can increase the resistance by progressively increasing the number of repetitions and sets they do. We did not start athletes training in the weight room with free weights or machines until they were at the junior varsity level (15 or older). Strength training should be commensurate with the athlete's age, experience, body development, and future growth pattern.

As players develop, improve their skills, and gain experience, the volleys between two competitive teams increase in speed, quickness, and duration. Players must therefore increase their aerobic capacity and strength in order to handle these situations while at the same time adding power to their game. Training sessions should be designed to include situations that require a time limit or other contact goals that can allow players to measure their success. After a warm-up that has increased athletes' heart rates as well as their oxygen intake, players can put their muscles, connective tissue, and joints through exercises that duplicate game movements. Players should not only prepare for the throwing motion of serving and attacking but also for jumping. The latter can be done by hopping and skipping. Finally, players must stretch their bodies using game-like techniques while preparing to play the ball in the unique extension, sprawl, and roll positions.

the ball several times before the play is over. In 2004-2005, Ashley Pederson, a graduating senior from Penn State University, attacked the ball nine times during the course of one rally in a game against Wisconsin. That one rally alone lasted 54 seconds. This does not count the number of times she jumped to block in that rally or moved into coverage. During the course of one match, players are continuing to be aerobically conditioned and to undergo strength training. Lifting one's body weight vertically numerous times over the course of a practice or match is *work*.

In addition to the principles of conditioning, players should create a healthy lifestyle that prevents injury and enhances overall health. This lifestyle should include eating properly, managing stress effectively (including using relaxation techniques), managing time efficiently, getting proper rest, avoiding destructive habits, and following appropriate medical advice when warranted.

Warming Up

Before athletes start any conditioning session or practice, they should warm up to increase their body's core temperature and the flow of blood to their muscles. Breaking a sweat is a good indication that the core temperature is elevated.

I have noticed in the past couple of years that there are two basic approaches that have emerged regarding how to warm up. The newest approach, which I don't buy, is to use Pepper, ball-control drills, or team transitioning drills. It seems that this might kill two birds with one stone, providing repetitions of ball control skills and position movements while warming up. My concern with this type of warm-up is that players will go for a ball and end up using the muscles before they have been properly stretched. I do, however, recommend using some of these gamelike drills *after* an initial warm-up for additional conditioning.

My coaching staff and I always tried to set aside 15 to 20 minutes for a combined warm-up for our team. We used the following 10 components in varied durations before every practice:

1. Warm-up jog.
2. Stretch while moving. Players walk and stop in positions designed to isolate some initial stretching positions for the Achilles tendons, calves, ankles, hips, legs, and shoulders.
3. Agility movements, such as shuffling, carioca, skipping (easy, for height and distance), hopping left and right, spike approach jumps, high knees–quick heels, skater strides, increasing the length of the stride, backpedaling, ladder agilities (after practice), and sprints.
4. Flexibility. During static stretching of the muscles and joints, athletes should work from the head to the neck, arms, shoulders, trunk, legs, and ankles. Each stretch should be done using good mechanics and held (not bounced) at a point of mild discomfort, not pain. After each stretch, players relax and hold again to progressively increase the muscles' length around a joint. A good goal is to increase and maintain joint mobility.
5. Flexibility. Players perform stretches that incorporate the gamelike body positions used in extensions, sprawls, rolls, and dives.
6. Sit-ups and push-ups.
7. Jump work.
8. Use of elastic tubing to isolate deltoid and rotator-cuff muscles.
9. Lateral and diagonal footwork at an easy pace followed by increased quickness.
10. Throwing a ball with a partner to prepare the shoulder, elbow, and wrist joints used in the serving and attacking motions.

After this warm-up, the front-row players would work on attack and block jumping while the back-row players worked on game movements from position. Athletes playing all the way around would do reps of both.

Once the warm-up session ended, my players would play some six-on-six movement and coverage volleyball. This required three gamelike contacts, with the third contact being a definite tip, a controlled arm swing, or a two-handed jump-set to a player on the opposite side of the net. The goal was to keep the ball from hitting the floor.

Flexibility Training

Putting a warmed-up muscle through a static stretching position before the body assumes that position during technical training and intense competition helps that muscle avoid injury and improves the performance and quickness of muscle memory and the speed of muscle contraction. Moreover, consistently training flexibility is a key component to increasing the overall range of motion of a joint and thereby decreasing the risk of future injury. By-products of improving flexibility include enhanced sensory receptors in the muscles, improved kinesthetic awareness, and increased power output. In my experience, a lack of kinesthetic awareness—the ability to know one's place relative to his or her surroundings—is most detrimental in the culminating roll of a lateral extension, especially on the player's non-dominant side.

While flexibility training is an important part of warming up before a practice or competition, it is also important to do so within 5 to 10 minutes after normal or intense training activity or competition. The increased muscle temperature after a workout or game facilitates maximum gains in a player's range of motion. This stretching cool-down also helps to return the muscles to their normal resting position and length thereby helping to prevent sore muscles. Other important stretching guidelines include the following:

- Stretch the entire body. Perform at least one stretch for 10 to 30 seconds for each major muscle group. Include stretches for the neck, back, shoulders, chest, hips, quadriceps, hamstrings, calves, and feet.
- Perform each stretch with the proper form.
- Stretch slowly; move into the correct position slowly and then increase the intensity for 10 to 15 seconds. Stretch to the point at which you may feel mild discomfort. Don't bounce; instead, make the stretch a static hold throughout which you are breathing slowly, comfortably, and rhythmically.
- Perform each stretch one to three times per workout.

Table 9.1 lists the flexibility exercises I used with my teams and includes the muscles each stretch targets.

Table 9.1   Flexibility Exercises for Specific Muscles and Structures

Stretch	Muscles and structures targeted
Neck flexion and extension*	Trapezius, sternocleidomastoid, and ligaments of cervical spine
Side stretch	Latissimus dorsi, trapezius, and muscles and ligaments in pelvic area
Deltoid stretch	Posterior deltoid and latissimus dorsi
Pec stretch	Pectoralis major, pectoralis minor, and deltoids
Lats and triceps stretch	Triceps, latissimus dorsi, and posterior deltoids
Hamstring stretch	Hamstrings, spinal erectors, gastrocnemius, low back, and ligaments of lumbar spine
Lower back and gluteal stretch	Erector spinae, gluteus maximus, and gluteus minimus
Standing adductor stretch	Hip adductors, hamstrings, and (with back toe toward the ceiling) calves
Sitting groin adductor stretch	Adductors and sartorius
Calf stretch	Gastrocnemius and soleus
Dorsiflexor stretch	Tibialis anterior and the gastrocnemius
Achilles stretch	Achilles tendon, gastrocnemius, and soleus
Trunk rotation	Lateral (outside) of the hip, thigh, trunk, and lower back

* I have noticed setters doing this stretch after long repetitive setting sessions when they are forced to track many balls.

Cardiovascular Exercise

Rather than relying on general cardiovascular conditioning like jogging or swimming, I preferred to use more sport-specific methods to increase my athletes' cardiovascular endurance. I did this by incorporating endurance drills into our individual, group, and team training sessions. These drills were always done for a specified number of repetitions, a given amount of time, or as a consequence for improper performance. All sprint work had a built-in finishing factor: the player who lost a sprint was required to do one more full rep of the same. This finishing factor helped to ensure that players gave all-out efforts to avoid doing that additional sprint. Of course, over the years I had four different setters who seemed to always lose these sprints. But on the court, in practice, and in games, these players were able to set every ball and beat teammates to balls that they shouldn't have. These players had game quickness and closing speed, if not sprinter's speed.

While I do not recommend that varsity-level players or above run conditioning sprints after practice, players in the younger age groups who don't participate in rallies of the same length and intensity during practice as older players do need postpractice conditioning. The postpractice conditioning can include sprints but also should emphasize court coverage movements as well as jump conditioning for those who play at the net. All our players did do agility-ladder movements after practice, although more often in the preseason for our junior varsity and varsity players. We did not do them during postseason playoff training, as these practice sessions were short, crisp, and to the point. During the off-season, players may train for another sport or run or bike on their own to increase their cardiovascular conditioning.

Agility and Footwork Training

Volleyball is a game of quick, precise, and explosive movements. When a team's opponents play the game at a faster speed than a team can handle, mistakes are made more frequently. Players can learn through vision and recognition training to better anticipate what type of ball is coming at them, but they still must learn to move more quickly. The best players not only have quick feet but also are usually more balanced and natural in their movements. Even when quickness is natural, players must still be trained to handle gamelike situations. This includes using steps that permit them to close a block, transition off the net, or accelerate to a ball that is going to hit the floor or go out of bounds. Coaches can provide opportunities to increase foot quickness with gamelike repetitions, line drills, combination drills that include vertical movements, floor drills, and ladder drills. Players who increase muscle memory through specific work subsequently react faster in game situations.

A team can incorporate this type of training in combination with its daily sessions or during preseason or off-season training. This training is intense, so it is especially important that players warm up adequately before doing any agility or footwork drills. Players can build up the intensity throughout training by doing such things as increasing the number of repetitions or the distance of drills, decreasing the time to attain the distance, or decreasing the rest time. This sort of training also develops players' overall conditioning and therefore should be done at maximal effort for each set.

The drills should also help stimulate all the muscle groups. Players can have a core set of drills that are specifically designed to promote some of their weak areas. For example, if a player moves slowly off the net after a block attempt, he or she should use a drill that incorporates a lateral movement, followed by a vertical movement, a diagonal movement, and another vertical movement. While players jog around the perimeter of the court, a coach can call out commands for them to switch their footwork (for example, turning inward, outward, slide-stepping, and so forth). Players can use a diagonal hip opening drill followed by a forward sprint and jump. Players can run the drills around or across the court, along the net, or from an end line to the net and back. The number of repetitions depends on how many players are involved or the time limit placed on the drill. My experience has been that when I set an arbitrary reps, say 10, players often would bottom out after six or seven reps. I have also had players go beyond their limit and go into exercise-induced asthma. Four or five consecutive reps are usually a good start, though. The learning climate must facilitate open discussion so that players are comfortable in discussing their limits.

The following drills are some of my favorites, but there are many others that can work athletes' agility and the speed of their footwork.

LADDER DRILL

FOCUS

This drill improves foot speed, push-off, plantar flexion, and muscle and aerobic endurance.

PROCEDURE

Players can use a specially purchased commercial ladder for this drill or use lines that are taped on the floor in an area that won't interfere with other courts or be a safety concern. I've also had players perform this drill on the school's steps.

1. Players step forward with each foot between the rungs of the ladder with perfect steps and as quickly as possible. Players step first with the right foot and then the left such that both are within the space between the rungs before stepping with the right again.

2. Players repeat the drill—jumping in and out from between the rungs—facing sideways, backward, and forward.

3. Sequences can be performed to use lateral as well as forward and backward footwork. We let each player in the group lead footwork movements for their teammates to follow.

LINE DRILL

FOCUS

This drill provides players with numerous opportunities for moving forward diagonally and opening their hips and retreating diagonally.

PROCEDURE

1. Coaches start by setting up an X pattern on the court. Each line of the X, from the center of the X outward, should be 4 feet (1.2 meters) long.

2. A player starts in the center of the X and steps to the right front, back to the middle, to the right back, to the middle, to the left front, back to the middle, to the left back, and back to the middle as quickly as possible

3. While in the middle of the X, players should be in a balanced position with their hips and shoulders parallel to the net before opening the hips and going diagonally in one of four directions.

ON-COURT AGILITY DRILL

FOCUS

This drill involves a figure-8 weave that works on lateral and diagonal movements that players use to cover the court. It emphasizes players using three or more steps to cover their responsibility. Players move at a different angle each time.

PROCEDURE

1. The drill starts in zone 6 of the court (the back middle). Divide the squad into three groups, each with an odd number (between three and nine) of players so that each player performing the drill can stay in the exact same order and can go the opposite way every other time. The remaining players retrieve the balls or hand them to the person running the drill.

2. A coach or coach's assistant stands with his or her back to the net at the center of the court and tosses the ball to each player in turn. Players begin from the end line. Each player passes the ball and then circles back to the starting point on the side to which he or she passes The angle and distance of the pass is determined by the coach or tosser and is designed to increase the player's ability to move to the ball with speed, balance, and control.

3. Once the player reaches the front of the rotation, he or she passes to the next angle and repeats until he or she has passed to seven different angles, three to the right, three to the left, and one straight ahead.

4. If the passed ball is out of the close range of any particular player, that player may have to use an emergency lateral extension and roll in order to play that ball back to the desired target.

5. The duration of the drill can be determined by the objective. For example, if the goal is to drill movement and conditioning, it can proceed for a certain amount of time or a designated number of individual player contacts. When the objective is to improve the passing, the goal may be a specific number of perfect passes to target to end the drill.

6. The players rotate clockwise once they have met the objective of the drill.

BLOCK MOVEMENTS

FOCUS

This drill works on improving the movements blockers make along the net.

PROCEDURE

1. The middle blockers involved in this drill work one at a time, alternating with their teammates. Blockers can begin their movement when the coach smacks a ball, or they can start after the completion of the previous player's movements. All players start at the middle of the net on the nonworking side.

2. Each player, in turn, ducks the net, ready to begin the block and attack movements.

3. Following each player's initial steps to block, the middle hitter can use a diagonal movement first away from and then toward the net to attack.

4. The middle hitter performs footwork patterns (see pages 87 to 88 for ideas), alternating to both sides for a predetermined number of repetitions. As each player makes the move back to the net to attack, he or she must call for the ball and jump as if to hit a quick set.

5. This drill can continue by adding a tossed ball to a setter who sets the quick ball.

6. Players can continue the drill with the blocker taking three steps left, jumping to block (ball will be tossed over the blocker), transitioning off the net, and approaching the setter to attack the set ball.

APPROACH MOVEMENTS

FOCUS

This drill trains the front-row players to approach the net and begin their subsequent attack from different areas of responsibility on the court.

PROCEDURE

This drill works one group of hitters at a time (i.e., the left-side hitters).

1. Players wait their turn in a line of teammates to receive a ball 8 feet (2.4 meters) in from the left sideline. After making a pass to the setter, the first player in the line releases to the outside while calling for a 4 ball.

2. Each player approaches, jumps, and attacks the ball before returning to the line to begin again.

3. The drill continues with each player releasing from the net on a free-ball call to a point 12 to 15 feet (3.7 to 4.6 meters) from the net. Once the distance off the net has been reached, the player makes a set call, such as for a 4, and approaches and attacks the ball.

4. He or she makes a block attempt at the net and then transitions off the net to the 12- to 15-foot (3.7- to 4.6-meter) mark and swings out to make an outside-in approach. Once again, each player must call for and attack the set ball.

5. A final approach can be made from an inside (off-blocker) coverage position to the outside at 12 to 15 feet (3.7 to 4.6 meters) before approaching and attacking the ball.

Jump Training

There are many options available to train players to jump for efficiency of movement, correct footwork, full-range arm lift, and explosive takeoffs. Realistically, the player's genetic inheritance dictates most of his or her vertical jumping ability, but additional gains in vertical jump can be made through strength and jump training. In addition to athletes jumping rope or performing hop sequences over cones, I provide several other jump-specific training exercises in the following section; strength training is discussed later in this chapter.

BROAD JUMP

FOCUS

Players should concentrate on jumping with proper form. The technique used in this drill duplicates the lifting and explosive jump of the spike approach but on a horizontal rather than a vertical plane. Doing consecutive jumps over the length of the gymnasium will not only produce some sore muscles the next day but also a better understanding of the effort it takes to lift one's body vertically off the ground.

PROCEDURE

Players can perform this drill with or without the arms assisting the jump by following these steps:

1. The player stands with the feet shoulder-width apart.

2. Using the arms to assist the jump, he or she reaches both arms back while dropping quickly into a flexed position.

3. The player brings both arms forward to jump, generating momentum for maximum lift and drive.

4. He or she lands softly with balance and is able to immediately repeat the move. Upon landing, he or she maintains a good body position with the head up, knees bent, and feet shoulder-width apart and balanced.

5. Continue this jumping activity to reach the specified distance.

This jump can also be performed as a long jump without the arms. To do so, the athlete places the hands on the hips or on top of the head as he or she drops quickly into a flexed position before exploding up and forward.

SKATER STRIDES

FOCUS

These strides simulate the movement of a speed skater. They work the adductor and abductor muscles (that is, the inside and outside of the thighs), which are important for total leg strength when combined with the strength of the quadriceps and hamstrings.

PROCEDURE

1. Players stand with their feet approximately shoulder-width apart and their knees slightly flexed.

2. The right arm drives from below the outside of the right hip diagonally across the body to the upper left while the athlete pushes off the right leg and leads with and lands on the left foot. Players should try to hold their balance momentarily on that left foot before initiating the next stride.

3. On the next stride, the left arm drives across the body while the athlete pushes off the left leg and leads with the right foot.

ELASTIC-BAND JUMPS

FOCUS

Consecutive side-to-side jumps over elastic bands improve leg strength while forcing the athlete to maintain balance and emphasize quickness.

PROCEDURE

Waistband elastic can be purchased at a fabric material supply store, or athletes may use surgical tubing. The waistbands are preferred, however, as there is less chance for injury when players either don't jump high enough or don't bound far enough from one side to the other and miss clearing the band. Players follow these steps:

1. Players participate in groups of seven or more. Two players hold the band and are then replaced as teammates alternate holding each end of the band and jumping. You can also tie one end of the band to the volleyball standard so that the coach can hold the other end and give directions and encouragement.

2. Two players sit approximately 20 feet (6 meters) apart with each one holding one end of the band. Start the band approximately 4 inches (10 centimeters) off the ground.

3. Players start at one end of the band and hop or jump over it from side to side for a previously determined number of jumps or however many jumps it takes to get to the other end of the band. Players should start with right-foot hops, emphasizing quickness. On the next trip, players hop on the left foot. Following that, they jump using both feet.

4. Players raise the band after each set of the single- and double-foot jumps. Once the band is over knee height, each player jumps only three times when using one leg and five or six times when using both legs.

5. When the band reaches waist height, each player jumps one time using an angled spike approach to get over the band. Players can do a tuck jump with their knees pulled up to the chest to clear the height.

BOX JUMP

FOCUS

Players can do plyometric training, such as this exercise, using sturdy wooden boxes between 1 and 3 feet (30.5 and 91.4 centimeters) high; these can be constructed or purchased. The goal, using speed and strength training, is to generate the greatest amount of force in the shortest amount of time

PROCEDURE

1. Coaches should choose box heights that challenge the vertical jumping ability of their athletes.

2. Players stand in front of the box with their feet balanced and shoulder-width apart.

3. Players jump as high as possible and land softly on the box with the head and shoulders up.

4. They step down and continue until they have accomplished a set number of repetitions.

Another way to perform this drill is to jump down off the box and immediately back up, rebounding as quickly as possible on each jump to take advantage of the muscles' elongating and contracting—that is, of the muscles recoiling.

Strength Training

In the following discussion of strength training, I focus on ways to improve strength specifically for the sport of volleyball. Coaches should realize that there are many theories about the best way to undertake strength training and incorporate the ideas of others that best fit into their particular situation—that is, those that work given the age group of the players being coached and the type and amount of equipment that is available. The exercises I highlight in this section concentrate on the legs, chest, back, shoulders, arms, and torso.

An athlete's personal strength provides him or her with an advantage when assuming defensive positions, blocking, and balancing above the net. It also greatly contributes to explosive vertical takeoffs and subsequent arm swings above the net. By performing strength exercises and drills that focus on footwork movements, quickness, and agility, players develop their ability to control their bodies while moving at faster speeds.

Strength training should be designed to improve muscular strength and endurance by using both body weight and other forms of resistance to properly overload the muscles. Cardiovascular endurance can also be developed by using lower weights and higher repetitions. Being a dynamic sport, volleyball demands that players have power, speed, balance, and endurance. Players must train to play the game on the ground yet also quickly accelerate across the court and jump with strength and balance above the net. Increasing a player's strength can help prevent injuries to the shoulder girdle, torso, and legs. Players can play at a consistently high level for two hours after they begin a match, and sometimes even longer.

Many school programs for youths begin in the seventh grade. As I mentioned earlier, at these younger ages, rather than introducing them to weights, we used body-weight resistance training and provided overload by either increasing the number of repetitions of an exercise or adding an additional set so that our athletes were gradually increasing personal muscle strength and endurance. (This type of resistance training is also appropriate for teams that may not have access to a weight facility.) In our program, boys began lifting weights in ninth grade and girls in ninth or tenth grade. Regardless of the athletes' age or what facilities are available, however, it is important that safety and preventing injury while strength training be top priorities.

An important principle of effective strength training is the principle of overload. This refers to the progressive, week-by-week increase in workload that results in strength gains. To systematically provide the right amount of overload for athletes, coaches need to know each athlete's starting point. In my program, we handled this by using the first two weeks of our preseason or off-season training to teach the correct form for each exercise. Athletes would meet three days per week during these initial instructional sessions. Because we scheduled a day off between sessions, we worked the total body by alternating large and small muscle groups or upper- and lower-body work. Once players were comfortable with the techniques, we pretested for each exercise. Each player recorded his or her maximal lift for one repetition. Players then would start training on each exercise, starting at a weight that was 55 to 75 percent of their personal best lift. So, for example, if you have a player who bench presses 100 pounds for his or her one-repetition maximum, that player should begin with 8 to 10 repetitions at 55 to 75 pounds.

There are several ways to increase the amount of weight used in the athlete's overload progression. One way is to establish the standard of increasing the weight for upper-body exercises by 5 pounds (2.3 kilograms) per week and by 10 pounds (4.5 kilograms) per week for lower-body exercises. If this is not possible, an athlete can add additional repetitions from week to week. Should an athlete increase the number of repetitions from 8 to 11, he or she can add 3 pounds (1.4 kilograms) the next week. To increase strength, the ability to contract an individual muscle must be increased or an increased number of the muscle fibers must be recruited for contraction.

Lifting With Free Weights Versus Machines

Free weights can be more dangerous than lifting machine weights because with free weights there is the possibility that the weight plates are not balanced, a spotter is not paying attention, or the lifter cannot maintain the balance of the total weight throughout the range of motion of the lift. By the same token, lifting free weights can be an excellent option precisely because it forces an athlete to balance the weight throughout the full range of motion. This balancing of the weight not only works the intended muscle groups but also forces the body to recruit other muscle fibers to stabilize the weight (just as the body must also do during movements in sport). Machine weights can be best for beginning lifters because they assist the athlete in maintaining correct form.

Once a player's strength has been developed, maintenance lifting can be implemented to maintain strength during the season. To determine if the weight being used is actually correct for increasing strength, athletes must feel a difference in lifting the last two repetitions of a set over the first six or eight reps. If the last two repetitions are as easy or comfortable as the initial six to eight, the weight is not heavy enough to produce strength gains. This does, however, help to maintain strength. Lowering the resistance and increasing the repetitions can accomplish training for muscle endurance. Muscle endurance training is also accomplished using the player's body weight while he or she goes through the rigors of the training and practice sessions of the season.

In undertaking a strength-training program, make sure that athletes follow these lifting procedures:

1. Use the correct form for each lift, whether on a machine or using free weights.
2. Make sure that during the lift the weight goes through a full range of motion.
3. Continuous breathing during lifting is accomplished by exhaling upon exertion and inhaling when returning the weight to the starting point.
4. Keep the weight close to the body throughout the lift.
5. Spotters are a vital and mandatory component of lifting free weights. Spotters not only support and encourage their partners but also have their hands in position to assist when needed.

Strength-training workouts are typically performed three times per week. This provides approximately 48 hours for the body to eliminate lactic acid and repair some of the minor damage done to body tissue. Typically, athletes alternate training days in their designed workouts. There are athletes who do train daily, but they do so by emphasizing different muscle groups on alternate days.

The following sections provide some brief exercise descriptions of upper- and lower-body lifts that are particularly beneficial for volleyball players. In addition to these lifts, players may incorporate push-ups, pull-ups, and abdominal crunches into their strength training.

Upper-Body Strength

Volleyball players must have strength in their arms, shoulders, chest, and back to maintain both serving strength and the power to play above the net when blocking and attacking. Several drills, listed in the next few pages, can help athletes develop strength in the pectoralis, triceps, and deltoid muscles. These exercises can be alternated or used in the order in which they are presented.

BENCH PRESS

FOCUS

This exercise works the pectoralis, triceps, and deltoid muscles.

PROCEDURE

1. The player lies down on a bench with his or her head by the bar. A good starting point is to align the body with the eyes directly below the bar. A spotter stands behind him or her.

2. The player bends the knees and puts the feet on the floor on either side of the bench. Some players prefer to bring their feet up on the end of the bench with their knees bent.

3. He or she grasps the bar with the hands balanced equally from the center of the bar.

4. On the count of three, the player lifts the bar from the rack and extends the arms completely above the chest.

5. While inhaling, he or she lowers the weight to the chest, touching the bar to the chest for a full range of motion but not bouncing the bar off the chest.

6. While exhaling, he or she presses the weights upward in a controlled motion (without arching the back) until the arms are completely extended.

For younger athletes, when the safety of using the bench press is a concern, the seated bench press using a vertical chair machine is a great exercise to perform.

DUMBBELL INCLINE PRESS

FOCUS

This exercises works the pectoralis, triceps, and deltoids, which are especially needed when blocking above the net.

PROCEDURE

1. The player sits comfortably on an inclined bench with the knees bent and the feet alongside the bench. The spotter stands behind the bench with one hand above each of the lifter's elbows to assist, if needed, in the full extension of the arm.

2. The spotter hands each dumbbell separately to the player and he or she rests the weights on the side of the chest. The weights are turned so that the balled ends face the front and back.

3. The player exhales as he or she simultaneously presses both arms directly above the head. At full extension, the weights are turned so that the balled ends touch each other.

4. The athlete then rotates the balled ends back and lowers the weight to the chest area while inhaling.

5. Once repetitions are completed, the partner can take the weights or the lifter can lower them to the ground.

Since this lift requires each arm to balance and stabilize independently, the spotter must watch the lifter's nondominant arm as this arm tends to have less control.

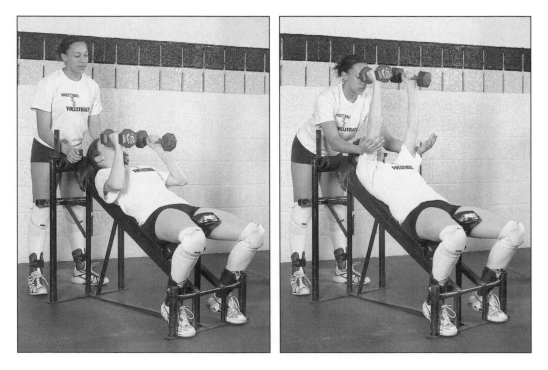

DUMBBELL TRICEPS EXTENSION

FOCUS

This exercise concentrates on the triceps to assist in the arm-extension action used in the serve, set, and attacking full arm swing.

PROCEDURE

1. From a standing position, a player grasps a dumbbell and holds it in a vertical position. He or she moves the weight behind the head with the elbows bent.
2. He or she stands in a balanced vertical body position with the feet shoulder-width apart and the head up.
3. While exhaling, the player presses the bent arms into a straight vertical position.
4. While inhaling, he or she returns the dumbbell to the starting position and repeats.

DUMBBELL SET

FOCUS

This drill works the pectoralis, triceps, and deltoids in such a way that it is of particular benefit for setters.

PROCEDURE

1. From a standing position, a player grasps both ends of one dumbbell with open hands.
2. While exhaling, he or she takes a short "setter's step" to an imaginary target and pushes the arms to full extension from a position 4 to 6 inches (10.1 to 15.2 centimeters) above and in front of the forehead.
3. Upon inhaling, the player returns the weight to the starting position.

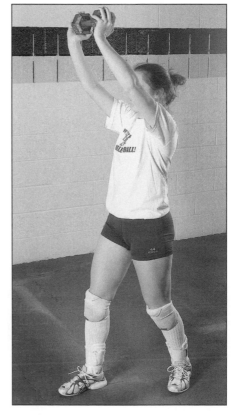

DUMBBELL DELTOID RAISE

FOCUS

This exercise focuses on the medial, anterior, and posterior heads of the deltoid (also called the deltoid cap) to help prevent shoulder injuries.

PROCEDURE

1. The player selects a pair of dumbbells and stands upright.
2. For lateral raises, he or she holds the arms with the elbows locked and the palms facing the side of the hips. He or she exhales as the arms are lifted straight out from the side (the palms now facing the floor) and upward until the arms are extended slightly higher than parallel to the floor *(a)*.
3. The player inhales as he or she returns to the starting position.
4. For front raises, he or she stands with the feet slightly staggered and the palms facing backward. He or she exhales as the arms are raised forward and up until they are slightly higher than parallel to the floor *(b)*.
5. The player inhales as he or she returns to the starting position.

6. Rear raises are more difficult since the athlete needs either to lean forward so that the chest is flat or kneel on a bench in order to isolate one arm at a time.

   a. For standing rear raises, the athlete exhales as he or she raises the dumbbells back and away from the side with the palms facing backward until the arms approach the height of the shoulder.

   b. For kneeling rear raises, place the left knee on a bench, keeping the right leg straight and the right foot on the floor. The right arm is straight and moves backward during the lift. Switch knees to lift with the other arm.

7. The player inhales as he or she returns to the starting position.

Players can also perform this set of exercises using elastic bands or surgical tubing for resistance. Our athletes integrated the use of surgical tubing, after our daily warm-up, into every practice. One end of the tubing is stabilized under the athlete's foot. But players should use caution to ensure that the stabilized end of the tube does not pull out from under an athlete's foot and snap through the air.

PEC DEC, OR CHEST PRESS

FOCUS

This exercise works the pectoralis major and deltoids.

PROCEDURE

1. The player sits on a pec-dec machine or a chest-press bench and selects the desired weight.

2. He or she starts with the arms to the side and the elbows bent at a 90-degree angle. The hands hold the handle or rest on top of the arm pad.

3. While exhaling, the player presses both arms together at the same time until they touch in front of the body.

4. He or she inhales as the weight is returned to the starting position.

SHOULDER DIP

FOCUS

This exercise works the pectoralis major, triceps, and deltoids.

PROCEDURE

1. The player starts on a dip station in a vertical position with the arms straight.
2. He or she inhales as he or she lowers the body until the arms are at least at a 90-degree angle.
3. The player exhales as he or she presses the body upward until the arms are straight *(a)*.
4. Players may also use an assisted dip machine that permits the addition of weight plates to counteract the player's body weight. This permits players who have not been able to do a dip with their body weight to employ this drill using a full range of motion.

It is very important that the athlete does not use a leg kick or kip action; the body must be kept from swinging. Dips can also be done using three chairs *(b)*. Each hand is placed on the seat of an adjacent chair while both legs are straight with the heels placed on a third chair. The player lowers his or her body until the elbows are bent at a 90-degree angle and then presses up to straighten the arms.

WRIST ROLLER

FOCUS

This exercise works the forearms, wrists, fingers, and shoulders.

PROCEDURE

1. To perform this exercise, the player needs weight plates that are attached by a rope to a handle.

2. The player starts with the back against a wall so that no levering action takes place.

3. He or she places the hands on the handle and raises the arms straight out in front without any arch in the back.

4. He or she rotates both hands over the handle to wind the rope around the handle until the plate reaches the handle.

5. The player can slowly unwind the handle (which is difficult) or allow the plate to spin back to the starting position (which is easier).

ROTATOR-CUFF EXERCISE

FOCUS

This exercise works the muscles of the rotator cuff. The amazing shoulder joint differs from the other joints in the body in the wide range of movements that it can make. While volleyball players use this joint for serving, it is used most prominently with the attacking arm swing. Players take arm swings at different speeds and (at times) different angles that place a great deal of torque on the shoulder. The internal stabilizing mechanism of the shoulder girdle must be able to withstand the repetitive or overuse injuries caused by the numerous swings taken during the course of the season.

PROCEDURE

Players can perform this exercise, using tension tubing or elastic bands, as a preventative measure before or after a workout. Before using the exercise bands or tubing, players should check them for rips, tears, or worn spots so that they don't break during the exercise. Players should also make sure the band is anchored under the center of the shoe so that it doesn't slip out when under tension and snap the user or a teammate. The band can never be too long because the excess can be held above the hand, but it can be too short. A player should stand normally with the shoulders parallel to the ground. With the arm hanging normally down, the player should have enough band to be able to anchor a portion under the shoe plus a few inches of excess in the hand. To increase resistance, the player can choose a firmer band or lower his or her hand holding it. Players work on the right shoulder for all the exercises before switching to the left shoulder.

1. The player starts by standing with one end of the band secured underneath the right shoe while the other end is held in the right hand with the palm facing the side.

2. He or she stretches the band up and bends the arm to a 90-degree angle so that the elbow is at the height of the shoulder.

3. The player holds the band vertically behind the arm and two or three inches (5 to 7.6 centimeters) in from the elbow *(a)*. While the hand maintains control of the band, he or she pulls it down so that the palm is facing the ground and is parallel with the elbow *(b)*. The pull is made against the resistance of the band on the way down.

4. The player resists the contraction of the band as he or she moves the hand back to the starting position and repeats this movement 10 times.

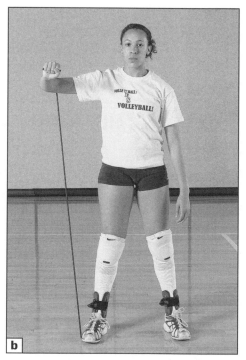

5. Next, he or she puts the band in front of the elbow, two to three inches (5 to 7.5 centimeters) in, while holding it in the hand *(c)*. In this situation, the contracting band pulls the hand and forearm down as the player resists the pulling action bringing the arm to a 90-degree angle.

6. He or she pulls against the resistance of the band, moving back and forth to the starting position, always keeping slight tension on the band *(d)*.

7. The player repeats the action with the other arm.

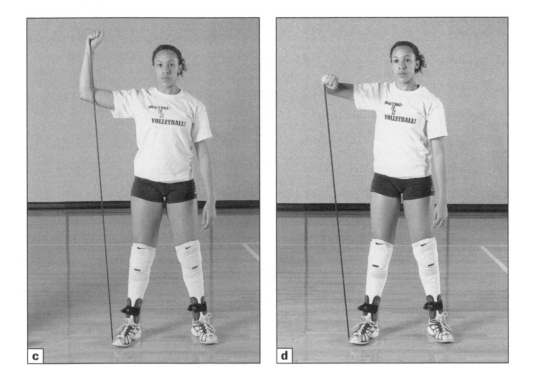

This exercise requires the player to be disciplined in maintaining proper form because the elbow constantly tries to move out of the 90-degree angle in which it is held.

Lower Body

Many players are concerned about their vertical jump (or lack thereof). While the jumping ability of most players can be traced to their genetic inheritance, increases can be made through progressive overload while engaging in lower-body strength exercises such as the leg curl, leg extension, and the others listed here.

FREE-WEIGHT SQUAT

FOCUS

This drill works the quadriceps and gluteal muscles.

PROCEDURE

This exercise requires spotters and perfect body position to prevent injury. Although the quadriceps and buttocks are being worked, the player uses many muscles to maintain balance and proper form throughout the lift.

1. The player stands facing the free weights that are resting on a rack. He or she may want to place a pad or a towel at the base of the neck to absorb some of the pressure from the bar. A spotter should stand on each side of the lifter with the hands cupped under, but not touching, the ends of the bar.

2. The lifter steps under the bar by bending at the knees, not by leaning over at the waist.

3. Using the legs and buttocks, he or she extends up to place the weight on the shoulders and steps back to get away from the support rack.

4. With the feet shoulder-width apart, the lifter inhales as he or she lowers the weight by bending or squatting at the knees to an angle greater than 90 degrees. The back should be straight throughout the lift and the head facing forward.

5. He or she exhales while returning to the starting position by extending the legs and places the weights back on the rack using the same form as when taking up the bar at the beginning.

An alternative exercise to the free-weight squat is using the leg-press machine. When performing leg presses, the athlete should not allow the buttocks to raise up from the seat because this changes the leverage angle.

HEEL RAISES

FOCUS

This exercise works the gastrocnemius and quadriceps.

PROCEDURE

1. This drill can be performed on the leg-press machine, using the squat rack, or standing with a dumbbell in each hand.
2. The player starts with the feet flat on the floor and legs together.
3. He or she raises and lowers the body, flexing at the ankle joint and lifting the balls of the feet.

DUMBBELL LUNGE

FOCUS

This exercise works the gastrocnemius and quadriceps.

PROCEDURE

1. The player stands upright holding a dumbbell in each hand.
2. He or she steps or strides forward so that the front knee bends at a 90-degree angle and is aligned over the front foot. The back knee should not touch the ground.
3. While exhaling, the player pushes back to a vertical position and continues the exercise, alternating front legs.

Nutrition and Rest

With any discussion of conditioning, the importance of nutrition and rest in enhancing the physical well-being and health of the athlete cannot be overlooked. In fact, proper nutrition and adequate rest can be just as important as cardiovascular conditioning and strength training.

What a player takes in is what his or her body uses for energy and maintenance. The body requires food to provide energy, to build and repair tissue, and to regulate metabolism. Proper nutrition is important before a workout to provide the energy necessary to properly train and is also important 30 to 60 minutes after a workout to provide the nutrients to repair tissue and restore energy. Good preworkout nutrition tends to include foods that are high in carbohydrate and easily digestible, such as bagels, pasta, energy bars, trail mix, and cereal bars. Postworkout meals should consist of foods from the major food groups with a balance of carbohydrate, protein, and some fat. Before matches, players should allow one to three hours to digest a meal. Smaller meals can also make for easier digestion.

Another important part of fueling the body for training is keeping it hydrated. The need to stay hydrated must never be taken lightly. Players should not wait until they feel thirsty to start replacing fluids because thirst is not the first indicator of need. Body cells function best when they are in a solution of water. The muscles work hard to create energy, and with that energy comes the production of heat. The heat is dissipated through the circulation of blood, which circulates the heat to the skin in the form of sweat.

Since players sweat at different rates, some athletes need to replace fluids more often than others. Players must be trained to replace fluids. Although there are variations, players generally should replace between 5 to 8 ounces (150 to 240 milliliters) every 15 to 20 minutes. It is even better if players bring their water bottles to a place off the court for ready use. Coaches should design practices so that short and long water breaks are available for the athletes. Some players may wish to enhance their fluid intake by drinking a sport drink. These products offer some of the electrolytes that the body eliminates in sweat, and they are flavored. This may encourage athletes to take in more fluids.

My team's water breaks during practice would follow a match-type schedule (that is, one-minute breaks, the same amount of time as allotted for timeouts during games). We generally planned a minimum of three minutes of rest for every 45 minutes of practice, not including water breaks. Players were also able to have hydration and recovery periods when not directly involved either in a drill or retrieving balls. Players were encouraged to have water bottles off the court near the drill so they could rehydrate without losing focus or interfering with the drill.

CHAPTER 10

Practice Sessions

Coaches need to consider several factors when they plan, design, and implement a practice session. These factors include the background and experience of the players, the number of coaches and facilities (including courts) that are available, and the equipment that the team has on hand. Coaches need to also keep in mind how much time they have available for practices and if they will include strength and conditioning programs, such as those described in chapter 9. The age and skill levels of the participants also have an impact on the number of coach-directed versus player-directed drills that can be planned. Related to this is whether there is staff available to assist in player instruction. Some programs have several courts available and are able to divide players into groups based on their roles and responsibilities or the position they play. Other programs have one or two courts and limited space surrounding those courts. But they are able to hold nonball training drills outside the gymnasium in foyers, hallways, and wrestling rooms, thereby freeing up court space for ball-control drills. Having the flexibility to schedule special individual training may depend on when other activities take place during the school year and what other sports use the gymnasium for training.

In addition, the players' perceptions of the coach's attitude toward practice and the amount of energy the coach brings into the gymnasium are factors in the growth, learning, and productivity of individual players and the team. The coach's personality, demeanor, and ability to relate to players of different age groups and ability levels are important. Observation and feedback skills must combine with patience to help players benefit from each practice session. In all my seasons, if I could do it over again, I would try to be more patient but no less demanding of my athletes. Players must feel that their coach is supportive and caring. Trust and respect are earned rather than demanded. Knowing that the coach is honest, fair, firm, and consistent can alleviate conflicts among players. The coach's personality has to be his or her own, and it has to show through both inside and outside the gymnasium.

Depending on whether you are involved with a club or scholastic program, there are different guidelines that affect training and competitive play. Scholastic programs, while staying within the local, state, and federal mandates, must adhere to the academic guidelines and the athletic philosophy of the school district. Club programs do not have academic standards but instead rely on the parents' discretion and guidance. Each state has written guidelines that mandate the starting date, the number of scrimmages that can take place, the first and last legal playing dates, and the total number of competitions that can be played.

Understanding Training Cycles

There are four basic cycles of training throughout the year: preseason, in-season, postseason, and off-season training, The *preseason* is the developmental phase of a training program before competition begins that establishes the foundation for the technical training related to on-court skills, boundary awareness, verbal communication, and tactics. These skills will continue to be enhanced and fine-tuned as learning increases and the season progresses. At the entry levels of play, such as in junior high programs, basic conditioning and strength training are initiated during this phase. (Players competing at the junior varsity or varsity level or in club programs for older players are often involved in off-season conditioning programs that incorporate both strength training and aerobic conditioning.)

During preseason training, coaches need to make sure that they are sticklers for efficient movement, sound all-around technique, correct body and court positioning, and court awareness. The preseason is also a good time for coaches to establish the use of video as a teaching and reinforcing tool by scheduling time for this into practices (see the related sidebar on page 199). While striving to build aerobic conditioning into our practice plan, my coaches and I also used the preseason for jump and agility training as well as strength training, which we alternated on a daily basis.

In-season (often called competitive-season) practices are designed to improve weaknesses, maintain strengths, and focus on rotations, player responsibilities, and the ability of players to transition from situations as they unfold during competition. Not only does technique training take place in-season but also the maintenance of strength through strength conditioning. During the in-season, my team would lift every other day (Monday, Wednesday, and Friday) and would incorporate some agility and jump training time into each day's postpractice activities. Our strength work consisted of one set of 8 to 10 repetitions, rather than the two or three sets we did during the off-season. Players and their partners rotated to each station as upper- and lower-body muscle groups were alternated. Partners spotted one another when necessary so that one worked and another recovered during the two minutes devoted to each station.

During the in-season, practices should be designed to focus on achieving specific objectives, such as trying to neutralize the strengths of the upcoming opponent or improving on a recently exposed weakness. One way to present a major objective is to give an overview by introducing the concepts early in a practice session (just before or after warm-ups) and showing the finished movements or team positioning that is expected. Coaches can create drills that establish individual responsibilities and follow these drills by working with the combinations of players who will be impacted by the projected adjustments. Then the team can work on learning to recognize, communicate, and respond to the triggers that dictate the flow of the required coverage. As the team is able to assimilate all the individual and team training, practice can become more efficient and effective. During my program's daily in-season practices, we devoted time to knowing boundaries (see pages 81 to 82), individual skill improvement or maintenance,

Using Video As a Teaching Tool

My program used early preseason practices to videotape individual players and groups on a daily basis. Once a group of players was taped, the members of the group would watch the tape while another group was being recorded.

We would also videotape a few intrasquad scrimmages and a lot of scrimmages, matches, and tournaments against other teams. A coach who videotapes matches must build extra time into practices to watch the videos, which my staff and I did before the start of the next day's practice session. I was fortunate to have a young man tape our matches; our players taped the practice sessions. We only taped actual play, and the tape was stopped between each play so that no unnecessary footage lengthened our viewing. The videographer would keep a verbal update of the score so we knew what portion of the game we were viewing. When I had time, I would dub in teaching action either in slow motion or repeat mode to show both good and bad play.

and group and team play. The continued in-season use of video, usually in the form of reviews of match or tournament play, provides visual reinforcement for proper court positioning and play.

Participation in a scholastic *postseason* competition—a district and or state tournament—is an earned reward. It is usually the result of achieving a team goal and often reveals the team development that has taken place. During practices in this phase of the season, the time devoted to specific review or learning depends on the early-round match-up. A coach's strategy may dictate working on a phase of the team's play that has been bothersome rather than purely preparing for the opponent. Emphasis may shift to visual awareness or recognition and also focus on mental toughness. Our practice time during the postseason was shortened to no more than 90 minutes—including lifting—with emphasis on skills, crisp movements, and team demands. The goal of these practices was to reduce the number of unforced errors. That said, I always added two similar drills to a couple of the postseason practices to improve players' reaction time, quickness, and focus. One drill, using three players, was to use a ball ricocheting off a surface such as a hand or wall (see page 153). The second drill used the gymnasium's dividing partition to simulate the opponent's block.

In this second drill, the coach tosses the ball to the team's setter to simulate a serve being passed. The setter sets to one of three hitters. The other team members immediately move into coverage positions as one of the hitters jumps and swing-catches the ball. A coach or another player who is not part of the team on the floor throws a ball off the wall to simulate a block. The coverage team plays the ball ricocheting off the wall and transitions into another attack. Players continue this sequence until the ball coming off the wall hits the floor. Then they begin the drill again with a set to a different player. This drill emphasizes focus on the blocking hands of the opponent, reaction (both verbally and physically) to the rebounding ball, and transition to the next set and coverage. Do this in all six rotations. Once the players get the feel for the drill, the attacking player does not catch the ball but instead attacks the ball off the wall using different angles and speeds. The players not involved raise the noise level by clapping or cheering to simulate the noise in a playoff match. Depending on the length of the partition and the number of players available, multiple teams can run the drill.

During the *off-season* phase of training, my first recommendation is for players to take time away from the sport to rest, recover, and recharge. A player can participate in other activities that he or she enjoys and vacation or travel, if it is possible to do so. The off-season, which spans the summer for scholastic programs and falls late in the summer for club programs, can be used to attend open gyms or community programs that are available for age-group training or to compete in pickup games. Attending summer camps for individuals and teams as well as playing on the beach (on sand courts) may also be possible.

Separate sessions may also be scheduled during the off-season for individual players to work on skills specific to their position. The off-season for boys in Pennsylvania occurs from late June through February. I isolated time for these players to lift weights with a continuous program from January through the end of February. Female athletes who were not involved in a second sport or had some open time away from their club team were also able to perform strength training at this time. It is generally easier for players to attend these sessions regularly during the school year than over the summer.

Each of these cycles of training complements and builds upon the others throughout the season. For example, a program's off-season training may focus on the foundations of conditioning, such as strength, agility, flexibility, and nutrition. This work makes players more fit to improve their skills later in the season, which helps them avoid injury.

Planning Practices

Setting goals is essential if a coach is to promote individual and team improvement. A team's long-term goals help to integrate newcomers into the system so that steady improvement in play occurs throughout the season, with the team peaking as it approaches the playoffs. Daily objectives on the other hand, focus on players' acquiring the necessary knowledge and skills and being able to transfer these trained elements to successful team play. For the coach, this means planning drills that isolate each player's role in the big picture and providing players with the repetitions they need in order to accomplish their own goals and those of the team.

Each year, I began the season by preparing a long-range training plan for each athlete. This plan was based on his or her background and experience and provided a timeline for the developmental sequence of skills, movements, tactics, and team play. I suggest that coaches prepare several drills to introduce or review specific skills. It is better to have more drills planned than can be executed than to feel uncomfortable when a drill isn't working and frustrated that you do not presently have the time to fix the situation.

Here is a possible sequence to follow for introducing skills to new or second-year players. As a part of every warm-up, the players start by performing footwork movements that they will need later on as their areas of coverage expand. Then I introduce the forearm pass because I believe the players will handle more balls from serve-receive and defense with their forearms than with any other technique. I follow the forearm pass with the overhead set, serve, dig, attack, and block. Beside each skill in a notebook, I listed all the individual, group, and team drills that could be used to introduce, teach, and train these skills. I then refined this list by adding any drills I would create or come across.

Most programs' preseason goals are centered on establishing and reinforcing efficient and technically sound fundamentals as the players increase their ability to move and control the ball. To compete at a higher level, players must be ready to play the game at a faster speed and with more power. Therefore, the intensity of the practices needs to increase over time, as should the level of skill that players strive to achieve.

When players enter the gymnasium to begin their daily training session, a coach needs to make them aware of the training or practice objectives of that day. These objectives might be associated with the improvement of a specific skill, the addition of a new technique to the players' repertoire, or the team training to overcome a weakness that was exposed by an opponent in the match the day before. Coaches should also explain how the day's training objective will increase the team's opportunities for success. Russ Rose, head women's volleyball coach at Penn State, uses the following list of ideas to help him determine what drills and lessons practices will incorporate:

• **Address the major components in player development.** Building on a solid base of fundamentals and getting players to use their skills to perform at the desired level is all part of player development. Coaches need to find ways for players to be able to apply the knowledge and skills they learn in practices. I have found ways to do this by asking players to *show me* how to correct a mistake without my providing the answer verbally. For example, if a player is making a dig but the dug ball is not going to the target, I might ask the player to show me how to correct the problem.

• **Emphasize technical skill development.** Simply put, players need to learn to continually improve their execution of technical volleyball skills to increase their success with the game.

• **Emphasize motor skills, body balance, and movement.** Coaches can incorporate drills with and without volleyballs to develop each player's ability to have great body position as well as the quick and efficient movements necessary to cover his or her court responsibilities. Once the players have developed the necessary ball control and movement skills, a coach should incorporate game like scrimmages, which require the ability to apply or transfer these skills to game situations.

• **Emphasize learning.** It is not what is taught that is important but rather what is learned. Not a day should go by in which learning fails to take place. Coaches learn about players, and players learn about themselves and the team. Each day, when players and coaches leave the gymnasium, they should be able to say *I am better at (x) than I was yesterday.* The level of challenge must be appropriate for the participants. I see this as one of the reasons for the development of club programs. Talented players, who may not have been able to raise their level of play with the school squad, can now receive the appropriate sorts of challenges in the club program as well as exposure to college coaches. Coaches should provide opportunities to let players play, and watch them play. There are players who can use their skills with positive results when isolated in a small group or one on one in a coach-directed drill, but then they struggle when doing the same skill in a team setting at game speed. These players need to receive feedback and repetitions that allow them to elevate their play in that team setting. Coaches need to make sure that they don't write off a player who drills poorly. I have seen many kids excel in a game situation even after they performed at a low level in their preparation.

• **Evaluate the cohesiveness and competitive ability of varying combinations of players.** Coaches need to identify and evaluate where players can best contribute to a cohesive team both now and in the future. The chemistry of the most productive team of players may differ from the chemistry of a group of players that has the best combined individual skills. Finding a way for a player to contribute and understand his or her role is a critical component of team integration. Coaches must challenge every player to produce while being evaluated, and encourage all players to make themselves indispensable to the team.

• **Develop the players' abilities to handle pressure and crises.** Using various individual and team drills, coaches need to challenge players to respond to their frustrations and adversity by refusing to allow them to get down on themselves. Coaches can introduce offensive and defensive pressure drills, such as Money Ball (see page 13) to challenge each player competitively in practices. Coaches need to encourage players to accept and meet the challenges they face, even if the players have to get angry to do so. Players must be challenged both physically and mentally. Winning is a by-product of the plan to develop excellence. Players must learn to make their individual contribution and bring focus and energy to the game. Coaches need to identify those players who relish a challenge.

Once coaches determine the main objectives of practices, they can prepare for the upcoming season by developing a comprehensive sequential outline of the training that encompasses each phase of the season—the preseason, in-season, postseason, and off-season. They can then keep these plans on file, whether in a three-ring binder or computer file, and use them as a reference. Each year a coach can take notes and monitor how effective the plan and individual training sessions are and make adjustments as needed. A coach should be prepared to use all methods of instruction to reach players in accordance with the way they learn best.

Coaches need to decide what their facility needs are compared to what is available to use. This includes determining how many courts are available, how much space there is around the outside of the courts, how much space is between the courts, and how much time is available to use the courts. Our teams, both male and female, were provided the time in their respective seasons to train players to be competitive locally and statewide. Female volleyball, in our state, plays during the fall and is the only scheduled indoor activity. The girls therefore had no conflicts over gymnasium space or time. During the preseason, before the first day of school for students, they were permitted the opportunity to schedule multiple daily sessions. The boys play volleyball in the spring; their court time is limited to two hours a day due to the conflict with outdoor sports that rotate to the indoor facility during inclement weather or winter sports teams that are in the playoffs. Table 10.1 shows a sample comparison of the time available for preseason training for females and males, and illustrates how a coach can structure practices based on facility availability. Even though the time available for the team may be limited, there are ways to fit in what is needed for effective training. Above all, the time spent in the gymnasium should be well planned,

Table 10.1 Comparison of Two Preseason Scholastic Seasons

Females	Males
Before the first day of school	School in session
Only indoor sport	Time rotated between playoff-qualifying basketball teams and outdoor sports (baseball and softball scheduled inside due to weather)
Practice time open-ended	Two-hour gymnasium time
6:45a.m.: setters arrive; stretch and drill until 7:30	4:30p.m.: team reports to foyer for warm-up and stretching until 4:45
7:30: rest of team arrives, warms up; setters watch videos and rest	4:45-5:00: team movements and introduction of day's objectives
7:50-8:05: movements and stretches using surgical tubing	5:00-7:00: ball usage; team practice, combining individual, group, and team training
8:05-10:15: individual training session	
10:15-11:30: break for lunch	
11:30-11:45: warm-up plus ball handling	7:00-7:30: lifting or jump training in weight room
11:45-1:15: group and team training sessions	
1:15-1:45: lifting, alternated with jump or water training	

should effectively produce the intended objectives, and should provide a sense of accomplishment.

The squad makeup can be a drag on the productiveness of a practice session. A large squad can certainly stimulate competitive situations, with players pushing each other for a starting position, but at the same time can limit the number of practice repetitions in drills for each player. Squads with young, inexperienced players create other concerns. Because these players can't initiate drills and control the ball for all the players to benefit from these drills, a coach may be limited in the number of goals he or she can set for the day. Also, the rhythm, intensity, and flow of a drill may be shorter due to the players' inability to keep a volley going because of limited ball control. This can lead to inconsistent rallies, which result in frustration and boredom. Small squads might not have the player talent in the second group to push or challenge the first team in practice. A possible solution is for coaches to design and implement "wash"-type drills in which a score from one team gets cancelled when the other team reaches its objective. This can help alleviate imbalances in ability. Another solution may be to have the best team produce consecutive side-outs to score a point, whereby the weaker team only needs one. These systems allow the bar to be set higher for one team and may be a good way to challenge the first team to produce under pressure or adversity.

The number of other coaches or staff available can also impact how a coach plans a practice. These individuals could be volunteer coaches, alumni who are home during college break, or team members who have played during the opposite season. Coaches (or a helper they recruit) should be able to place balls with a certain degree of accuracy when serving, hitting down balls, or attacking with topspin. These balls must be placed to get the desired results from each player, whether they are good serve-receive passes, digs to a target, or blocks on attacks. The most helpful coaches are also those with knowledge about teaching technique, court awareness, evaluating play, and the blending of players to get the best out of each player.

I did not have any assistants when I first started coaching, so all player development and feedback was based on my observational abilities. My focus continually drifted to the younger players who needed more attention at the expense of assisting the varsity players. Interestingly, the year our staff increased by adding a junior varsity coach was the year we qualified for the state playoffs for the first time.

A coach also needs to evaluate what equipment he or she has available, including how many net systems (and how to adjust them), how many balls are available (preferably one ball for every two players), and how many ball carts are at the team's disposal (three or four is ideal). It is also important to know if the team has a video camera, TV monitor, and VCR for video review; jump or teaching boxes; surgical tubing or bands for preventative or rehab work; ladders for agility work; and a weight room.

The following list can help coaches organize their training. Once a team begins competitive play, certain weaknesses or training needs will be exposed. Addressing these weaknesses in practice will help players to further improve their training.

Checklist for Planning Practice Sessions

Before practice

- Set out to review with individual players some aspect of their play. A coach may want to walk a player through a positioning concern or review and demonstrate a technique adjustment or correction.
- Review the latest team play during a practice session or match.
- Prepare the preseason goals for the week along with the overall skill sequence.
- Develop and keep a composite list of several teaching drills for individual, group, and team segments of practice.
- Add newly created drills to your composite list when new drills are designed as problem solvers to address a difficulty identified by play against an opponent.

- Keep a review of the players of opposing teams and the strengths and weaknesses of these teams. Include information regarding their offensive and defensive tendencies and plan practice sessions to prepare for them.

- Determine what time frame is available to teach on each training day and if this time includes watching videotaped play or videotaping part of practice.

- Determine if there are any special pieces of equipment needed for training.

- Decide if taped lines need to be added to the court to establish player starting or takeoff points.

- If more than one net is available, decide if the net height should be adjusted to work on a specific technique. For instance, a low net can assist with blocking work with the hands without the players actually jumping.

- Determine if any players are not available for practice or need treatment before practice.

- Post the day's practice plan for staff and athletes in the locker room, on the gym bulletin board, or on the net standard.

- Decide who is responsible for the court setup and for getting the ball carts, training equipment, ice, and water—players, coaches, or both?

During practice

- Write reactions to each drill right after players complete it, noting what went well, what drill did not produce the anticipated results, what drills were too ambitious, what drills athletes should repeat later in the week, and what needs to be reassessed or eliminated.

- Mark any drill that the team did not have time to do during practice. This will help determine if too many drills were scheduled, a particular drill took longer than expected, or if the objective perhaps was met in another way in a previous drill

- Note and add to your composite list a drill that was created on the spot to fill a need.

- Develop the ability to visually monitor more than one group at a time by stationing yourself in an appropriate spot on the court.

Practice Design

Once a coach plans out the objectives for the day or week, he or she is ready to design the individual practice sessions (see table 10.2). Each practice session should devote a portion of time to the development of each individual player's physical conditioning, including flexibility, muscle endurance, and aerobic enhancement. For example, a daily in-season developmental session will include the following:

- Warm-up and aerobic conditioning work (see pages 173 to 174)
- Agility and footwork movements (see pages 176 to 180)
- Flexibility exercises (see pages 174 to 175)
- Preventative exercises, such as rotator-cuff work with surgical tubing (see pages 191 to 193)
- Individual technical skill improvement
- Individual court awareness, technical team strategies, and player movements executed at game speed

Of course, the time allotted for practice can vary from team to team and day to day due to facility availability and other factors. I find it best to block time for each segment of practice into 5-, 10-, or 15-minute sessions. Then segments can be combined for a longer block of time. For example, if a coach finds that the team needs to emphasize team play, he or she can reduce some group or individual time segments in order to extend the time spent on team play.

The players are risking possible frustration and failure during each practice. It is important for coaches to structure sessions that provide real feedback, since players are asked to work their way through situations that range from slow learning to intense, competitive conditions. Coaches can emphasize that if a player is satisfied with where he or she is at present, learning is likely to cease. Coaches need to convince players that accepting structured, honest evaluation and constructive criticism permits them to grow and raise their level of play.

As I discuss in chapter 2, coaches can create a learning environment by encouraging returning players to model the energy, focus, and intensity needed to produce positive results. Teaching formats should take into consideration different players' learning styles and be sequentially planned. Coaches should provide honest and accurate feedback while being fair and firm with all players and remembering to acknowledge effort as well as results. Coaches can incorporate challenges into drills that force players to work through adversity and frustrations while developing mental toughness and the ability to work well with teammates. Coaches must be able to adjust the practice tempo from a patient learning atmosphere to a challenging and intense one with a mere look or voice inflection.

Table 10.2 Sample Blank Practice Form

Week #_____   (Circle)   Preseason   In-season   Postseason   Off-season   Lesson #_____

Day _____   Opponent _____   Date _____

Video Review   Yes   No

Objective(s)_____

Player(s) not available _____

Player(s) receiving taping or treatment _____

Player(s) receiving tutoring _____

Prepractice individual time 2:30-2:45 "short court" or one on one with coach

Video time 2:45-3:00

Time	Activity	Players involved	Objective	Feedback

From *The Volleyball Handbook* by Bob Miller, 2005, Champaign, IL: Human Kinetics.

As the season progresses, coaches can create drills or segments to address concerns with team play that are identified through scrimmages, matches, and tournaments. Some areas coaches may choose to emphasize are covered in the next section and in table 10.3.

Team Focus

As the season progresses, coaches can make adjustments in the practice design to address team or individual weaknesses that competition has exposed. For example, a coach can create a drill during practice to solve a problem a team may be having. Players should also be encouraged to openly discuss their own specific individual training needs with their coach. A practice can then include individual or group sessions to help those players improve their skills and gain confidence. As the season progresses, coaches can shorten practices and increase the quality of play required while practicing. If the team qualifies for postseason play, it can focus on intense, short drills with higher expectations and focused

Table 10.3 Comparison of Various Training Cycles

Element of instruction	Preseason: two-a-days, 7 hours with *70* minute break	In-season: 190 minutes	Postseason: 90 minutes	Postseason lifting time: 90 minutes	Off-season: open gym, 120 minutes
		(Before practice 15 minutes)	(Before practice 15 minutes)	(Before practice 15 minutes)	
Specialty session	30 minutes				
Warm-up agility and bands	20 minutes	20 minutes	15 minutes	15 minutes, including bands	15 minutes
Movements	5 minutes	5 minutes	5 minutes		5 minutes
Water break	5 minutes				
Individual technique work	135 minutes	45 minutes	20 minutes	15 minutes	35 minutes
Lunch break	70 minutes				
Group training	50 minutes	40 minutes	20 minutes		15 minutes
Water and rest break	5 minutes				
Team sessions	70 minutes	50 minutes	30 minutes	30 minutes	50 minutes
Strength training, M/W/F	30 minutes	30 minutes		30 minutes	

team play. Shorter individual drills can be scheduled during this phase of the season to maintain great ball control, body balance, and movement.

A coach can prepare his or her team to face a highly skilled opponent by having a good sense of the team's current level of play as well as the opponent's strengths and weaknesses. A good way to undertake this sort of preparation is to refer back to the preparation used for an opponent that employed a similar style of play (see the sample scouting report on page 217 for ideas). This is a good approach to take if the team has two or more days to prepare for this opponent. Coaches need to keep in mind how much information the players can process, internalize, and transfer consistently into action. If preparation time is short, a coach may choose to prepare the team by simply having players continue to train by doing what they do well and correcting or improving on weakness.

For example, let's say that an opponent's strengths lie mainly in that they have two strong and very consistent topspin jump servers who are likely to impact your team's normal first and second rotations. A coach can develop player confidence or ability by increasing the number of topspin repetitions his or her team gets during practice. Or he or she may decide to start in the fourth and fifth rotations to neutralize these servers. If an opponent has one extremely accomplished serve-receive passer, your own team's players may be instructed to serve short so that this player doesn't get to pass. Forcing other players to pass may limit the offense that the opposing setter can run.

Individual Skill Focus

Individual skill work includes the introduction of skills and drills during the preseason as well as a sequenced progression of skills during the competitive season. After a warm-up segment, practices can begin with an individual instructional segment designed to establish or review efficient body position, balanced movement, and correct skill technique. As the season progresses, individual work will be used for review and to work on making positive touches. If there is adequate help present at

Passing the serve using the forearm pass technique.

practice, one group can be training and the other reviewing video. Players need to practice for perfection by setting a high level of expectation for the drill, such as trying to make a specific number of perfect contacts, achieving progressive scoring (that is, having a rally), or completing a timed goal like keeping the ball in play for a minimum of 55 seconds. The drills should progress such that players play at game speed and with high intensity.

Group Skill Focus

Group sessions should be designed to work combinations of players in areas where they must synchronize their movements and coordinate their areas of responsibility. Coaches can use drills that isolate players who are responsible for a portion of the court. Those players who cover the right side, for instance, must coordinate their movements from front to back, back to front, and outside to inside. Another movement that needs to be coordinated among multiple players starts with the transition release of the setter to distribute the ball among the attackers from serve-receive, defensive, and free-ball situations. A similar situation involves the way the players respond when the setter plays the first ball and responsibility to set is thereby transferred to the designated help setter. Another example is the coordination of steps between the middle and outside teammates to block as well as their efforts to transition off the net to run an offensive play after a dig by a teammate.

Teamwork Focus

Players will mesh better and function well in team situations the more often they play together. As they play, coaches can watch and get a better feel for how individual players respond to a variety of situations and what needs they might have. They can also get a good sense of the team chemistry. Once the small groups have coordinated their play, players can be combined to see how well they play as a team. Coaches can then design drills to address any identified concerns with the team's play so that all players can work well together in scrimmages, games, and tournaments. Coaches should set the standard for the successful completion of drills but must make sure to set challenges that will enhance the mental conditioning of the players by having them face gamelike pressure and the demands of perfection. It is important that coaches find ways to demand that their players give more than they think they can and do so more often than they think is possible. This allows a team to work and struggle together to overcome limitations, eliminate unforced errors, and experience the satisfaction that comes with knowing all members of the team have done their best.

Support for the *team first–me second* concept by players as well as their parents can be that all-important element in forging team cohesiveness. We have entered an era of perceived entitlement: whether players have earned the right to be on the court or not, they or their parents think that because they made the team that they should be guaranteed playing time. Individual players' goals can then overshadow the combined effort of all the players on the team. Having players and parents buy into the concept of making individual contributions for the betterment of the team as a whole, as opposed to simply focusing on starting or playing time, is critical for your team to move forward and compete at its highest level.

CHAPTER 11

Match Preparation and Tactics

As I discuss in chapter 2, a coach's philosophy regarding player development, game preparation, and competitive tactics is exhibited and challenged each time the team takes the court. Some volleyball coaches have become reluctant to continue coaching due to the stress of being uncomfortable with feeling their success is measured only by wins and losses. Other coaches relish the challenges that are part of player and game management. The style of play a team employs, as well as the behaviors demonstrated by its players and coaches, strongly influence the climate within the competitive arena. Coaches and players who actively demonstrate a supportive, enthusiastic climate and model sportsmanship in their competitive challenges set the stage for strong spectator support.

Given the nature of volleyball, one's opponents are always separated from one's own team by the net. This seemingly minor point has figured heavily into the way I have approached the game. Volleyball involves no physical contact, few delaying tactics, no way to run a play sequence over and over again, and no time clock. Therefore, ball control, timing, rhythm, and teamwork on only one side of the net are all absolutely essential for a team's success. That is, it is more important how you play than who you play. Recognizing and anticipating what the opponent is attempting to do is important, but first a team must function together as a unit to make the opponent react. Developing a solid base of fundamentals that includes skills, movement, and court positioning has been discussed. From this foundation, it is paramount to work to establish confident players who can make the necessary adjustments during the sequence of ball contacts, during timeouts, and between games that will make them successful.

The philosophy behind the game preparation and tactics that a coach employs can be seen in player selection, squad makeup, and daily team training. My priorities were always ball control, defense, and a balanced attack at the net. Other coaches may look to dominate at the net by emphasizing attacking and blocking or by creating competitive match-ups by rotating the lineup forward or backward to place the team's best blockers against the opponent's best attacker. Coaches can also decide to put pressure on the opponent's best player to try to take that person out of rhythm. A couple of ways to do this are to serve tough serves to that player and to double block his or her attack while only setting a single block on the other attackers. Today's game, at the higher levels, not only has increased speed and power but also employs offensive tactics that rely on attacking combinations, various swing-hitting angles, and very effective back-row attacks. Coaches must find ways to neutralize the opponent's attack by blocking or using great defense to score points when serving.

In addition to the daily drilling of essential skills and tactics, coaches need to be ready to make the adjustments necessary to cover a weakness exposed during the match with either formation or personnel changes. Besides covering the scouting of one's own team, in this chapter I discuss how to scout an opponent, cover setting up a game-day routine, establish good prematch preparation, address lineup concerns and strategies, and make game adjustments.

Scouting One's Own Team

When preparing for competition, coaches have to realistically understand the strengths and weaknesses of their individual players and the team overall. Coaches should determine and articulate to their players what the starting lineup will be as well as how they will prioritize substitutions in order to maximize the team's opportunities for success. Players need to know and understand their roles so that the team develops chemistry and works to be successful as a unit. In daily training, coaches should try to provide verbal and visual feedback to the players when this is possible and appropriate. Finding 15 or 20 minutes before the start of practice to review the previous night's match or daily video footage should be a priority. From there, any technique inefficiencies that are causing players to have less success with ball control than is expected can be addressed and corrected.

During practice and games, coaches should watch the body language and facial expressions of their players to determine how focused and poised each player is. This can help the coach make appropriate comments that permit the player to refocus and move forward. During practice, coaches should put together a different combination of players to see if there is a better chemistry or team flow within a certain group. This can be worthwhile even if there is a noticeable difference in talent level among the players in the new combination. Game tactics may involve the use of a time-out to regroup a team or enter a substitute to change the dynamics of the team play.

Coaches should place nonstarters and substitutes into the game when there is the most opportunity for those players to experience success. I always placed the third middle on our depth chart onto the court for two rotations to start each game. This permitted that player to gain some experience and comfort without the pressure that often comes at the end of a tight game. The chemistry of the team can also dramatically change due to injuries and illnesses when a new player is thrust into the mix. As such, spot-playing, or entering a player here and there for a couple of plays, allows the next player on the depth chart to provide a cushion for that emergency substitute. When attempting to provide experience for nonstarters, a coach's strategy should be to ensure that the best team is on the court at the end of the game.

Scouting an Opponent

A team's ability to scout an opponent before a game depends on several factors. Sometimes a coach or players have already played the opposing team that season or have watched a videotape of its play against another opponent. Teams in the same region gain a feel for the players and systems run by opponents they regularly meet. But if it is the first match of tournament pool play or the first time one's team is playing an opponent during the season, a coach and team may not have had the opportunity to see the opponent play at all. If that's the case, the team will at least be able to watch the opponent during the warm-up before the match. This allows players to identify and gather some information about the opposing team's setter, the hitting styles of its attackers, its serving techniques, the speed and height of the various sets it uses, and if it has any left-handed players. If the warm-up is the only scouting opportunity a team has available, then the coach should take the opportunity to watch the opponent while his own team is warming up. Some teams even forgo some of their own team's warm-up to watch their opponent go through attacking and serving drills, although I always made sure our players had opportunity to receive repetitions before we watched an opponent. When a coach knows the strengths and tendencies of opponents, he or she can then anticipate how they may try to attack his or her team and force errors.

When seeing a team for the first time, the factors that a coach and players should look for include the following (also see figure 11.1):

- What offensive system does the opponent seem to use?
- What are the setter's tendencies in terms of the height and quickness of the sets?
- Are there any left-handed players?
- Which players receive warm-up sets from all zones and also attack out of the back row?
- Which players receive the most serve-receive training?
- If the opponent has players who jump-serve or serve with topspin, which players do so exclusively?

Once a team has played a game against an opponent, its players have a better feel for that opponent's attacking strategy and the speed of the offense; the team can make adjustments to the blocking scheme and rotations between games to neutralize the type of attack they are facing. Once a team has seen the opponent's defensive coverage, the coach can give more specific instructions as to where to place off-speed shots. Until that identification has been made, a coach can instruct players to put off-speed shots into the middle of the court. This accomplishes two things: it always keeps the ball in play, and it keeps the opposing players moving to contact the ball. This strategy may also force the opponent's setter to play the first ball, making the help setter run the offense. Any lack of communication or hesitation on the opponent's part will be an advantage to the team.

The information collected about the opponent will be used differently depending upon the age, talent, and experience of the players one is coaching. Junior high programs should concentrate more on their own individual and team play to maximize strengths and minimize weaknesses. In scouting other teams they should, however, identify the opponent's offensive system, including the setter's number, the toughest servers, and whether there are any left-handed players. This can be done during the pregame warm-up.

Generally, junior varsity programs should emphasize their own play. But if he or she does have knowledge of the opponent's personnel and tendencies, the program's coach can reserve time the day before the game for review of this information. The team can make blocking, serving, and defensive adjustments during the game according to the offensive system of the opponent, its serving tendencies, and its attacking players. Any other adjustments can be discussed during time-outs and between games.

The amount of necessary preparation increases dramatically with the experience level of a team's players and the ability of the upcoming opponent. Based

Team: _____ Date: _____

Opponent: _____ Game scores: _____

*Enter the uniform numbers of the opponent's starting players in the order in which they start the game. Use this wheel to keep track of the players as they rotate.

*Look to see who starts in the 4 position to determine if he or she is the opponent's best player. This player could be the swing hitter who gets the most sets or the best middle blocker.

net

*Use six half-court sections to diagram the serve-receive patterns for each rotation.

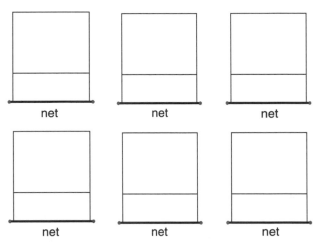

net   net   net

net   net   net

*Write specific comments on each of the opponent's players by player number. Reference the angle of flight for most of the opponent's attacks. For example, you could enter something like the following:

> #7 right-handed; quick middle attack; best on serve-receive, topspin serve
> #21 left-handed opposite; jump-serve with topspin; hits combos and hits well from back row
> #11 setter; jump-sets but does not tip often; jump-serve
> #3 very quick middle; also attacks slide sets well
> #17 quick defensive specialist; do not serve to this player; great passer
> #31 hard-hitting swing hitter; make him pass going to his left

Figure 11.1   Sample scouting report

From *The Volleyball Handbook* by Bob Miller, 2005, Champaign, IL: Human Kinetics.

on the talent and court awareness of players at the varsity level or higher, adjustments can be made in the practices leading up to the contest, during the pregame warm-up, and during the course of game action. I liked to focus on an upcoming opponent's tendencies by comparing its personnel and style of play to a recent opponent or to the manner in which our own team played.

During the preseason and into the competitive season, the team establishes a good foundation for play that prepares players to use various blocking, receiving, and defensive-coverage patterns. Developing a way to implement the needed tactical changes at any time without creating doubt or hesitation is a key learning objective for any team preparing for an opponent. When you have significant information on the opposing team, either on videotape or by having played them, it is important to design sections of practice to cover the strategy for the match ahead. Critical to the game plan is determining how much the players can process and transfer to the court in a short period of time in order to play effectively individually and as a team. Coaches should develop tactics that permit players to use their strong points without causing them to make changes that reduce their effectiveness. Then, as the game progresses, both the coach and the players can get a sense of the opponent's serving strategies and serve-receive patterns and use this information to serve to weaker receiving patterns or players.

Many high school, club, and college coaches have trained their teams to start games from any rotation in order to be comfortable in any match-up they face. This flexibility allows a team to match their best block against the opponent's attacking strength without causing confusion or discomfort.

Preparing for matches should also include giving specific instructions regarding serving, blocking, and defensive coverage; serve-receiving priorities; and offensive attack pointers that are focused on hitting to the opponent's weakest blockers or away from its blocking strength. Defensive coverage can begin in the base coverage with adjustments and combination movements designed for neutralizing one of the opponent's specific players made from there.

My goal was to have our players commit to a smart, aggressive effort through the course of each game and match. We did not want the scoreboard to dictate whether we relaxed or pressed but strove to focus just on the next play. Once one play was over, *that play was over*. Our goal was to adjust and respond as the match progressed.

The following is an example of a brief scouting report that came to me from a state semifinal match 30 minutes before the start of the finals. Both semifinal matches took place simultaneously with little opportunity for scouting and no time for retraining or simulating the opponent's strengths and weaknesses. At the conclusion of the semifinal matches, two colleagues who had watched our upcoming opponent play approached me separately. The information they passed on was that the opponent's best attacker had maximum success hitting the ball to a certain spot on our court. As our team met, I indicated to the player who would be playing back-row defense against this attacker that we needed her to be involved in a special coverage. This was a trained defensive coverage that we had used earlier in the season but had not employed recently. The rest of the team would stay in the middle-back defense, while this player would only rotate to the 5 corner. Every time this set occurred during the match, we called "red 5" to reinforce to her where she should be positioned on the court. Needless to say, she had success digging the attack and was able to transition to offense from this defense. We defeated this team to win the state championship.

Establishing a Game-Day Routine

On a daily basis during the preseason and again during the in-season, players should go through preparation routines for their matches. My program's formal game preparation procedures actually started at least a practice session or day ahead of the match. When preparing for a tournament that included multiple teams, we reviewed the blocking and defensive adjustments that we would make based on the various offenses that we could face. Game day is different from practice days in that the match may be played in the evening while practice generally occurs right after school. Players must also plan time for dinner, schoolwork, and transportation to school either for a bus trip or for a home match.

Even though our overall game preparation centered on technically preparing our players to be physically efficient, their need to be mentally resilient, poised, and visually focused also needed attention. To this end, I asked our players to take some time during the day to visualize themselves playing the ball in different situations, such as after moving from their base position with balance and confidence, placing a serve to a certain area, blocking an opponent's attacker, and attacking off the block or into a weak coverage area. Once the team got together, I wanted each player and the team as a whole to establish a sound preparation routine for the match. This included being seen by the trainer (if necessary), changing for the match, and performing any warm-ups that were needed before stepping on the court.

Prematch Warm-Up

Before the actual on-court warm-up, teams can find an open area in which to stretch and do agility work. The amount of time and court space allotted for prematch warm-up activities varies depending on the format used in tournaments and match play. For actual court warm-ups before our high school matches, we set aside a 20-minute block of time: eight minutes, with each team using one-half of the court, for work on ball handling and ball control, and six minutes for each team to use the entire court and net while the other team either watched or used an area off the court to continue warming up.

The on-court warm-up should accomplish several things. First, it should allow time to go over the movements and body positions that each player will use during the course of a match, such as specific steps that are involved in blocking and the movements and techniques needed to go to the floor. Second, it should provide each player the opportunity to touch and control the ball in situations similar to those that will be duplicated during the match. The players who will receive the opponent's serve should get the most contacts, with either floaters or topspin serves, to replicate the opponent's strategy. Third, the attackers should work on all their different attacking angles and controlled shots during the warm-up instead of just hitting hard. Fourth, players should spend time visualizing their serving and then try to duplicate that visualization by placing the ball correctly during their actual practice attempts. Fifth, players can receive contacts during individual or perimeter digging drills that duplicate expected shot, tip, and roll angles. Finally, if time permits, some teams (especially when a second net is available) can take several serves from teammates in the exact rotation patterns that will be used during the match.

The Lineup

When starting a match and between every game, the coach enters a starting rotation onto a lineup card. The starting rotation lineup has been thought out and may be set to permit your team's strength to come to the front rather than to try to better match up against and thereby neutralize the opponent's strength. The coach may alternate starting a couple of players from game to game, as my coaches and I did, due to the limit on team entries and the basic restriction of being able to only substitute at two of the six positions, not including the libero.

During my coaching career, I started the game with our team's most familiar rotation 99 percent of the time, rather than attempting to match up specifically against the opponent we were facing. I did this basically because we were fortunate to have enough athletes to keep a pretty balanced rotation of attackers and blockers at the net at all times. That does not mean that we did not have go-to players; we definitely did have one or two players each year who fit into this category. When possible, I preferred to run a 5-1 offense. In order to do that, we had to be aware of the blocking ability of our setter. When the setter was not a good blocker, we made adjustments to our coverage or blocking responsibilities to compensate so that we still could use the 5-1 system.

Coaches may choose to adjust their players' starting positions by moving them either forward or backward for a few rotations. The idea is to neutralize the other team's most effective players so as to create an advantageous match-up. The only thing to keep in mind is that both coaches could be moving their rotation forward or backward as they enter the lineup for the next game. How a coach sets up the initial lineup can be based on his or her team's serving strengths, blocking strategy, player entries, the availability of the libero, or the team's best attacker getting the most rotations across the front row. Among my most important decisions were where to start the setter and whether the setter would lead a middle attacker or an outside attack through the rotations. Check the diagrams on pages 121 to 128 that show the patterns used when a single setter (a 5-1 offense) moves through all six rotations and leads the middle hitter. I also set my lineup to get our best servers the most attempts per game. (However, this strategy has been neutralized by the rules that permit players to receive serve with their hands without the fear of getting called for a double contact. The deep serve has basically been taken away, but a short serve away from the opponent's middle hitter can still be a good strategy.) Even though we substituted liberally, we always wanted our best team on the floor at the end of the match and constantly emphasized solid and consistent blocking.

Prematch Talk

During my prematch talk, I actually reviewed the information covered in our last practice as we prepared for the current opponent. Before each away match, we took time on the bus on the way to the match to set the climate for the match and identify the important focal points. Before home matches, we met as a team before our pregame warm-up. My pregame talk usually summarized the main points that had been discussed and implemented at the practice the day before. Since the lineup must be handed in a few minutes before the start of the match, all players, especially any that alternate, should know who will start. When a coach takes the time to individually convey the starting lineup to each player before the game, it shows support and adds a personal touch that fosters trust and respect, especially if the lineup includes any changes from the norm. The final pregame talk with players should be short, simple, and positive.

Coaching During Games

The amount of coaching that takes place during game play depends on the individual inclinations of the coach. Positive feedback, even if it entails only acknowledging the player's effort or court position, can be very meaningful. Some coaches want to be involved in every play, while others interact when concerned about player basics, loss of focus, or lack of poise. Some coaches get involved when it is necessary to interrupt the opponent's momentum.

Once the lineups are in and the game begins, players and coaches have the opportunity to impact the flow of the game. Players are the major component and, of course, by staying within themselves and executing the game plan can strive to be competitive in all their matches. Coaches can provide a positive influence by observing, acknowledging, and supporting the responses of the players to what is happening to or around them. Other options available to coaches for influencing the flow of the game revolve around dealing with the personnel on the floor, the substitutes available, and time-outs. Substitutes can be entered to raise the level of play either in the front or back row, or a coach can enter a substitute for the express purpose of breaking the momentum of the other team by temporarily stopping the game action. This can be done when an opponent's server has run three straight points or when the opponent is approaching game or match point. Two time-outs are available for the coach to use at his or her discretion, either to stop the other team's momentum or to rest and return

© Human Kinetics

Demanding, gamelike practices prepare players for the pressures of competition.

confidence to his or her own players. Players as well have been known to subtly and intentionally slow down play when their team is struggling. Some examples of this include tying a shoe, wiping water off the floor, asking for a lineup check, or discussing a call.

My personal goal was to prepare my team as well as possible to compete intelligently and aggressively in matches. My practices were intense, pressure-packed, and demanding, both physically and mentally. My thought process was that if players could handle any stressor that was dished out during training, game situations would not seem as tough or stressful to them. I was constantly aware of trying to maintain my poise during games but was not opposed to raising everyone's level of concern when it was warranted. With regard to officiating calls that, in my opinion, were suspect, I definitely tried to pick my battles.

My coaching strategy was to assist the players with recognizing what situations might arise and where opposing players were positioned on the court before the start of play. My coaches and I also worked to continue teaching during games, but we discouraged players from looking over to the bench on every play. Rather, we simply reminded them of how to proceed while a substitution was being made or between plays when the need to focus or refocus was necessary. When a player rotates out, the coach can use this time to acknowledge the positives of that player's play as well as to correct any concerns.

Many years ago, I was reading an article that provided the viewpoint of a young player. She indicated that her coach either acknowledged each player or shook her hand when she came out after a positive performance but ignored players who didn't fare as well. Yet, the players who need the most support and encouragement from the coach are those who made a mistake or are struggling. *Every* player should be acknowledged *every* time he or she comes off the court. On our team, after my acknowledgment, each player was likewise acknowledged with a hand touch by every team member on the bench. When there was a need for one-on-one discussion, I would ask the player to return and sit beside me for a few moments.

Charting

During each game, the three items that I personally tracked were the opponent's rotation by player number, our time-outs, and each player's performance. The last item was followed with coded notes. I would chart the opposing team's rotations and call out the numbers of their three front-row players, making sure my team knew when the opponent's setter was in the front row. Also, by charting the rotations we knew which of the opposing team's players was the next server and we could tell immediately if they were out of rotation. The coded notes on our players were done so that I wouldn't forget to personalize any comments that I needed to make during time-outs or between games. Charting his or her own team can help a coach maintain stats regarding decisions made, reinforce a decision, and build up information to pass on to the media.

During game play, it is not uncommon for coaches to be thinking a couple of plays ahead. Coaches should continue to visualize substitution entries to allow new players to gain some experience. Substitutions can also be made to remove a player from the game who seems to be uncomfortable or unsteady. I personally tried not to remove a player immediately after a mistake. This only seemed to magnify the situation. We would try to make adjustments and cover for the struggling player by giving another player more area to cover. If it was necessary to remove the player, we would wait for the next rotation (if possible) to make a substitution. On the other hand, when the number of total individual and team entries permitted, I always tried to insert a player to take advantage of his or her strength. I did my best to put designated players in to serve, block, dig, or attack when the team needed them on the floor. I also tried to put new players in when the situation provided the most opportunity for success.

Game management follows the ebb and flow of the game and is strongly influenced by a coach's "gut feeling" that evolves during the action. The score or a run of points may be a factor in the coach doing his or her part to slow, stop, or reverse the momentum that the opponent has built. But judging the play and the composure of the competitors on the court or reading the nonverbal communication of a team may be more of a governing factor than the score in a coach's decision to get involved. The team's effort may be exactly what a coach is looking for, and it just may be a matter of time before the entire effort taking place on the court swings the momentum. Unfortunately, with rally scoring, a coach's decision to make a move may have to occur earlier than it would with the side-out format.

Handling Time-outs

Time-outs are limited and should be used for a specific purpose. Before taking a time-out to slow down the other team, a coach can instead try changing a pattern, giving a player more responsibility, or putting in a new player. As a last resort, a time-out can be called to stop the opponent's momentum when three or four consecutive points have been scored. For example, if an opponent's jump server's effectiveness is causing the team to be aced or giving the opponent a free ball, he or she may be forced out of the jump-serve rhythm and need to start serving floater serves—or may even mistime his or her next toss—after being interrupting by a timeout. Opponents are also using this strategy to disrupt your servers' momentum. Other occasions for calling a time-out include providing a team with a chance to catch its breath, rehydrate, regain focus or poise, and communicate with the coaching staff.

My staff and I have called time-outs specifically to talk to one player. Most often when we did this, we separated the setter to go over strategy and any concerns we might have; we also spoke separately with the floor captain or a player who was struggling. When a program is fortunate enough to have an assistant who can either talk to the rest of the team or one who has built up rapport with a player, it may be possible to achieve a couple of goals within one time-out. When the coach is on his or her own, he or she may use half of the time-out for one or a couple of players and the rest of the time-out for the entire team.

During time-outs a coach can also call on charts to reaffirm what he or she believes is occurring on the floor. For instance, the attacking chart might confirm that the distribution of sets is heavy on the left side and light in the middle. This could indicate that passes are off-target or off the net, thus prohibiting the team from forcing play to the middle of the court. The coach may thus suggest that the team continue with the strategy it is currently using but advise that players keep their chests down longer to direct the ball further to the net. Coaches need to emphasize their concerns without giving so much information that the players can't process it all. They also need to provide as much positive reinforcement as possible.

Coaches need to decide how they want to handle the team huddle. I always thought it was best to have all the players focused on the coach, who is standing along the sideline of the court. By doing this, players don't have the opportunity to check out who is in the bleachers. I wanted to see my players' eyes, and I wanted them to either focus on my face or what was being written on the clipboard. Coaches should break the huddle with one reminder, such as the location of the opponent's best player or setter. I also liked to use easy-to-remember initials that the team repeated together in order to refocus on a situation. Two such examples are PBD for "play better defense" and CTB for "control the ball."

Postgame Talk

After an evening's match or tournament play, I tried to bring closure to the events of the day by emphasizing one or two points. On many occasions I would culminate the postgame comments by acknowledging the players who worked especially hard during the team preparation but who did not get as much playing time as any of us would have liked. At all times, honesty, fairness, consistency, and firmness should be priorities in any discussion. A coach should not hesitate to talk to an individual player privately or off to the side if the situation merits such attention.

In many situations, I shied away from getting too deeply into what occurred in the match just played by saying, for example, "Let's look at the videotape tomorrow." I then concluded my comments with reference to the team's energy, intensity, and competitiveness. On two occasions during my career, I went beyond ranting and raving to what could be categorized as going ballistic. I am still upset and ashamed of how I handled those two situations. By keeping the postgame comments short, a coach has the opportunity to reflect on or process more of the factors that contributed to the outcome of the match rather letting one or two plays fuel the fire that is likely to be burning after a loss, a poor performance, or a disappointing play.

One strategy that I began to use in 1983 was to employ the travel time on the bus after an away match to talk to each player about the game. This did not happen all the time, but it happened when I thought it would do the most good. I remember one occasion on which the bus ride home was a four-hour trip and we had played poorly. The evening before the tournament we stayed in a motel and a few of the girls choreographed a dance routine that involved every member on the team. They taught a step, and the players with the most success were recruited to assist those who were the most uncomfortable. This went on for over two hours. We videotaped the final product, which was outstanding. However, our play the next day was not. On the way home, the players thought I was going to rip into them, but instead I referred back to the effort to organize the dance that had taken place the night before and compared it to the movement and rhythm needed by a team to be successful on the court. Seeing what they did earlier and comparing it to what my staff and I were trying to accomplish put a whole new perspective on teamwork for them.

INDEX

Note: The italicized *f* and *t* following page numbers refer to figures and tables, respectively.

ABOUT THE AUTHOR

Upon his 2002 retirement, Bob Miller had amassed a 950-150 (.864) record and 7 state championship titles in 55 seasons of coaching high school varsity boys' (35 seasons) and girls' (20 seasons) volleyball at North Allegheny High School in Pittsburgh, Pennsylvania, his alma mater. In 1994, he was inducted into the Pennsylvania Volleyball Coaches Association Hall of Fame, an organization for which he is currently a second-term president. He is also a member of the North Allegheny School District Athletic Hall of Fame and is an adjunct member on the Western Pennsylvania Interscholastic Athletic League (WPIAL) Volleyball Steering Committee.

As a court coach, Miller has trained players at Penn State University Camps, Volleyball Express Camps at Juniata College, and the Youngstown State Team Camp, as well as Wooster High School in Ohio and Butler High School in Pennsylvania. He has also spoken as a clinician at a University of Pittsburgh clinic and made several presentations for the Pennsylvania Volleyball Coaches Association clinics. Miller was instrumental in establishing the first club program in Western Pennsylvania, called Willow Pond, where he was involved in coaching a 16-and-under boys' team. He also coached the girls' teams twice in the Keystone Games.

Miller currently volunteers with both boys' and girls' volleyball programs and works with a senior women's team that captured its division title at the 2004 Pennsylvania Keystone Games while training for the Senior Olympics held in the summer of 2005. Miller's daughter, Julie, and son, Brian, both played at Penn State University, where Julie currently serves as director of volleyball operations. Both were also assistant coaches at North Allegheny High School. Miller and his wife, Margaret, live in Pittsburgh, Pennsylvania.

VOLLEYBALL Skills & Drills

American Volleyball Coaches Association

ISBN 0-7360-5862-1 • 208 Pages

To place your order,
U.S. customers call TOLL FREE

1-800-747-4457

In Canada call **1-800-465-7301**
In Australia call **(08) 8277 1555**
In New Zealand call **(09) 448 1207**
In Europe call **+44 (0) 113 255 5665**
or visit **www.HumanKinetics.com**

Developed by the AVCA!

Master volleyball's key techniques and elevate your performance in all facets of the sport with *Volleyball Skills & Drills*.

Developed by the American Volleyball Coaches Association, this book includes an introduction by Taras Liskevych and chapters from 10 of the game's top coaches on the topics they know best:

- Paul Arrington: Practicing
- Sean Byron: Setting
- Don Hardin: Blocking
- Jim McLaughlin: Attacking
- Marilyn Nolen: Receiving Serves
- Penn State assistants with Russ Rose: Playing Defense
- Tom Peterson: Serving
- Joan Powell: Digging
- Joe Sagula: Playing Offense
- Stephanie Schleuder: Transitioning

Featuring 90 of the sport's best drills, this guide will maximize both the rate and quality of learning to help you get the most out of each practice session.

HUMAN KINETICS
The Premier Publisher for Sports & Fitness
P.O. Box 5076, Champaign, IL 61825-5076